MODERN HUMAN
LIBRARY OF MED.

*General Editors*
NERYS ANN JONES
ERICH POPPE

# EARLY WELSH GNOMIC AND NATURE POETRY

Edited by
Nicolas Jacobs

LIBRARY OF MEDIEVAL WELSH LITERATURE

**Already Published**
(available from University of Wales Press)

*Welsh Court Poems*
edited by Rhian M. Andrews (2007)

*Selections from* Ystorya Bown o Hamtwn
edited by Erich Poppe and Regine Reck (2009)

**Forthcoming**
(available from www.medwelsh.mhra.org.uk)

*Historical Texts from Medieval Wales*
edited by Patricia Williams

*Hystoria Gweryddon yr Almaen:*
*The Middle Welsh Life of St Ursula and the 11,000 Virgins*
edited by Jane Cartwright

*A Selection of Early Welsh Saga Poems*
edited by Jenny Rowland

*Medieval Welsh Political Poetry*
edited by Helen Fulton

# EARLY WELSH GNOMIC AND NATURE POETRY

Edited by
Nicolas Jacobs

MODERN HUMANITIES RESEARCH ASSOCIATION
2012

Published by

The Modern Humanities Research Association,
1 Carlton House Terrace
London SW1Y 5AF

First published 2012

ISBN (hardback) 978-1-907322-58-7
ISBN (paperback) 978-1-907322-68-6

Copies may be ordered from www.medwelsh.mhra.org.uk

# CONTENTS

ER COF TEULU
BWLCHYSTYLLEN A LLETYLLWYD

# PREFACE

This book was undertaken some sixteen years ago in response to an invitation to provide for the use of students in Wales and beyond a new edition of the texts first edited in 1935 by Kenneth Jackson in his *Early Welsh Gnomic Poems* together with a few others which, for various reasons, he had not seen fit to include. Progress has been slow and intermittent, in face of the more pressing calls on my time which will be familiar to all academics at the end of the twentieth century and since, and I have often had my doubts whether the work would ever be finished. But the time has now come to let it go, with all its remaining errors, inconsistencies and other imperfections, for which I take full responsibility and invite constructive criticism.

My debt to Jackson's work must be immediately obvious. His intellectual energy and the breadth of his learning in all the Celtic languages remain awe-inspiring, even twenty years after his death; the task of editing the texts would have been immeasurably harder without the benefit of his pioneering work, and if I have on occasion felt obliged to disagree with his conclusions I have done so only with the greatest respect. But the world has in the meantime moved on. The philological expertise Jackson could take for granted among his students in the Cambridge of 1935 was already coming to be regarded as an eccentricity in Oxford thirty years later, and after forty more years it can be little more than a memory anywhere in the English-speaking world. My notes are accordingly much more detailed than his needed to be. Commentaries are made for students, not students for commentaries, and the editor who annotates only what he himself finds difficult does his readers scant service. If, to those already familiar with Middle Welsh, I have appeared to waste words on the trivial or the obvious, I plead in extenuation the difficulties my contemporaries and I had as beginners in using traditional Welsh editions, many of them, in contrast to Jackson's, as unhelpful as they were erudite; and I make no apologies for trying to make it as easy as possible for a new generation of students to become familiar with these curious but strangely attractive poems. For the same reason I have added a linguistic introduction, including the still neglected topic of syntax, and as comprehensive a glossary as I could compile.

My thanks are due to the staff of the National Library of Wales, Aberystwyth, the British Library, London and the Bodleian Library, Oxford, for their help over the years, and to the authorities of those libraries, to the Cardiff Libraries and Information Service and to Jesus College, Oxford, for permission to print from manuscripts in their possession. I am grateful to the Modern Humanities Research Association for their readiness to take over the series of which this volume is part, and to the Trustees of the Sir John Rhŷs Fund, University of Oxford, for offering a generous subvention, which was not in the event needed. I owe a personal debt in particular to Nerys Ann Jones for her constant help and encouragement, especially for her painstaking work in checking and correcting the whole text, and above all the glossary; but also to Rhian Andrews, Thomas Charles-Edwards, Tom Elias, Ellis Evans, Geraint Gruffydd, Marged Haycock, Dafydd Jenkins, Dafydd Glyn Jones and Erich Poppe, all of whom have been generous with their help and have saved me from many blunders.

I owe a further debt of gratitude to my friends for their patience in face of my frequent lack of it: to Carolyn Chapman above all and also to my colleagues at Jesus, among whom I would mention by name Niall Ferguson, Paulina Kewes, Peter Mirfield, John Walsh and David Womersley. I would also express my gratitude (though in many cases too late) to those who encouraged me in my early days in my love of Wales and its language: Cathrin Daniel and her children John and Anna (whose untimely deaths I particularly lament) and Iestyn; Idris Foster; Caradog and Mattie Prichard; Gwyn Thomas; and Dewi Thomas. But perhaps my greatest debt of all is to those celebrated in the dedication of this book. Theirs is a world I shall not see again, and no amount of regret will bring it back – *hiraeth am uarw ny weryt* – but I have understood the poetry and its context better for having known it, and I shall be grateful as long as I live.

N.J.

Bangor, St Tysilio's Day 2011.

# ABBREVIATIONS

The following abbreviations are used in the text, footnotes, and glossary; for full references to books and journals see Bibliography.

## Grammatical

| | |
|---|---|
| acc. | accusative |
| adj. | adjective |
| adv. | adverb |
| asp. | aspiration |
| coll. | collective |
| comp. | comparative |
| conj. | conjunction |
| distrib. | distributive |
| eq. | equative |
| f. | feminine |
| fig. | figurative |
| foll. | following |
| gen. | genitive |
| impf. | imperfect |
| impers. | impersonal |
| impv. | imperative |
| ind. | indicative |
| indef. | indefinite |
| interj. | interjection |
| intr. | intransitive |
| Lat. | Latin |
| m. | masculine |
| ModW | Modern Welsh |
| mut. | mutation |
| MW | Middle Welsh |
| n. | noun |
| neg. | negative |
| nom. | nominative |
| num. | numeral |
| obj. | object |
| OW | Old Welsh |

| | |
|---|---|
| perf. | perfect |
| pers. | personal |
| pers. n. | personal name |
| phr. | phrase |
| pl. | plural |
| poss. | possessive |
| pr. | present |
| prep. | preposition |
| pret. | preterite |
| pron. | pronoun |
| refl. | reflexive |
| rel. | relative |
| sg. | singular |
| subj. | subjunctive |
| superl. | superlative |
| tr. | transitive |
| v. | verb |
| vn. | verbal noun |

## Bibliographical

'Absolute Forms'   Simon Rodway, 'Absolute Forms in the Poetry of the Gogynfeirdd'.

| | |
|---|---|
| *ASE* | *Anglo-Saxon England* |
| ASPR | The Anglo-Saxon Poetic Records |
| *BB* | *Brut y Brenhinedd*, ed. Brynley Roberts |
| *BBCS* | *Bulletin of the Board of Celtic Studies* |
| *BBGCC* | Marged Haycock, *Blodeugerdd Barddas o Ganu Crefyddol Cynnar* |
| BL | British Library |
| *CA* | *Canu Aneirin*, ed. Ifor Williams |
| CBT | Cyfres Beirdd y Tywysogion |
| *CLlH* | *Canu Llywarch Hen*, ed. Ifor Williams |
| *CMCS* | *Cambrian* (formerly *Cambridge*) *Medieval Celtic Studies* |
| CUP | Cambridge University Press |
| 'Cystrawennau'r Cyplad' | T. Arwyn Watkins and Proinsias Mac Cana, 'Cystrawennau'r Cyplad mewn Hen Gymraeg' |
| DIAS | Dublin Institute of Advanced Studies |
| *ECNP* | Kenneth Jackson, *Early Celtic Nature Poetry* |
| *EWGP* | Kenneth Jackson, *Early Welsh Gnomic Poems* |
| *EWSP* | Jenny Rowland, *Early Welsh Saga Poetry* |

| | |
|---|---|
| *GBGG* | *Geirfa Barddoniaeth Gynnar Gymraeg* |
| *GDG* | *Gwaith Dafydd ap Gwilym*, ed. Thomas Parry |
| *GMW* | D. Simon Evans, *A Grammar of Middle Welsh* |
| *GPC* | *Geiriadur Prifysgol Cymru* |
| *HGC* | Henry Lewis, *Hen Gerddi Crefyddol* |
| Jarman, *Gododdin* | A. O. H. Jarman, *Aneirin: Y Gododdin. Britain's Oldest Heroic Poem* |
| *JCS* | *Journal of Celtic Studies* |
| *LHEB* | Kenneth H. Jackson, *Language and History in Early Britain* |
| *LlC* | *Llên Cymru* |
| *LlDC* | *Llyfr Du Caerfyrddin*, ed. A. O. H. Jarman. |
| *MA*² | Owen Jones, Edward Williams and William Owen [Pughe], *The Myvyrian Archaiology of Wales*, 2nd ed. |
| Cavill, *Maxims* | Paul Cavill, *Maxims in Old English Poetry* |
| NLW | National Library of Wales |
| OUP | Oxford University Press |
| *PBA* | *Proceedings of the British Academy* |
| *PKM* | *Pedeir Keinc y Mabinogi*, ed. Ifor Williams |
| *SC* | *Studia Celtica* |
| *SW* | Robert Borsley, Maggie Tallerman and David Willis, *The Syntax of Welsh* |
| *TYP*³ | *Trioedd Ynys Prydain*, ed. Rachel Bromwich. |
| UWP | University of Wales Press. |

# BIBLIOGRAPHY

BARTRUM, P. C., *A Welsh Classical Dictionary*, Aberystwyth: National Library of Wales, 1993.

BLOOMFIELD, MORTON W., 'Understanding Old English Poetry', *Annuale Medievale*, 9 (1968), 5–25.

BORSLEY, ROBERT, TALLERMAN, MAGGIE and WILLIS, DAVID, *The Syntax of Welsh*, Cambridge: CUP, 2007.

BRAMLEY, KATHERINE ANNE, JONES, NERYS ANN, OWEN, MORFYDD E., MCKENNA, CATHERINE, WILLIAMS, GRUFFYDD ALED and WILLIAMS, J. E. CAERWYN, eds, *Gwaith Llywelyn Fardd I ac Eraill o Feirdd y Ddeuddegfed Ganrif*, CBT II, Cardiff: UWP, 1994.

BROMWICH, RACHEL, ed., *The Beginnings of Welsh Poetry: Studies by Sir Ifor Williams*, Cardiff: UWP, 1972.

——, ed. *Trioedd Ynys Prydain*, 3rd ed., Cardiff: UWP, 2006.

CAVILL, PAUL, *Maxims in Old English Poetry*, Woodbridge: D. S. Brewer, 1999.

CHARLES-EDWARDS, T. M., OWEN, MORFYDD E. and WALTERS, D. B., eds, *Lawyers and Laymen: Studies in the History of Law presented to Professor Dafydd Jenkins on his seventy-fifth birthday*, Cardiff: UWP, 1986.

CHARLES-EDWARDS, T. M., 'A Note on Terminology', in Charles-Edwards, Owen and Walters, *Lawyers and Laymen*, pp. 10–12.

CURTIUS. E. R. (tr. W. R. Trask), *European Literature and the Latin Middle Ages*, London: Routledge and Kegan Paul, 1953.

DAVIES, HUGH, *Welsh Botanology*, London, for the author, 1813.

DAVIES, SIONED and JONES, NERYS ANN, eds, *The Horse in Celtic Culture: Medieval Welsh Perspectives*, Cardiff: UWP, 1997.

DICKINS, BRUCE, ed., *Runic and Heroic Poems of the Old Teutonic Peoples*, Cambridge: CUP, 1915.

DOBBIE, E. VAN K., ed., *The Anglo-Saxon Minor Poems*, ASPR VI, New York: Columbia University Press and London: Routledge and Kegan Paul, 1942.

EVANS, D. SIMON, *A Grammar of Middle Welsh*, Dublin: DIAS, 1964.

——, ed., *Historia Gruffudd vab Kenan*, Cardiff: UWP, 1977.

EVANS, J. GWENOGVRYN, ed., *The Black Book of Carmarthen*, Pwllheli: privately publ., 1906.

——, ed., *Facsimile and Text of The Book of Aneirin*, Pwllheli: privately publ., 1908.

——, ed., *The Poetry in the Red Book of Hergest*, Llanbedrog: privately publ., 1911.

GAMESON, RICHARD, 'The origin of the Exeter Book of Old English poetry', *Anglo-Saxon England*, 25 (1996), 135–85.

HALSALL, M., *The Old English Rune Poem: A Critical Edition*, Toronto: University of Toronto Press, 1981.

HASKINS, C. H., *The Renaissance of the Twelfth Century*, Cambridge, Mass.: Harvard University Press, 1927.

HAY, WILLIAM, *Diarhebion Cymru*, Liverpool: Gwasg y Brython, 1955.

HAYCOCK, MARGED, *Blodeugerdd Barddas o Ganu Crefyddol Cynnar*, Llandybïe: Cyhoeddiadau Barddas, 1994.

HUWS, DANIEL, *Medieval Welsh Manuscripts*, Aberystwyth: UWP and National Library of Wales, 2000.

IRELAND, COLIN, *Old Irish Wisdom Attributed to Aldfrith of Northumbria: An Edition of Bríathra Flainn Fhína maic Ossu*, Tempe: Arizona Centre for Medieval and Renaissance Studies, 1999.

ISAAC, GRAHAM R., 'Gwarchan Maeldderw: A "Lost" Medieval Welsh Classic?', *CMCS* 44 (Winter 2002), 73–96.

—— 'The old- and early Middle-Welsh "future" tense: form and function of a moribund category', *JCS*, 4 (2004), 153–70.

JACKSON, KENNETH H., *Early Celtic Nature Poetry*, Cambridge: CUP, 1935

—— *Early Welsh Gnomic Poems*, 2nd ed., Cardiff: UWP, 1960.

—— *Language and History in Early Britain*, Edinburgh: Edinburgh University Press, 1953.

JACOBS, NICOLAS, 'Sylwadau pellach ar *?im bluch* (≡ *ymlwch*) "yn foel"', *LlC*, 21 (1998), 162–65.

—— '"Englynion" y Misoedd: Testun B neu Fersiwn Llansteffan 117 a Pheniarth 155', *Dwned*, 6 (2000), 9–24.

—— 'The "Stanzas of the Months": maxims from late medieval Wales', *Medium Ævum*, lxx (2001), 250–67.

—— 'Englynion Calan Gaeaf a'r Misoedd o "Englynion Duad"', *SC*, 36 (2002), 73–88.

—— '"Englynion" y Misoedd: Testun C neu Fersiwn Nyffryn', *LlC*, 25 (2002), 1–11.

—— '*Lledwag kronffair*: What Kind of Fair and Why So Little Frequented?', *CMCS*, 44 (Winter 2002) 97–101.

—— 'Nodiadau ar y Canu Gwirebol. I: "Englynion" y Misoedd: Testun A neu'r Fersiwn Cyffredin', *Dwned*, 9 (2003), 65–80.

—— '"Gossymdeith Llefoet Wynebclawr": Canu Gwirebol o Lyfr Coch Hergest', *LlC*, 27 (2004), 1–29.

—— 'A Jacksonian Emendation Revisited: RBH 1030.21–22 *bit granclef glew*', *CMCS*, 48 (Winter 2004), 101–06.

—— 'Nodiadau ar y Canu Gwirebol. II: Y Penillion Tymhorol o Beniarth 182', *Dwned*, 11 (2005), 9–18.

—— 'Animadversions on Bastardy in the Red Book of Hergest: *Early Welsh Gnomic Poems* IV.6', *CMCS*, 55 (Summer 2008), 51–59.

—— 'A Fresh Look at *Gwarchan Adebon*' in Stefan Zimmer, ed. *Kelten am Rhein: Akten der XIII. Internationalen Keltologiekongresses, Bonn 2007, II. Teil: Sprachen und Literatur*, Beihefte der Bonner Jahrbücher 58.2 (Mainz: Verlag Philipp von Zabern, 2009), pp. 105–09.

—— '*Geufel*: An Unidentified Plant in the Red Book *Gorwynion*', *CMCS*, 62 (Winter 2011), 81–87.

JARMAN, A. O. H., *Llyfr Du Caerfyrddin gyda Rhagymadrodd, Nodiadau Testunol a Geirfa*, Cardiff: UWP, 1982.

—— *Aneirin: Y Gododdin. Britain's Oldest Heroic Poem*, Llandysul: Gomer, 1990.

JENKINS, DAFYDD and OWEN, MORFYDD E., eds, *The Welsh Law of Women*, Cardiff: UWP, 1980.

JENKINS, DAFYDD, 'Property Interests in the Classical Welsh Law of Women', in Jenkins and Owen, *The Welsh Law of Women*, pp. 69–92.

—— 'The Horse in the Welsh Law-Tracts', in Davies and Jones, *The Horse in Celtic Culture*, pp. 64–81.

JONES, OWEN, WILLIAMS, EDWARD and OWEN [PUGHE], WILLIAM. *The Myvyrian Archaiology of Wales*, 2nd ed., Denbigh: Gee, 1870.

KRAPP, G. P. and DOBBIE, E. VAN K., eds, *The Exeter Book*, ASPR III, New York: Columbia University Press and London: Routledge and Kegan Paul, 1936.

LARRINGTON, CAROLYNE, review of D. A. H. EVANS, ed., *Havamál* (London, 1986), in *Saga-Book of the Viking Society*, 22 (1987), 127–30.

—— *A Store of Common Sense: Gnomic Theme and Style in Old English and Old Icelandic Wisdom Poetry*, Oxford: OUP, 1993.

LEWIS, HENRY, 'Diarhebion ym Mheniarth 17', *BBCS*, 4 (1927–29), 1–17.

—— *Hen Gerddi Crefyddol*, Cardiff: UWP, 1931.

—— *Yr Elfen Ladin yn yr Iaith Gymraeg*, Cardiff: UWP, 1943.

LLOYD-JONES, J., *Geirfa Barddoniaeth Gynnar Gymraeg*, Cardiff: UWP, 1931–63.

PARRY, THOMAS, ed. *Gwaith Dafydd ap Gwilym*, 3rd ed., Cardiff: UWP, 1979.

PARRY-WILLIAMS, T. H., *The English Element in Welsh*, Cymmrodorion Record Series 10, London: The Honourable Society of Cymmrodorion, 1923.

—— ed., *Canu Rhydd Cynnar*, Cardiff: UWP, 1932.

—— *Hen Benillion*, Llandysul: Gomer, 1940.

RICHARDS, MELVILLE, *Cystrawen y Frawddeg Gymraeg*, Cardiff: UWP, 1939.

—— ed., *Breudwyt Ronabwy*, Cardiff: UWP, 1948.

ROBERTS, BRYNLEY F., ed., *Brut y Brenhinedd: Llanstephan MS 1 version*, Dublin: DIAS, 1971,

RODWAY, SIMON, 'Absolute Forms in the Poetry of the Gogynfeirdd: Functionally Obsolete Archaisms or Working System?', *Journal of Celtic Linguistics*, 7 (1998), 63–84.

ROWLAND, JENNY, ' "Englynion Duad" ', *JCS*, 3 (1981), 59–87

—— *Early Welsh Saga Poetry*, Cambridge: Boydell and Brewer, 1990.

SHIPPEY, T. A., *Old English Verse*, London: Hutchinson, 1972.

—— *Poems of Wisdom and Learning in Old English*, Cambridge: D. S. Brewer, 1976.

SIMS-WILLIAMS, PATRICK, *Irish influence on Medieval Welsh Literature*, Oxford: OUP, 2011.

SISAM, KENNETH, *Studies in the History of Old English Literature*, Oxford: OUP, 1953.

STANLEY, E. G., 'Old English Poetic Diction and the Interpretation of *The Wanderer, The Seafarer* and *The Penitent's Prayer*', *Anglia*, 73 (1955), 413–66.

—— ed., *The Owl and the Nightingale*, London and Edinburgh: Nelson, 1960.

THOMAS, ALAN R., *The Welsh Dialect Survey*, Cardiff: UWP, 2000.

THOMAS, GRAHAM C. G., 'An Early Welsh Seasonal Poem', *BBCS*, 34 (1987), 61–65.

THOMAS, R. J. and OTHERS, eds, *Geiriadur Prifysgol Cymru: A Dictionary of the Welsh Language*, Cardiff: UWP, 1950–2002; 2nd edition in progress 2002-.

THOMSON, R. L., ed., *Branwen uerch Lyr*, Dublin: DIAS, 1961.

TOLKIEN, J. R. R., 'Beowulf: The Monsters and the Critics', PBA, 22 (1936), 245–95.

WATKINS, ARWYN and MAC CANA, PROINSIAS, 'Cystrawennau'r Cyplad mewn Hen Gymraeg', BBCS, 18 (1958–60), 1–25.

WEST, M. L. ed., HESIOD, Works and Days, Oxford: OUP, 1978.

WILLIAMS, IFOR, 'Y Diarhebion yn y Llyfr Du o'r Waun', BBCS, 3 (1926–27), 22–31.

—— ed., Pedeir Keinc y Mabinogi, Cardiff: UWP, 1930.

—— 'The Poems of Llywarch Hen', PBA, 18 (1932), 269–302, repr. in Bromwich, ed., Beginnings of Welsh Poetry, 122–54.

—— ed., Canu Llywarch Hen, Cardiff: UWP, 1935.

—— ed., Canu Aneirin, Cardiff: UWP, 1938.

—— Lectures on Early Welsh Poetry, Dublin: DIAS, 1970.

WILLIAMS, J. E. CAERWYN, LYNCH, PEREDUR I. and GRUFFYDD, R. GERAINT, eds, Gwaith Meilyr Brydydd a'i Ddisgynyddion, CBT I, Cardiff: UWP, 1994.

WIRTJES, HANNEKE, ed., The Middle English Physiologus, Early English Text Society 229, Oxford: OUP, 1991.

WMFFRE, IWAN, Language and Place-Names in Wales: the Evidence of Toponymy in Cardiganshire, Cardiff: UWP, 2003.

# INTRODUCTION

## Gnomic and Nature Poetry

### A. Wisdom Poetry: Precepts, Proverbs and Maxims

'Gnomic poetry' is the conventional term for a compilation of sententious verse concerning human life and the natural world; as thus defined, it is particularly typical of the cultures of North Western Europe in the early middle ages, being best exemplified in Mediaeval Welsh and Old English, together with some slight remains in Old Norse and some prose parallels in Old Irish. It may be viewed as a subdivision of the wider category of wisdom poetry,[1] but is distinguished by its preference for sententious statement over moral instruction and by its pervasive interest in the natural world, which in the case of the Welsh texts extends to the inclusion of much natural description which is not gnomic at all.[2] Preceptual poetry of a moral and religious kind is well exemplified in Welsh and even more in the two Germanic languages,[3] but in general in Welsh a clear distinction can be drawn between it and the gnomic poetry; the blurring of the generic distinction between it and saga poetry[4] is in practice much more problematic.[5]

Gnomic poetry is nevertheless often easier to recognise than to define. The difference between a gnome or maxim and, on the one hand, a proverb or, on the other, a general observation which happens to be true is fairly clear; every proverb is a maxim, and every maxim is an observation, but not every

---

[1] For a wide-ranging survey of such poetry, see Hesiod, *Works and Days*, ed. M. L. West (Oxford, 1978), pp.3–25.

[2] Pure nature poetry, as opposed to incidental references to the natural world, does not survive in Old English and is rare in Mediaeval Welsh before the fourteenth century, but it is well exemplified in Old Irish: see Jackson, *ECNP*, for discussion and translated examples.

[3] For Germanic preceptual poetry, see Shippey, *Poems of Wisdom and Learning*; Larrington, *A Store of Common Sense*. The Welsh preceptual matter is briefly discussed by the present author in Nerys Ann Jones, ed., *A New Guide to Welsh Literature*, I (Cardiff, forthcoming).

[4] In using this convenient term I follow Rowland, *EWSP*, though, as she makes clear, it cannot be taken for granted that all such poetry represents the verse element in a saga of mixed prose and verse such as Ifor Williams postulated as the origin of *Canu Llywarch Hen*.

[5] There is a unique instance of overlap between gnomic poetry and heroic elegy in *Gwarchan Adebon* (X in this edition). This text has traditionally been regarded, following Ifor Williams (*CA*, pp. lviii-lix) as a fragment of a rhymed collection of proverbs, and is edited here for that reason, but on closer examination it proves to be a heroic elegy, or part of one, with substantial gnomic elements. This would occasion no surprise in Old English, but seems unparalleled in mediaeval Welsh.

observation is a maxim nor every maxim a proverb. One distinction is that the first two are intended to be remembered and that a memorable element can be recognised in them, whereas the validity of a general observation does not require it to be committed to memory. A proverb may also be distinguished from a maxim by its tendency to include moral as well as descriptive elements. In addition, the same statement may appear as a maxim if taken literally, but as a proverb if read figuratively; and if the latter interpretation clearly has more point than the former, then that statement can be regarded as a proverb.[6]

Kenneth Jackson, in what remains the classic analysis of the type,[7] distinguishes between three kinds of statement characteristic of the texts edited in his collection: two types of *gnome* or maxim, which he defines as 'a sententious statement about universals, whether about the affairs of men ("human-gnome") or about external nature ("nature-gnome")', and what he characterizes as 'descriptive statements about nature relating to particulars ("nature-description" As examples he cites, respectively, *bit wreic drwc ae mynych warth* 'a bad woman causes frequent scandals', *gnawt nyth eryr ym blaen dar* 'usual is the nest of an eagle in the top of an oak') and *eiry my[ny]d gwynn to tei* 'mountain snow, white are the house-roofs'.[8] Jackson's taxonomy, which further distinguishes the *gnome* from the *proverb* more or less as defined above and the *precept* with its element of advice or exhortation, has stood the test of time and is followed in this edition; the symmetry is completed by reference to some descriptive statements about the affairs of men comparable to those about nature. These are rare: *baglawc bydin* 'serried (*or* 'armed with staves') is the host'[9] is perhaps the best example. The relation between these four types, and in particular the reason for the frequency of the third in contexts where its relevance to the gnomic material is far from clear, remains to be investigated. Jackson distinguishes usefully between true gnomic poetry, where almost all the references to nature are gnomic, what he calls 'quasi-gnomic poetry', where there is a substantial admixture of pure natural description, and those texts which comprise a mixture of the two, but since poems of these various types are copied together without distinction in the Red Book of Hergest it is not clear that a contemporary audience would have differentiated between them.

Inevitably, in the definition of what is or is not gnomic there will be borderline cases, and how these are to be interpreted must depend on the context. Context, for example, can transform a general observation into a maxim; almost every observation about human life and society in the saga poetry is a maxim, as with the oldest example we have, from the Juvencus *englynion: dou nam rigeus unguetid* 'two lords can converse; one speaks'[10] or, from 'Llym awel', *meccid*

---

[6] For a more elaborate attempt at drawing such distinctions, see Cavill, *Maxims*, pp. 41–81.
[7] *EWGP*, pp. 1–4.
[8] *Ibid.*, VII.16.iii, IV.7.i, III.35.i (= III.16c, IV.7a, II.35a in this edition)
[9] VII.1a in this edition (= *EWGP* II.1.i.)
[10] See *EWSP*, pp. 466–67, 3c.

*llvwyr llauer kyngor* 'a coward hatches many excuses'.[11] The full significance of such observations appears only from reading them as general statements about the moral and physical nature of the world, as well as in their dramatic context. And such statements are so common in much of the saga poetry as to oblige the reader to be alert to a gnomic tone wherever there is a general observation, even when it refers directly to the story itself. In the great exclamation of Heledd, *dygystud deurud dagreu* 'tears wear away the cheeks'[12] the character is not only describing her own tribulations but stating a general truth about the nature of grief and its effect on the sufferer's appearance and demeanour. This blurring of the distinction between the particular and the general is not unique to early Welsh poetry; there is a comparable tendency in Old English elegiac poetry[13] and even in *Beowulf*, which is formally a heroic narrative but could be characterized, in the light of its recurrent expressions of mutability and its pervasive tone of regret, as an elegiac as well as a heroic poem.[14]

A maxim can also be recognised, to some extent, by its form. Metre tends to add dignity or authority to any statement, and the compact form of the seven-syllable line of the *englyn* may well have suggested its suitability for the purpose quite early on. When poetic ornament is added, the gnomic force of the line is strengthened. 'Claf Abercuawg' provides some examples: first of all, a line which may be read either as a general observation about the world from which the sick man is excluded, or as a human maxim: *llawen gwyr oduwch llad* 'men are merry over their beer'. In another line the general truth behind the personal experience is emphasized by *cynghanedd sain*, with the same verbal juxtaposition as in Heledd's words: *ni chel grud kystud kallon* 'the face cannot hide the heart's anguish'. A similar effect is gained by repetition with variation between the end of one *englyn* and the beginning of the next, in a kind of extended stanza-linking (*cyrch-gymeriad*): *ni at Duw da i diryeit | da y dirieit ny atter* 'God does not grant good to the hapless man; to the hapless man no good shall be granted'[15] or by incremental repetition, as in the Juvencus *englynion*: *nit guorgnim molim trintaut* 'it is no great labour to praise the Trinity', *nit guorgnim molim map meir* 'it is no great labour to praise Mary's son',[16] or, in 'Claf Abercuawg' again, in a rhetorical pattern where the defective *cynghanedd* is compensated by a semantic parallel, *cas dyn yman cas duw fry* 'hateful to man here, hateful to God above'.[17]

Equally evident here is the tendency to use particular syntactical patterns to give gnomic force to a statement, especially the 'pure nominal sentence':[18] *amlwc*

---

[11] I.10c in this edition.

[12] *EWSP*, pp. 429–47, 25c.

[13] See in particular E. G. Stanley, 'Old English Poetic Diction and the Interpretation of *The Wanderer*, *The Seafarer* and *The Penitent's Prayer*', *Anglia*, lxxiii (1955), 413–66.

[14] The classic statement of this, which has by now become a scholarly commonplace, is in J. R. R. Tolkien, '*Beowulf*: The Monsters and the Critics', *PBA*, xxii (1936), 245–95.

[15] *EWSP*, p. 451, 26b, 28c, 29c, 30a.

[16] See Haycock, *BBGCC*, no. 1, 8c, 9c.

[17] *EWSP*, p. 452, 31c

[18] For an account of this, see below, on 'Language', C (1) (a).

*golwc gwyliadur* 'clear is the sight of him who watches',[19] *kadir yscuid ar yscuit glew* 'fine is a shield on a brave man's shoulder',[20] or *dricweuet llyvrder ar gur* 'cowardice is a poor endowment for a man'.[21] The same pattern is very common in the gnomic sequences: *trydyd troet y hen y ffon* 'a third foot to the aged is his staff',[22] while sentences of this type beginning with *gnawt*, or, less frequently, its antonym *odit*, for instance *gnaud gwydi traha trangc hir* 'usual after arrogance is lasting death', clearly represent a formulaic pattern.[23] This line occurs in a sequence of incremental repetition in the saga *englynion* associated with the story of Seithennin, and reappears in '*Englynion*' *y Misoedd*.

Another syntactical pattern found in several gnomic lines (though not exclusively so) is the 'hanging' construction:[24] *da y dirieit ny atter*, already quoted from 'Claf Abercuawg', is an instance, or, in a stray *englyn* printed by Jenny Rowland in *Early Welsh Saga Poetry*, *ar na wrandawer tawai* 'he who is not listened to is a silent fellow'.[25] This pattern corresponds to that in the gnomic *englynion*, as for instance in *rybud i drwch ni weryt* 'a warning to a bad lot has no effect', a line somewhat proverbial in its tone, which appears more than once;[26] the type is especially common in that extensive collection of wisdom, morality and maxims, *Gossymdeith Llefoet Wynebclawr* ('The Provision of Llefoed the Leper').[27] But perhaps the most striking example is from the Heledd saga: *vn prenn ygwydvit a gouit arnaw | o dieinc ys odit* 'one tree in a wood with sickness upon it: if it escapes it is a rare thing',[28] where a nature-maxim about a diseased tree is turned into a proverb by being applied to the fall of Cynddylan, an image which recurs later in the sequence in the line *ny elwir coed o vn prenn* 'one tree is not called a wood'.[29]

Many of these instances are proverbs, and indeed the characteristic syntactical patterns are common to the two classes of statement, as where *gwell* takes the place of *gnawt*: *gwell corrawc no chebyd* 'better a spendthrift than a miser'[30] and, though less clearly, with *gwae*: so *gwae ieueinc a eidun brotre* 'woe to the young who yearn for a bed-cover *or* brother's house'.[31] The boundaries of these different kinds of statement in the early *englynion* are fairly tenuous. It seems, however, that the difference was evident to those who composed or compiled the gnomic sequences towards the end of the twelfth century, since, whereas proverbs are comparatively infrequent in these sequences, there is an extensive

[19] *Ibid*, p. 450, 21a.
[20] I.7c in this edition.
[21] I.15c in this edition.
[22] II.30c in this edition.
[23] *EWSP*, p. 464, 4c; cf XII.4h in this edition.
[24] For an account of this, see below, on 'Language', C (3).
[25] *EWSP*, p. 467, 1c.
[26] II.33c, VI.2c in this edition.
[27] IX in this edition.
[28] *EWSP*, p. 429, 2a-b.
[29] *Ibid.*, p. 431, 16c.
[30] *Ibid.*, p. 448, 4c.
[31] *Ibid.*, p. 429, 1d.

collection of them in the roughly contemporary poem known as *Englynion y Clyweit*.[32] There are also sequences of moralistic or preceptual *englynion* with little or no proverbial element, such as *Kyssul Adaon*[33] and some parts of *Englynion Duad*. The so-called *Englynion y Misoedd* ('Stanzas of the Months'), which are not *englynion* at all but eight-line heptasyllabic stanzas,[34] are also full of proverbs as well as maxims in the broader sense and moral observations; this is a late composition, but a comparable mixture is to be found in *Gossymdeith Llefoet Wynebclawr*, a text in rhymed sections (*caniadau*) of irregular length probably dating from the twelfth century. It is possible that there were two parallel traditions,[35] and that the authors or compilers of the *englyn* sequences were more reluctant than the others to accept too much mixture of material, but if so the reason for the difference remains unclear, and the fact that gnomic and moralistic sequences occur side by side in *Englynion Duad* suggests that the compilers at least did not always regard the distinction as significant.[36]

### B. Gnomic, Proverbial and Saga Poetry

According to Kenneth Jackson's hypothesis some kind of pure gnomic poetry, with no admixture of natural description, must have already existed before the composition of the saga *englynion*. This, in his view, is the source of the gnomic lines with which these *englynion* are peppered.[37] Unfortunately, no such text survives, but only a number of collections of proverbs, beginning with that in the Black Book of Chirk towards the middle of the thirteenth century.[38] Since the gnomic *englynion* of the Red Book of Hergest are to be dated at least half a century, if not a century earlier, and the partly gnomic sequence *Llym awel* in the Black Book of Carmarthen probably some time before that, there is no means of proving that any such proverb-collection was in existence before the mixed gnomic poetry which survives, and, as Jackson himself showed, we find among them the occasional proverb which derives from a misunderstanding of a line from the gnomic or saga poems.[39] On the other hand, there is no need to assume that all the maxims in the proverb-collections are late: though there is no evidence for gnomic poetry as such at an early date, it is hard to believe that there were no maxims at all in Welsh before the composition of the saga *englynion*. We may compare the situation in Irish, where a number of collections

---

[32] For a text of this poem, with modern Welsh translation, see *BBGCC*, pp. 313–37.

[33] For this and related poems, see *BBGCC*, pp. 283–96.

[34] XII in this edition.

[35] Jackson, *ECNP*, p. 147, suggests that the late *Eiry mynydd* poems in long stanzas (not edited here), and, by implication, '*Englynion' y Misoedd*, represent a conflation of these two traditions.

[36] The gnomic elements of this collection are printed as VI and (in part ) III in this edition; the rest are edited with translation by Jenny Rowland, '"Englynion Duad"', *JCS*, iii (1981), 59–87.

[37] *ECNP*, pp. 135, 141.

[38] See Ifor Williams, 'Y Diarhebion yn y Llyfr Du o'r Waun', *BBCS*, iii (1926–27), 22–31. A valuable alphabetically arranged collection of proverbs from various sources may be found in William Hay, *Diarhebion Cymru* (Liverpool, 1955).

[39] *ECNP*, pp. 142–43.

of maxims and proverbs are preserved, some as early as the eighth century if the arguments of their latest editor are correct.[40] These collections are not in verse, but many of them exhibit alliteration, an aid to memory which may be regarded as half way to full metrical form; and even if no comparable collections existed in Welsh as early as that, a number of maxims must have been generally known, even without any formal arrangement. It might be expected that some of these might have had six or seven syllables in their original form, and thus have been suitable for use in an *englyn milwr* or an *englyn penfyr*. The great number of Irish proverbs of the type *tosach féle fairsinge* 'generosity is the beginning of nobility' or *ferr carae cormaim* 'a friend is better than ale' afford a parallel to the numerous pure nominal sentences in the Welsh poems and especially *gwell corrawc no chebyd* 'better prodigal than a miser' in 'Claf Abercuawg'.

At first sight, there is no reason to expect pure nature descriptions in the gnomic sequences, and their presence needs explanation. Since Jackson was arguing on the supposition that the sequences derived from pure gnomic poetry, he was obliged to assume that the saga sequences also played a part in their development. In these poems natural descriptions are used to provide a background and an appropriate atmosphere for the words of the characters in the same way as in the Old English elegies; they are thus obviously relevant in a way in which they are not in the gnomic poetry. According to Jackson's hypothesis, saga *englynion* of this type were incorporated in the gnomic sequences because the two types of *englyn* were so similar in their general structure — the one beginning with a nature-maxim, the other with a natural description, but both continuing with concise observations about human life in its practical or moral aspects. This pattern was generalised, it is suggested, to provide a pattern for the mixed gnomic poetry of the Red Book and other collections.[41] The argument could be supported by reference to the device of incremental repetition, which is probably to be traced back to the saga poetry where it is so prominent and has an evident rhetorical function.

It is difficult to prove a negative, and it would be rash to claim that no such sequence of events as Jackson suggests could ever have happened. But if so great a degree of influence from the saga poetry on the gnomic tradition be accepted, there may be no need to assume a primitive tradition of pure gnomic poetry at all. On the principle of the simplest explanation it may be argued that the sequences of gnomic stanzas are a secondary development on the base of certain elements in the saga poetry. Nor is it necessary to assume, as Jackson suggests,[42] the influence of a supposed tradition of seasonal poetry connected with popular observances celebrating the coming of summer and mourning its departure, though the possibility cannot of course be ruled out; once the formal pattern was established, it would be perfectly natural to give unity to a sequence with

[40] Colin Ireland, ed., *Old Irish Wisdom*, pp. 34–38.
[41] *ECNP*, pp. 181–190.
[42] *ECNP*, pp. 149–62

some such formula as *Kalan gaeaf* 'First day of winter'. More plausible, though Jackson is more sceptical about it, is the influence of the tradition of calendar poetry exemplified in Old Irish and, to a smaller degree, Old English, and based originally on ecclesiastical calendars.[43] Whereas the series of *englynion* beginning *Calan tachwedd* 'First of November'[44] could be a secondary development from a *kalan gaeaf* series, especially since the two phrases refer to the same day, and a similar origin is possible for the eight-line stanzas of *Neud kalan Ionawr* 'It is the first of January', and, ultimately, *'Englynion' y Misoedd*,[45] the calendar tradition remains a possible influence on all three.[46]

Rather strangely, saga elements are occasionally found in the gnomic sequences as well as the converse. These are on the whole personal exclamations, for instance in the compound sequence *Baglawc bydin*, where the flow of ideas is suddenly interrupted with the words *Duw reen, py bereist lyvwr* 'Lord God, why did you make a coward?'[47] or in the *Eiry mynyd* sequence, quite unexpectedly: *Och rac hiraeth fy mrodyr* 'Alas for my grief for my brothers!'[48] Such saga elements are to all appearance wholly irrelevant to the main matter of the poetry, and because they are so infrequent it is easy to see them as extraneous elements. By an extension of Jackson's hypothesis, some such elements could have been drawn into the gnomic poetry in the same way as those of pure natural description: perhaps, at its simplest, because an extraneous stanza begins with the same formula as the rest, as in the case of the *Eiry mynyd* series. On the other hand they could be explained according to the alternative hypothesis as the remains of saga poetry which happened to survive the process of selection and expansion which gave rise to the gnomic sequences.

Part of this process may have left traces in three texts: in the sequence 'Claf Abercuawg', which stands in the Red Book of Hergest between the gnomic poems and the Llywarch Hen series, as if the compiler saw it as a bridge between the two; in the sequence *Baglawc bydin* in the same manuscript, and in the compound sequence *Llym awel* from the Black Book of Carmarthen.[49] There is no doubt about the saga content of the first of these, a monologue put in the mouth of a sick man whose illness prevents him from fighting and keeps him in isolation on a remote farmstead. But the natural descriptions in it are so

[43] *Ibid.*, pp. 162–70: Jackson makes a very fair case for the hypothesis before finally rejecting it. For an Old English calendar poem, see *The Menologium*, in *The Anglo-Saxon Minor Poems*, ed. E. van K. Dobbie (ASPR VI, New York and London, 1942), pp, 49–55.

[44] VI. 8–18 in this edition, following on from seven *Calan gaeaf* stanzas and concluding with another. On metrical grounds the second part of this composite sequence seems slightly earlier than the first, but not so much so as to affect the argument. See Jenny Rowland, '"Englynion Duad"', at 64–65; Jacobs, 'Englynion Calan Gaeaf a'r Misoedd', at 74–76.

[45] XI and XII in this edition.

[46] XII A 9a-b provide slight evidence for the influence of ecclesiastical tables or calendars at least in the last stages of the tradition; see note to those lines, and, for detailed discussion, Jacobs, 'Nodiadau ar y Canu Gwirebol. I', at 73–74.

[47] VII. 9c in this edition.

[48] II.21c in this edition.

[49] VII and I respectively in this edition.

extensive and so memorable that they often quite overshadow the saga material, and there are also gnomic sections where the character and his story seem virtually forgotten.

This evident shift of emphasis may be reflected in the rather more complicated structure of the sequence *Llym awel*. This poem contains extensive elements of pure natural description as well as of pure saga poetry, with a mixture of the two together with some human maxims in some of the stanzas. Three separate sections are apparent here. In the first the description of winter is used as a background for a dialogue on cowardice between two unnamed characters; this section is associated with the story of Llywarch Hen by the presence of a stanza which both Kenneth Jackson and Jenny Rowland reasonably regard as extraneous.[50] In the second section, which Rowland, perhaps rightly, sees as a continuation of the first, there is another winter dialogue, this time between a character named Pelis and another unnamed hero, who speak of a night expedition to free Owain ab Urien from captivity. In the third section we find an account of the death of Mechydd, son of Llywarch Hen. In this section there is no reference to the winter except in one stanza, which appears in fact to belong to the second section, while a further complication arises from the presence of two further stanzas which Rowland has identified as belonging to yet another saga concerning Rhun ap Maelgwn.[51]

On one view this mixture is merely an example of the tendency for the débris of lost stories to accumulate like a terminal moraine at the foot of a glacier, with no clear purpose behind their juxtaposition. But there may be an element of editorial intention behind the series: the connexions between themes, characters and descriptions could have drawn together a number of fragments not originally associated. Moreover, the connexion between the anonymous dialogue and the story of Pelis may be seen from a different standpoint again: the tendency to mix natural description with gnomic or moral observations may have already become so strong a poetic convention that the narrative content of the two sections had become comparatively unimportant to whoever grafted them together. Whether the copyist transmitted the sequence more or less as it came down to him or was himself responsible for putting it together, this composite sequence may exemplify a shift from pure saga poetry towards gnomic poetry, though any decision as to where one ends and the other begins is evidently quite arbitrary.

The evidence of the sequence *Baglawc bydin* in the Red Book of Hergest points the same way. Here the last four stanzas, beginning *Glaw allan* and containing the line *Duw reen py bereist lyvwr?* 'Lord God, why did you make a coward?', are similar in subject-matter to the first section of *Llym awel*, while three of the four beginning *Marchwieil* have evidently, as Jackson suggests, been drawn in from a

---

[50] Stanza 19: see *EWGP*, p. 45; *EWSP*, pp. 233, 634.
[51] *EWSP*, pp.236–38.

lost saga.[52] This sequence, accordingly, is not gnomic poetry in the full sense, but its place in the manuscript — between *Kalan gaeaf* and *Gorwynion* — suggests that the compiler of the Red Book of Hergest considered it of a kind with the other gnomic sequences. The mixture of gnomic poetry and natural description may thus have become important in itself at the expense of the coherence of the saga material, until it finally displaced it altogether to give rise to the gnomic sequences that have come down to us.

## C. Biblical, Old English and Scandinavian Parallels

The possibility of external influences on this process must not be disregarded. The most obvious potential source is the Bible. Yet, though occasional passages of nature poetry occur in the wisdom literature of the Old Testament, they are used either as examples of the glory of God the Creator or as moral images:[53] these passages are strikingly dissimilar to Welsh gnomic poetry. What are more usually found are moral precepts; but though some lines in the gnomic poetry are similar to these, and sequences like *Kyssul Adaon* or the moralistic sections of *Englynion Duad* closer still, the Book of Proverbs and similar texts are unlikely models either for the form or for the content of the gnomic poems. The closest parallel is perhaps the juxtaposition of cosmology and law in the composite text of the eighteenth Psalm (the nineteenth in the English Bible and Book of Common Prayer), *Caeli enarrant gloriam Dei* 'the heavens declare the glory of God'. But no early commentary on that psalm drawing attention to this aspect of it has yet come to light.

Line by line, there are frequent similarities between Welsh texts and Old English gnomic poetry,[54] yet, when the respective poems are taken as a whole, the Old English poems provide even less of a model for the Welsh poems than the wisdom poetry in the Bible. The most recent editor of the Old English texts, Thomas Shippey, suggests that 'gnomic poetry' is in this case too limiting a term,[55] and it is true that these poems contain a greater proportion of moral advice and abstruse knowledge of the mysteries of the universe than is to be found in those Welsh poems generally considered as gnomic; much of their material is in fact closer to that found in the Book of Taliesin.[56] There are, nevertheless, some purely gnomic sequences — three of them, by Shippey's

---

[52] *EWGP*, p. 46.

[53] The most striking examples are in Job xxxv-xli; compare also Psalms civ and (in part), cxlvii, together with Ecclesiasticus xlii:15 — xliii: 27.

[54] Jackson, *EWGP*, p.2, compares Old English 'a bear is to be found in the woods' and 'a gadding woman gives rise to comment' to Welsh 'usual is the nest of an eagle in the top of an oak' and 'a bad woman causes frequent scandals' respectively.

[55] *Poems of Wisdom and Learning*, p. 12; all relevant texts are edited here with modern English translation, see especially pp. 64–79, 130–34. As Shippey had earlier suggested (*Old English Verse* (London, 1970), p. 67), they are better viewed as 'wisdom literature' in the broader sense. See also Morton W. Bloomfield, 'Understanding Old English Poetry', *Annuale Medievale*, 9 (1968), 5–25.

[56] These texts are edited, with Modern Welsh translations, by Haycock in *BBGCC*.

account, in the celebrated tenth-century anthology known as the Exeter Book,[57] and a fourth, which as it stands belongs to the eleventh century, in British Library MS Cotton Tiberius B. I. These may form a basis for comparison with the Welsh gnomic *englynion*.

Once again, there is some similarity between the Welsh and the English texts as regards subject-matter: both mix nature-maxims and human maxims in such a way as to suggest a purpose or concept common to both. But that is the only similarity between them. It would be rash to claim, given the frequent difficulty of distinguishing between them and nature-maxims, that there are no pure natural descriptions in the English poems; but there are certainly fewer examples which cannot be read as general observations on the nature of the world than in the Welsh poems. Indeed, the structure of the poems in the two languages is entirely different. Instead of a series of independent stanzas, with almost every stanza constructed on a regular pattern which would permit the development of lines of pure description as an element in them, we find in Old English sequences of short observations on widely varied matters following no particular pattern. For instance, the poem called by Shippey *Maxims* I A presents a fairly coherent discussion of the social order in the context of God's purpose; *Maxims* I B a largely disconnected series of brief statements on various subjects; *Maxims* I C a similar series but one given some coherence by an general overtone of fear and existential gloom, and *Maxims* II a sequence of human and nature-gnomes unsystematically jumbled up together. Some of these appear at first sight disorganized, yet within each of them there is some kind of conceptual connexion, however arbitrary or fanciful, which results in some sort of sequential statement.[58]

In short, where Welsh gnomic poetry is disconnected and concise, Old English gnomic poetry is connected and discursive. It would be very hard to imagine that either could have provided a model for the other, unless indeed there is some Old English influence on *Gossymdeith Llefoet Wynebclawr*, which exhibits a similarly disorganized mixture of human maxims and moral and religious precepts, together with the occasional reference to the natural world. But both chronology and cultural history are against this supposition; the Welsh poem was probably composed in the twelfth century, at a time when classical Old English poetry had ceased to be accessible except to the rare antiquarian and when any cultural influences from beyond the border would have been Anglo-Norman rather than Anglo-Saxon. If there is any foreign influence on this poem,

---

[57] See Gameson, 'The origin of the Exeter Book of Old English Poetry', who gives, at 166, a date of c. 960–980. Sisam, *Studies in the History of Old English Literature*, p. 97, argued that the MS 'was transcribed continuously from a collection already made'; however that may be, the *Maxims* are evidently a compilation, and the constituent material can hardly be later than the first half of the century, considerably earlier, that is, than any of the Welsh poems can be demonstrated to have existed.

[58] On the difficulty of identifying the function of these poems, see Shippey, *Poems of Wisdom and Learning*, pp.18–19. Shippey's expression of honest puzzlement is addressed, but not satisfactorily answered, by Cavill, *Maxims*, pp. 156–83.

it is more likely to have been Norse than English, in view of some similarities with the Old Norse *Havamál*, some parts of which may be as early as 960 and thus could have circulated in oral form in the period of Welsh-Norse political contacts associated with the career of Gruffudd ap Cynan (c. 1055–1137).[59]

Indeed, even in the case of the stanzaic gnomic poetry, the closest parallel is not in Old English but in Old Norwegian. There is one instance each in Old English, Old Norwegian and Old Icelandic of a rune-poem, an alphabetic poem, that is, with one stanza for each letter of the runic alphabet.[60] The English and Icelandic examples are of no relevance here, since they contain nothing beside observations on the objects after which the letters are named, but in the case of the Norwegian poem there is a regular pattern of two-line stanzas, the first naming the letter with a short description, the second giving a moral or religious maxim in a manner very similar to that of the third line in the Welsh gnomic stanzas. Unlike the Old English gnomic poems, this series is considerably later than most of the Welsh gnomic poetry, and since there is only one instance to set against the comparative wealth of texts in Welsh, it is unlikely to represent a long tradition which could have influenced the development of the Welsh material earlier on (in the time of Gruffudd ap Cynan, for example) so as to generate such gnomic sequences as those in the Red Book of Hergest. Influence in the other direction remains a possibility.

## D. Welsh Gnomic Poetry: Development and Function

It seems, then, that the existence of Welsh gnomic poetry as we have it cannot be accounted for to any significant extent by the influence either of the Bible or of the vernacular literature of adjacent cultures. The causes of the development must be sought and the function of the poetry explored within the Welsh tradition.

Two stanzas from 'Claf Abercuawg' may serve to illuminate the process. The first runs as follows:

> *Gordyar adar; gwlyb gro.*
> *Deil cwydit; divryt divro.*
> *Ny wadaf, wyf claf heno*

'Clamorous are the birds; wet is the gravel. Leaves fall; disconsolate is the man with no homeland. I do not deny it, I am sick tonight'. There are two natural descriptions in the first line, followed by a nature-maxim and a human maxim in the second. The logic of the connexion between the nature- and human maxims

---

[59] For an account of these contacts, see D. Simon Evans, ed. *Historia Gruffudd vab Kenan*, pp. lxxv-lxxxi, xciv-xcix. On the *Havamál*, see Larrington, *A Store of Common Sense*; also her review of D. A. H. Evans, ed., *Havamál* (London, 1986), in *Saga-Book of the Viking Society*, xxii (1987), 127–30.

[60] See Dickins, ed., *Runic and Heroic Poems*; for more recent editions of the English poem, Shippey, *Poems of Wisdom and Learning*, pp. 80–85, 135–36; M. Halsall, *The Old English Rune Poem*.

is the first and easiest step. It is the nature of leaves to fall; it is natural for an exile to lose heart. The two propositions follow naturally from the order of the world; one is as inevitably true as the other, and the fundamental truths of human life have a status comparable to that of the motions of the sun and moon or the cycle of the seasons.

A further development may be seen in another stanza:

> *Alaf yn eil; meil am ved.*
> *Nyt eidun detwyd dyhed.*
> *Amaerwy adnabot amyned*

'Cattle in shelter, mead in the cup. The happy man does not desire trouble. Patience is the girdle of understanding *or* self-knowledge'. Though these lines can be applied to the situation of the sick man, this is essentially a gnomic stanza. Rather than the pure natural descriptions in the first line of the earlier stanza, this is an observation about living creatures in their relationship with the human world together with one about the behaviour of men as social beings. But whereas the second line, as in the previous case, states a truth about human nature, in the third the limits of the discussion are extended to embrace a moral observation. Patience is the girdle of understanding: when patience fails, there is an end to a man's efforts to know himself. Numerous similar collocations, elsewhere in the poetry, of human maxims of a factual and a moral kind imply that truths regarding the moral order were perceived as having the same status as those concerning human nature and the nature of the world.

The principle can be extended to the particular observations about nature and human behaviour in the two stanzas. It is not an eternal truth that birds are noisy or that gravel is wet, but it is in the nature of birds to compete in singing early on a summer morning, and gravel becomes wet from the evening or morning dew, from the rain or from the overflowing of streams, all of which are part of the order of the seasons. It is not in the nature of cattle to be in a byre, but it is good husbandry to keep them in shelter against the winter weather; cups are not always full of drink, but the long evenings of winter are both a cause and an opportunity for revelry. In the context of the saga it may be little consolation to the sick man of Abercuog that his sufferings are as inevitable as the seasons and part of the often inscrutable workings of Providence. But as far as the gnomic element is concerned, every natural description may be seen as a concrete example of the order of the world; its characteristic combination of different sorts of observation about the world emphasizes the unity of the physical and the moral universe, and to some degree celebrates the purpose of God, both in the creation which, as we are told in the first chapter of Genesis, He saw was very good, and in the moral order which determines the position of humanity within that creation. Given that the sequences which have come down to us probably developed by a process of accretion, it is not necessary that everyone who added to them had so conscious a motivation. The nature of the sequences, with their pattern of incremental repetition, is such as to encourage the incorporation of similar stanzas, and their mere existence is sufficient motivation for the composition of more such stanzas.

This, then, is a possible conceptual motivation for the gnomic poetry. If so, there is no need to consider the elements of pure nature poetry in it as an alien intrusion to be explained only by reference to its function in the 'saga poetry'. Even if such an origin were to be accepted, it would be necessary to allow that their function has changed. They no longer set a context, as they still do in *Llym awel*, but have come to illuminate the general through the particular. And thus, if Jackson's hypothesis of an original tradition of pure gnomic poetry unconnected with the saga poems proved after all to be correct, there would be no difficulty in accepting that elements of nature poetry had been part of it from the beginning. On the other hand, the existence of texts such as 'Claf Abercuawg', *Llym awel* and *Baglawc bydin*, which may be seen as representing an intermediate stage between saga and gnomic poetry, suggest that the concept of the unity of the physical and moral universes gained ground only by degrees, gradually shifting the emphasis in these texts from the story itself towards meditations on the order of the world and so providing a rationale for the gnomic poetry which reached the height of its popularity around the twelfth century.

One possibility of influence from outside Wales remains, in the shape of the principle of interpreting the whole world as a book in which the nature of God could be read. This idea is given expression for the first time, as far as is known, in the first half of the twelfth century in the work of Hugh of St Victor and his circle.[61] If the sequences in the Red Book of Hergest were to be dated, as is possible, in the second half of the century, they could be considered, tentatively, as a poetical response to the notion. But, as has been suggested earlier, these texts are better seen as the product of a gradual development, whose first stages may be observed in sequences such as 'Claf Abercuawg' and *Llym awel*, both of them probably considerably earlier than *Eiry mynyd* and the like or the supposed Victorine influences on them. If so, these influences would merely have confirmed an already evident tendency to emphasize the gnomic elements and finally to concentrate on them.

For the desire to read moral lessons in the natural world was not unfamiliar even before the twelfth century, as can be seen in the development of the *Physiologus* or Bestiary tradition. This tradition goes back to a Greek composition (as its title implies) of the early Christian period; the Latin versions circulated widely in the West, and one, at least in part, was known in England by the tenth century, for a version of parts of it survives in the Exeter Book.[62] Though there may be no need to seek a specific literary or philosophical source, the popularity

---

[61] See Curtius, tr. Trask, *European Literature and the Latin Middle Ages*, pp. 319–26.

[62] For a full account, see Wirtjes, *The Middle English Physiologus*, pp. lxviii-xci, to whom I am indebted for the previous reference.

of the *Physiologus* suggests that the idea of the natural world as a mirror of the moral world could have stimulated the increasing tendency to select and develop the gnomic elements in the poetry. It is possible, too, that the influence of the *Benedicite*, which is evident in the nine Juvencus englynion and the poem 'Gogoneddog Arglwydd' from the Black Book of Carmarthen,[63] is at work here; this canticle, drawn from the apocryphal portion of the book of Daniel, calls on a wide range of natural objects and phenomena to bless and praise the Lord.[64] If it can be accepted that the gnomic sequences in the Red Book of Hergest are a product of this process, it is possible to appreciate them not only, or indeed primarily, as examples of the unpretentious excellence of folk wisdom but also as part of the harvest of the intellectual movements of the Middle Ages. If, further, the philosophical developments of the school of Paris are allowed to have had a part in the process, some at least of the gnomic stanzas in the Red Book may be thought to take their place in European cultural history as an echo, if only a distant echo, of that intellectual revolution which has come to be known as the twelfth-century renaissance.[65]

## Language and Date

### A. Orthography

Three spelling systems appear in the texts edited here: the standard late Middle Welsh system exemplified by the Red Book of Hergest;[66] that associated with the Black Book of Carmarthen, a system apparently prevalent in Deheubarth in the second half of the thirteenth century;[67] and the Early Modern Welsh system found in manuscripts of the sixteenth century and later. A monograph on the subject is much to be desired; what follows is merely an attempt to provide a basic guide.

(1) Characteristic of all three systems are the following:

    (a) the use of <k> where ModW has <c>. This is almost universal before *e*, *i* and *y* and very common before *a*, less regular before other vowels and before consonants.

---

[63] See *BBGCC*, nos. 1 and 5.

[64] Dan. iii: 57–90 in the Vulgate; Song of the Three Children 35–68 in the English Bible. It is most conveniently accessible in English in the *Book of Common Prayer*, where it appears as the *Benedicite* as part of the Order for Morning Prayer; compare also Psalm cxlviii.

[65] As defined originally by Haskins, *The Renaissance of the Twelfth Century*.

[66] Also, some decades earlier, in the White Book of Rhydderch, though no text edited here appears in that MS. For a detailed account of mediaeval Welsh poetic manuscripts, see Daniel Huws, *Medieval Welsh Manuscripts*, especially pp. 65–83.

[67] A further spelling-system used in North Wales at the same time is described in Roberts, *Brut y Brenhinedd*, but is not used in any of the texts edited here.

(b) the frequent use of <u> or <v> where modern Welsh has <f>. This is particularly clear in the standard system, though even there <f> is usual at the end of a word; <f> is beginning to encroach in the Early Modern Welsh system, but is not yet dominant. For the use of <w> in the Black Book, see below.

(c) the use of *i* or *y* for the third person possessive pronoun (ModW *ei*).

(2) Characteristic of the two earlier systems are the following:

(a) The diphthongs in monosyllables or final syllables written in ModW as <ai>, <au> are always written <ei>, <eu> respectively.

(b) The lenited and unlenited forms of *r* are not differentiated.

(c) What is historically the lenited form of /g/, which normally disappears altogether in Middle Welsh, may be written occasionally after a final consonant as <y>, as in I.5a, II.1a etc. *eiry*. This later became a vowel, as in ModW *eira; gwala*, or was lost altogether, but in at least some cases it is a non-syllabic consonant, perhaps similar to the glide heard in French *Le Havre* etc. In VIII.1c the variant readings *bronnwaly* and *brongwala* show respectively the above development and the failure to mark the mutation of /g/ at all; this suggests an exemplar in an older spelling-system.

(d) The treatment of the nasal mutation is not consistent, but varies with the place of articulation of the radical consonant:

   (i) The mutation of *p* and *b* after *yn* is quite regularly shown merely by the change of *n* to *m*, the following consonant being left as it stands: IV.2b *ym plith*; I.3c *im bluch*, II.30a *ym bronn*, IV.7a, VIII.1b *ym blaen*. IX.17 *ymro* is an exception, and cf. II.21c *vy mrodyr*.

   (ii) The texts have no example of nasal mutation of a dental, unless IX.71 *yntywyll* and II.18b *yn diddos* are to be so interpreted. If so, the pattern would correspond to that of the labials.

   (iii) The representation of the mutation of *k* and *g* is complicated by varying representations of the relevant sounds. For ModW <ng> (/ŋ/) the Black Book has <g> (I.10b *llog*, 20c *dieigc* (ModW *llong, diainc*); for <ngh> it has <gh> (22c *kighor*, cf. ModW *cynghori*). *Yn* is reduced to its vowel, giving <ig-> for ModW <yng ng-> and <ig k/c-> for <yng ngh->; so I.12a *igogaur*, 14a *ig keithiw*, 15a *ig klidur*. In the standard orthography, outside the context of mutation, <ng> is written as in ModW. So is <ngh> in IX (33 *anghyfaelywr*, 59 *enghit*, 67 *trenghyt*, *denghyn*), but in the *englynion* it appears as <gh> (VIII.17c *aghywir*, 30c *agheluydyt*). For ModW <yng ng->, <yg g-> or <yngg> is written, so IV.5b *yg gweunyd*, IX.44 *ynggnif*; for <yng ngh-> most commonly <yg k->, but also <y gh>, <yn gh>, so IV.7b *yg kyfrdy*, II.15c *y gherwyn*, III.5b *yn gheudawt*.

(e) Where the groups *rm, rf, lm, lf, df* (≡ ModW *ddf*) or any consonant followed by *l, n,* or *r,* occur at the end of a word (or of an element in a compound), a 'parasitic' or 'anaptyctic' vowel is commonly written between the two consonants. This is normally 'obscure' *y* and so written, but in monosyllables it comes increasingly with time to be assimilated to the preceding vowel and takes the appropriate form: so, in the Red Book, II.8 *daraf, araf, corof* for *darf, arf, corf.* This evidently represents a development in pronunciation, since a corresponding vowel appears in spoken ModW, especially in Southern dialects, but the vowel is never counted in scansion in the mediaeval period.

(3) The standard orthography is used in extracts II, III (with the exception of those stanzas which do not occur in the Red Book), IV, V, VII, VIII, IX and X, though sporadic traces of the Black Book system appear in many of these. The chief characteristics of this orthography are as follows:[68]

(a) The voiceless plosives *c/k, p* and *t* are written thus at the beginning of a word. Intervocalically they are usually doubled to <ck>, <pp> and <tt>: so II.29c *meckyt,* 6c *dywetter,* but in our texts single <p> is written, as in II.35b *gwypo.* These voiceless intervocalic consonants are not common, but occur where a voiced consonant was originally followed by *h,* most commonly in verb forms (especially subjunctives and the third-person present forms in -*it*). The spellings <c>, <p>, <t> at the end of a word, where unvoiced plosives never occur, represent the corresponding voiced sounds; see the next paragraph.

(b) The voiced plosives *b, d* and *g* are spelt thus at the beginning of a word, as in ModW. Within a word, they are written as <b> (always), <d> (always) and <g> (usually): II.13b *uabolaeth,* 20b *hebawc;* 9b *dywedeis;* IV.4a *dygyuor,* 4b *uagu* (II.20b *bacwyawc,* IV.3a *gocled* are evidently survivals of an older spelling-system). But at the end of a word (or of an element in a compound) they appear respectively as <p> (often), <t> and <c>: so II. 36b *pop* (but 36c *pob*), 3c *odit, dirieit,* 6d *atwen,* 9c *anhebic* (ModW *pob, odid, adwaen, diriaid, annhebyg*).

(c) The lenited forms of *b* and *d,* /v/ and /ð/, written <f>and<dd> in ModW, are written as <u> or <v> and as <d> respectively. It will be seen that in consequence <d> in initial or intervocalic position is ambiguous and may initially cause confusion, and that the soft mutation of /d/ cannot be shown even where it occurs.

(d) <sc> occurs side by side with <sg> within a word (II.1c *trachyscu,* 8c *ysgynnu;* <sc> finally (20a *pysc*). <sb> does not occur in any of the texts here

---

[68] A feature of this and other manuscripts of the period is the frequent use in place of <w> of a letter resembling the figure 6. This is reproduced by Jackson in *EWGP*, but or the sake of simplicity <w> is printed in this edition, as it is by Rowland in *EWSP*.

printed (contrast III.14a *diaspat*, VIII. 28a *yspydat*), but the combination is rare and its absence may not be significant. It is by no means clear that these spellings have any phonological significance; the second consonant may have remained unvoiced in all cases.

(e) Exceptionally in II.10a *hellawt*, <ll> stands not for *ll* as in ModW but for a double consonant resulting from *l* plus earlier lenited *g*; see above, 2(c).

(4) The Black Book system is used in extract I, and occasional traces of it elsewhere suggest that a text has been copied from a manuscript in which it was used. Because it retains a few characteristics of Old Welsh orthography it has a notably archaic appearance and is at first sight puzzling; it is indeed older than the standard system, but not all texts in this spelling are necessarily older than one in the Red Book spelling. The chief peculiarities of this system, and those most likely to cause difficulty, are as follows:

(a) The use of <i>, <u>, <v> and <y> is confusing and often ambiguous; there is unfortunately no short cut to its understanding.

   (i) <i> is used commonly but not exclusively instead of standard <y> as well as for *i* : 1a *brin, clid,* 1b *llin,* 4a *pisscaud,* 6b *iscuit,* 15a *ig klidur* for ModW *bryn, clyd, llyn, pyscawd, ysgwydd, yng nghlydwr* etc; but note 3a *brythuch,* 7a *ysguid,* 11b *llyri,* 18a *mynit* where 'obscure' *y* is written <y>; and conversely <y> for *i* in 5c *llyu* for ModW *lliw*.

   (ii) <u> is used commonly but not exclusively instead of standard <w> as well as its functions in the standard orthography (vowel or consonant, ModW <u> and <f>): 1a *llum, anhaut,* 1c *gur,* 5a *guin,* 9c *annuyd* for ModW *llwm, anhawdd, gwr, gwyn, annwyd*. But initially <w> is used for *w,* not <u> or <v>, and <u> does not replace <f> finally: 7a *gwarthaw* for *gwarthaf.* 7a *reo* for ModW *rhew* is an exceptional OW spelling.

   (iii) <v> can replace <u> for any of these sounds: 1c *vn,* 4c *gvyrhaud,* 9a *dv, riv,* 10c *llvwyr,* 14c *divlit,* 15c *lyvrder* for ModW *un, gwyrhawd, du, rhiw, llwfr, diwlydd, llyfrder*.

(b) The treatment of dental consonants is quite distinct and at first sight eccentric, but is easily understood. <d> stands for /d/ in whatever position, never for /ð/ (ModW <dd>) as it does, other than initially, in the standard system. The latter sound is represented by <t>: 1a *anhaut,* 2b *gwaetev,* 6b *iscuit,* 9b *goruit,* 10a *mynit,* 11a *eurtirn* for ModW *an+hawdd (anodd), gwaeddau, ysgwydd, gorwydd, mynydd, eurddyrn*. 9c *hawdit* appears to be an exception: *hawtit* would be expected, and 12b *diulith* written for ModW *diwlydd* (instead of *diulit* or *-vlit* as in 14c) is exceptional. Initially, however, <t> represents its normal sound, which is represented intervocalically (where it derives from *d + h*) as <tt>: 5a etc. *ottid*.

(c) The treatment of *c/k*, *p* and *t* is much as in the standard system, except that <cc> is preferred to <ck> (10c *meccid*) and <pp> occurs (13c *dyppo*). The same may be said for that of *b* and *g*.

(d) <w> is used with great regularity finally instead of <f> (≡ /v/): 1c *seiw*, 3a *gaeaw*, 8c *aw*, *anaw* for ModW *saif*, *gaeaf*, *af*, *anaf*; and less consistently within a word for the same sound, whether before or after another consonant or intervocalically: 9c *hawdit*, 15b *ewur*, 15c *dricweuet*, 17c *llyw*, 18b *treuit* for ModW *hafddydd*, *efwr*, *drygfeuedd*, *llif*, *trefydd*.

(e) <sc> is regularly written where ModW has <sg>: 4a *pisscaud*, 6b *yscuid*, etc., and <sscc> in 23c *ffissccau*; but note also 7b *gosgupid*.

(5) The Early Modern Welsh system is used in extracts VI, XI and XII; in the last of these the language is itself EModW, the other two are much older. The system is essentially that still in use today, with the special features listed under (1), but a few older features are still found. Those occurring in VI and XI may have been carried over from earlier copies, but in the case of XII they may be genuine survivals.

(a) <c> still occurs for final /g/: so XII.1d *gwac*, 3a *rhyfic*, 5f *koc*, 8h *drwc*.

(b) It is only in the EModW period that <rh> comes to be used for unlenited *r*, and for some time the spelling is not stable, <rr> being sometimes found, presumably on the analogy of <ll>. So XII.6g *anrrydedd*, (B)12a *rragfyr*.[69]

(c) The spelling of some diphthongs has not yet stabilised. Note in particular VI.1a *gauaf*, XII.3g *ddaiar* for ModW <ae>; 7f *mowrair*, (B)10c *llownfras* for ModW <aw> (this may represent a dialectal pronunciation, cf 4f *kowir* for ModW *kywir*);[70] 12g *hoydl* for ModW <oe>.

(d) <v> is often used where <u> appears in the earlier orthography, and may stand for the vowel *u* as well as for the consonant *f*. These spellings are particularly characteristic of the manuscript used as the base of the text of XII.

## B. Phonology and Accidence

(1) The main grammatical difficulty lies in a number of old verbal forms. Almost all of these, understandably in view of the nature of the texts, are third person

---

[69] Conversely, <lh> occurs in some sixteenth-century MSS for /ll/, but not in any of those used as a base for the editions in this volume.

[70] Iwan Wmffre, *Language and Place-Names in Wales*, demonstrates (pp. 334–35) that /yw/, /aw/ in penultimate syllables were already becoming /ow/ in most if not all dialects by the sixteenth and seventeenth centuries respectively. In monosyllables such as *mawr*, *Mawrth*, the pronunciation with /ow/ has today, with one or two odd anomalies, a decidedly south-western distribution; see A. R. Thomas, ed., *The Welsh Dialect Survey* (Cardiff, 2000), nos. 441, 586, 594. The exact significance of the spellings is thus unclear.

singular, and most are present indicative; they are treated at greater length by D. Simon Evans in *GMW* §§129–31.

(a) Forms in *-id* and *-yd* (the so-called 'absolute' form), spelt thus in the orthography of the Black Book, *-it, -yt* in the standard system (see A 3(b), 4(b) above); see *GMW* §129 (d)(1). In the Black Book, and sporadically elsewhere, this termination appears as *-hid*; the effect of this *h*, whose origin is disputed, is to unvoice /b/, /d/, /ð/, /g/ to /p/, /t/, /th/, /k/ respectively: these, unless they precede another consonant, are normally, with the exception of <th>, doubled in spelling, see A 3(a), 4(c) above. So in the Black Book system, I.1b *llicrid, reuhid,* 5a *ottid, gosgupid, meccid*; cf. ModW *llygru, rhewi, odi, gosgubo, magu*. In the standard system, the nature of the spelling means that the presence of *h* or its effects can be demonstrated only sporadically: so II.32c *chwenneckyt,* XI.1e *pericklid. h* is written in IX.67 *trenghyt* but not 1 *eyt.* II.18b *kysgyt,* III.8c *gwesgyt* appear not to show unvoicing, but the appearance may be misleading, see A 3 (d) above. The corresponding consonants in II.16a *kyrchyt,* III.6b *twyllyt,* VIII.9b *gwesgerit,* IX. 67 *torrit* are not subject to unvoicing. It is arguable that *bit* in III is the corresponding form of the consuetudinal present of the verb 'to be'. XII.7e *dielid* is a rare instance in early ModW. For the use of these forms, see C.2(b) below. I.30c *rothid* is probably imperative rather than indicative, and the same may be true of some of the instances of *bit* in III (see *GMW* § 140 (b)); but the phonology is as above.

(b) An old impersonal present indicative in *-itawr* or *-itor* occurs in I.35a *rewittor,* VI.9a *pesgitawr,* IX.7 *llemittyor* (probably an error for *llemittor*); see *GMW* §131(a).

(c) An old impersonal present indicative with future sense in *-awr* occurs in VI.10b *diangawr,* VIII.29c *garawr.*

(d) An old third plural present indicative in *-int* occurs in a non-gnomic line: I.8b *diuryssint.*

(e) The subjunctive terminations originally began with *h* (corresponding to Irish *s*); this causes the unvoicing of the final consonant of the stem which is a characteristic mark of the mood; see A 3(a), 4(c) above.

(f) The third singular present subjunctive may end in *-wy* as well as in *-o*: III.4b *rodwy,* IX.68 *brynw[y],* XI.6h *derllyddwy.*

(g) The regular Middle Welsh third singular preterite of *dywed* is *dywawd,* see *GMW* §133(c)(1); this appears as XII.1g, 7g *ddyvod,* 8g *ddyfod,* with spelling variants in different manuscripts.

## C. Syntax

A survey of some aspects of the historical syntax of Middle Welsh is given by David Willis in the ninth chapter of *SW*, but almost all his examples are taken from prose texts and much that is relevant to the gnomic poetry is passed over. Some cases where points of phonology or accidence relevant to the topic arise are discussed in detail in *GMW*. The various types of sentence in Welsh are helpfully analysed by Melville Richards in *Cystrawen y Frawddeg Gymraeg*, though not with special reference to Middle Welsh. In consequence of the nature of the subject-matter, not all the typical features of MW syntax are exemplified in the gnomic poems; what follows represents a sketch of the characteristic types of sentence found there.

(1) The nominal sentence.

(a) In the typical sentence of this type (the 'pure nominal sentence') the predicate consists simply of a complement: this directly precedes the subject, which may be a noun or a noun phrase: I.1a *llym awel, llum brin, anhaut caffael clyd*, II. 7b *clyt y ogo*. An extended complement may be split, as in II.1b *kynneuin bran a chanu*. The complement is normally an adj. or adjectival phrase, but may be a noun or noun phrase: VIII 1c *bronnwaly hiraeth y h[en]eint*, XII.1h *gorev kannwyll pwyll i ddyn*.

(b) In some cases the complement may be preceded by *ys*, a form of the third person singular of the verb 'to be' (in the function of 'copula'; see *GMW* §145): II. 34b *ys odidawc wyneb ku*, VIII.6b *ys odit ae digawn*, IX.26 *ys gwac bro ny vo crevyd*, or, in a 'hanging' construction (see 3 below), IX.116 *a vo da gan duw ys dir*. This is rare in MW,[71] but the corresponding form *is* is regular in Irish of all periods, and its use in Old Irish corresponds fairly closely to that in the nominal sentence in MW. The implication is that this use of the copula was inherited from Common Celtic but was obsolescent in Welsh from an early stage, presumably because it was felt to be redundant,[72] but this tendency may have coincided with a desire for brief or laconic expression in the gnomic tradition, given that a different type of sentence, that expressed in ModW with *y mae*, may be reduced in an analogous way: see below, (g-h).

(c) In sentences of this type with the preverbs *ni* (negative) and *neu* (affirmative) the function of the copula is expressed by *nit* (*nid*, as still in ModW) and *neut* (*neud*) respectively: I.9b *nid annuyd hawdit hetiv*, XII.8f *nid teilwng iddo i fara*; I.18c *neud gueilgi gueled <yr> eluit*, XI. 11c *neud byrr dylif dydd*.[73] The semantic distinction between the unmarked sentence as

---

[71] See Arwyn Watkins and Proinsias Mac Cana, 'Cystrawennau'r Cyplad' for a list of instances in Old and Middle Welsh. It survives as late as the Four Branches, but there most commonly in the set formula *ys + adj. + a + noun*, as in *PKM 7. 16 ys glut a beth yd ymdidanyssam ni*, where it represents a fossilised idiom rather than a normal construction.

[72] When the copula is expressed (except, as here, in 3 sg. pres. ind.) it is not generally differentiated *formally* from the substantive verb (*GMW* §145 N.2), as it is in Irish at least after 600. Even *ys* may have substantive function, but rarely and then only with an infixed pronoun (*GMW* §147(d)).

[73] *Neut* in this sense must be distinguished from the composite affirmative particle *neut* from *neu + yt* (*GMW* § 190 N.): this is followed by the soft mutation, as in XI.11d *neud orffowys llynges*; see notes on XI. 1d, 11b for apparent exceptions. By contrast, both *nit* and *neut* as copula are followed by the radical.

in (a) and that with *neud* is not clear; the latter may represent a stronger assertion.

(d) The copula may also take the form *bit,* which is followed by the soft mutation. This form may according to context be either a third person singular imperative or a consuetudinal present; it is always used in generalisations rather than statements about particulars, and is the dominant form in III. In a few cases the form of the sentence is *bit* + subject + adverbial phrase; here *bit* has the function of the substantive verb rather than the copula: see (h), below.

(e) The order of the elements in a nominal sentence (with no copula expressed) may on occasion be reversed: I.20b *brooet llum,* II.4a *hyd escut,* VIII.22b *geuvel crin,* etc. The origin of this construction is not clear; it may represent an extension of an archaic construction whereby a verb predicate is preceded by its subject (see (2) (a) below), or of the 'hanging' construction (see (3) below,) but perhaps is a spontaneous development within the gnomic tradition from the standard pure nominal sentence. In some cases it may represent a stylistic device, designed to create a chiastic pattern (complement, subject, subject, complement, sometimes with internal rhyme) within the line: I.3b *crin caun calaw truch,* II.17b *crin calaf alaf dichleic,* VII.10c *gwelwgan gweilgi heli hallt,* VIII.14b *hir dydd merydd mall.*

(f) Common in comparable contexts in formal ModW (and usual for purposes of emphasis, which may explain its origin[74]) is what may be called a secondary copula placed after the complement, as in Acts xix: 28 *Mawr yw Diana yr Ephesiaid* 'great is Diana of the Ephesians'. This construction is already developing in the gnomic poems, especially where it is desired to express a tense other than the present, and becomes the normal unmarked order in Middle Welsh prose, but is far from being dominant in these poems. So with simple present VIII.6c *gweithret call yw caru yn iawn,* with consuetudinal present II.7c *kas vyd a oreilytto,* 8b *byrr vyd byt,* XII.3c *hwy vydd hindda no heiniar,* 10h *amau fydd y dydd y del;* with future I.16c *glau a uit hediw,* 17c *hinon uit* (with subject pronoun understood); with imperfect (in the sense 'would') II.4c *reit oed deall y alltut.* Similarly it may be used for clarity when the syntax is interrupted: II.10c *trwm, a wr, yw pechawt.*

(g) The construction with *y mae* + subject + *yn* + complement, which has in most contexts taken over the function of the copula in ModW, is never found in the gnomic poems.[75] But there are occasional traces of a similar construction with *bit,* see 1(d) above: III.2b *bit tawel yn deleit,* or without any verb at all: VIII.17b *geir teulu yn ysgwn,* 22b *gwenyn yn uchel.* Other

---

[74] See Watkins and Mac Cana, 'Cystrawennau'r Cyplad', at 7.
[75] The one instance of *y mae,* in XI.1f *Nid ydyw yn bryd man y mae addas,* is in function a substantive verb.

instances may be I.3c *coed im bluch*, 14a *guenin ig keithiw*, where *yn* appears to be followed by the nasal rather than the expected soft mutation: see *GMW* §25(a), N; alternatively these may be interpreted as adverbial phrases, see (h) below.

(h) A superficially similar construction in ModW, but one where the verb comes closer to the substantive function, is that where *y mae* + subject is followed by an adverbial phrase. The corresponding construction is common in the gnomic poems, but here the verb 'to be' is never expressed. So I.11a *eurdirn am cirn, cirn am cluir*, 17c *llyw in awon*, II.5b *hwyeit yn llynn*, 8a *hyd ar daraf*, V.1b *deil ar gychwyn*. Similar phrases are frequent after *gnawt* 'usual', which in effect takes the place of a verb, so V.2b *gnawt mwyalch ym mhlith drein*, etc., but here *gnawt* is strictly speaking the complement in a 'pure nominal sentence', see (a) above, and the adverbial phrase is an extension of the sentence.

(2) The verbal sentence.

(a) In sentences containing verbs other than the verb 'to be', the verb normally precedes the subject as in ModW; but there are traces of a yet older construction where the reverse is the case. The reason for the development remains to be explained. So II.2b *rac ruthur gwynt gwyd gwyrant*,[76] IX.11o *kyfa rann ry buchir*, X. 11 *en adef tangdef collit*; see *GMW* §199 N (c)). Again, the orders verb-object-subject and object-subject-verb can occur: so X.8 *ni cheri gyfofni gyvyeith*, 13 *rudvyt keisyessyt keissyadon*. The occurrence of these patterns in a single short poem, X, is notable.

(b) The gnomic poems preserve with great regularity the distinction between the 'absolute' and 'conjunct' forms of the third singular present indicative; see B1(a) above, and *GMW* § 129(d); also *SW*, pp. 298–99 and Rodway, 'Absolute Forms'. The absolute forms in *-(h)id* or *-(h)yd* are used when the verb stands by itself, the conjunct forms without termination, which give rise to those used in ModW, are used after the neg. particle *ny* (*ni*) and the perfective particle *ry*, which in this case most often has a sense of potentiality. Thus I.5b *nid a kedwir oe neges* beside IX.1 *golut byt eyt dydaw*;[77] 1b *llicrid rid reuhid llin* beside 1c *ryseiw gur* 'a man can stand'; XII.7e *llwyr dielid mefl mowrair*. The absolute form survives in proverb collections, though probably as a linguistic fossil, down to the seventeenth century.[78]

---

[76] Note also the archaic use of the plural verb here.

[77] *Dydaw* contains what is technically a conjunct form after the old preverb *dy-*.

[78] It never occurs in ordinary Middle Welsh prose, even in thirteenth century MSS; the celebrated instance in a poem of Dafydd ap Gwilym (*GDG* 76.23 *chwerddid mwyalch ddichwerwddoeth*) echoes a proverbial *englyn* quoted in the bardic grammars and possibly contemporary with the gnomic sequences: *chwerdit mwyalch mywn kelli; nit ard, nit erdir idi; nit llawenach neb no hi.*

(c) The so-called 'abnormal order' of subject + *a* (neg. *ny*) + verb, where there is no special emphasis on the subject, is not as common in the gnomic poems as it is in narrative prose, where it is actually the predominant type; see *GMW* §199, *SW* pp. 287–96. But several instances are to be found, especially in XII. So II.c-d *llawer deu a ymgarant | a phyth ny chyfaruydant*, VII.4a-b *Marchwieil bedw briclas | a dynn uyn troet o wanas.* (cf. 5a-b, 6 a-b), XII.3f *pob edn a edwyn i gymar.*

(d) The so-called 'mixed order', which is often formally identical with the 'abnormal order' but is distinguished from it by its use to emphasize the element which stands at the head of the sentence, is rare in the gnomic poems, with their preference for simple statement. Among the Red Book *englynion* II.22b *ystlys diffeithwch a dreid* is a possible instance, but the only certain cases are in 'Englynion' y Misoedd, late and untypical in this as in other respects: so XII.1g *gwir a ddyvod Kynvelyn* (cf.7g, 8g), 10g-h *angau i bawb sy ddiogel | amau fydd y dydd y del.*

(3) The 'hanging' construction.

Especially where either subject or predicate is a phrase rather than a simple noun or adj., the subject may be brought to the head of the sentence in a 'hanging' construction. In this edition, this construction is marked with a comma after the subject, after which 'it', 'he' is to be understood. In nominal sentences, at least in gnomic poetry, this construction is rare (examples are III.3b *a garo bardd, bit hard rodyat*, IX.112 *mevyl, ys gnawt o weddawt hir*, 116 *a vo da gan duw, ys dir*, in all three cases with copula expressed) but compare the Heledd sequences in *EWSP* p. 431–36, 18a etc. *Stafell gyndylan, ys tywyll heno*, 433. 34a etc. *Eryr eli, ban y lef heno*, and so on. In other types of sentence the idiom is commoner: II.28c *hiraeth am uarw, ny weryt*, 31c *diryeit, ny mynn gwarandaw*, 33c = VI.2c *rybud y drwch, ny weryt*, IV.12b *ymdiryet y Duw, ny'th dwylla*, VII.7a-c *Marchwieil dryssi a mwyar erni |a mwyalch [y ar] nyth | a chelwydawc, ny theu vyth.* In verbal sentences it is not always easy to distinguish between this construction and the archaic pattern noted in 2 (a) above. In some though not all cases the subject is represented in the latter part of the sentence by an epanaleptic personal pronoun (see *GMW* §200): so IX.6-7 *aglew, chwerit creu oe dinaw | pob llyfwr, llemitt<y>or arnaw*, 117 *a vo glew, gochlywir y glot*, XI.6h *ac nis derllyddwy, nis derfyd[d] dawn*, XII.10f *trychni, ni[d] hawdd i ochel.*

## D. Date

Like much anonymous mediaeval Welsh literature, most of the gnomic poetry is difficult to date with any accuracy. There has in the past been a presumption of an early date, and a tendency to assemble evidence with that conclusion in view.

Advocacy of this kind has no place in scholarly debate, but it has to be said that much of the evidence is equivocal.

(1) External evidence

(a) A latest possible date is given for all the poems by the date of the manuscripts. Extract I can be no later than mid-thirteenth century, the currently accepted date for the Black Book of Carmarthen;[79] the latest possible date for extract X, from the Book of Aneirin, may be a generation later. Extracts II, the greater part of III, IV-V and VII-IX, are not later than 1400, the approximate date of the Red Book of Hergest. Extracts VI, XI, XII and part of III survive only in manuscripts from the sixteenth or seventeenth centuries, though for other reasons all but XII must be much older.

(b) XII B 9c-f contain a rare astronomical or astrological reference which may point to a date in 1486 for the relevant section of the poem.

(c) The possibility of philosophical influences from the twelfth-century schools of Paris has been raised in the general introduction.[80]

(2) Internal evidence

This is of three main kinds: orthographical, linguistic and metrical. Each of these allows some more precise conclusions than can be drawn from the date of the manuscripts, but each has its own limitations and all share one major weakness: for the most part those features which are datable occur only sporadically in a group of poems which are not necessarily unified compositions. Those texts which are based on a clear structural scheme, such as XI and the second part of VI, are the most likely to preserve their original shape, but many of the *englyn* sequences (and poems such as IX in rhymed sections of varying length) are likely to have developed through a process of slow accretion, and in others, such as I and VII, there is evidence that two or more earlier poems or fragments of them have been combined to form a new entity. A feature which can be taken as evidence for an early or indeed a late date may be relevant only to a particular stanza or even a particular line, and such features rarely if ever occur consistently throughout an entire poem.

(a) Orthography. The appearance in the Red Book poems of occasional spellings where <u> is written for later <w> or where a mutated consonant is not shown was used by Jackson as evidence for an exemplar written in the twelfth or early thirteenth century:[81] the relevant examples are V.3b *bedu*, VI.24b *betuerw* and IV.3a *gocled*, II.20b,VIII.12b *bacwyawc*, VII.1c

---

[79] That is, not 1200 as Jackson supposed (see *EWGP*, p. 7). For the dating of the major manuscript collections of poetry, see Daniel Huws, *Medieval Welsh Manuscripts*, pp. 65–83.

[80] See pp. xxix–xxx, above.

[81] *EWGP*, p. 7.

*brongwala*[82] for *bedw, bedwerw, gogledd, bagwyawc, bronwala.* Spellings of the latter type, however, still occur in the Black Book of Carmarthen and in MS Peniarth 28 in the mid thirteenth century, and of the former type in the text of the Laws in British Library Cotton Titus D. ii, which belongs to the second half of the same century. The orthographical evidence thus does not in itself require a date for the Red Book poems before 1250, though, as Jackson observes, a stanza identical to VIII.31 (a version of which also appears in error in the Red Book after V.5) is copied in the lower margin of f. xlii in the Black Book, and this suggests strongly that other such stanzas may have already been in circulation some time before that date.

(b) Linguistic evidence

(i) Historical developments in phonology and accidence are not as firm a criterion as might be wished, since they can rarely be dated other than on the basis of their occurrence or otherwise in the work of the *Gogynfeirdd* or poets of the Princes, which is in turn dated by reference to the historical figures for whom it was composed. As the style of many of these poets is abstruse and often archaic, certain features may have survived longer in their work than in the simpler and perhaps more popular style of the gnomic stanzas; conversely certain innovative features may have appeared in the gnomic poems well before they became acceptable in the more formal poetry.

(ii) An instance of the latter is the practice of rhyming original *-aw* with *-o.* This development, which is supposed by Jackson to have begun in the spoken language in the second half of the eleventh century but not to have been fully established for a century or more after that,[83] is never found in the work of the *Gogynfeirdd,* nor does it occur in the Red Book *englynion,* but a comparison of the first and second stanzas of extract IX demonstrates that both forms were acceptable to the author of that poem, which is perhaps more likely to have been the case after 1150 than earlier. By this criterion the Red Book *englynion* appear somewhat older than extract IX, but some verb-forms point the other way, and all such evidence is sporadic.

(iii) Old verb-forms may provide some evidence of date. The frequency of the old absolute present indicative third singular in *-id* (see B (1) (a) above) is not conclusive, since present-tense statements in which it might be expected to occur are more common in the gnomic poetry than in other types of text. But such forms are particularly prevalent in extract I, a text which appears to draw on a pre-existing tradition of saga poetry and whose component parts may be supposed for that

---

[82] So in the Red Book; the somewhat later but related MS Jesus 20 has *bronnwaly,* a more modern form in this respect, though preserving older *-y* for *-a.*

[83] See Jackson, *LHEB,* pp. 296–99.

reason to be older than the Red Book poems, where the traces of such connexions are at best sporadic. It is interesting, too, that extract I exhibits *h* in this termination with greater consistency than the others, but since the reason for its presence is not clear this cannot be automatically assumed to represent the faithful preservation of an older form, and even here the historically incorrect use of the form after a preverb is found (I.7b *gosgupid*).

(iv) Among other present forms, the second singular in -*yd* (<d> ≡ /d/: IX.27 *gwneyd*) appears not to occur in any text securely datable after 1100, but is an isolated form in a loosely constructed poem which may contain lines of widely differing age.

(v) The third plural in -*int* is again for the most part typical of early texts; the one instance here appears to belong to an earlier saga sequence (I.8b *divryssint*).

(vi) Old future forms such as -(*h*)*awd* (third singular: VI.7a *rynawd*, IX.70 *gwisgawt*) and -(*h*)*awr* (impersonal: VI.10b *diangawr*, VIII.29c, IX.101 *carawr*), the passive in -*itawr*, -*itor* (VI.9a *pesgitawr*, IX.7 *llemitt<y>or*), the third singular imperfect in -*i* (X.8 *ceri* beside 5 *carei*) and the third singular preterite in -*essyt* (X.13 *keissyessyt*) still appear in the work of the *Gogynfeirdd* in the twelfth century, and some of them even in the early thirteenth; the third singular rel. in -*yd* (<d> ≡ /δ/: IX. 17 *gwneyd*) may survive later still. These may be deliberate archaisms in the often abstruse style of these poets and could have disappeared earlier in the less elevated language in which the gnomic poems were composed, but in themselves they are compatible with a date well on in the twelfth century.

(vii) One genuinely early feature is the disyllabic form *mäes* in XI.6c. In the work of Cynddelw Brydydd Mawr (c. 1155–1200) this word is always a monosyllable; as Ifor Williams observed, if so conservative a poet had been familiar with this pronunciation it is hard to suppose that he would not have made use of it. Any line which contains it is unlikely to be much later than 1100.[84] This poem, however, belongs to a different tradition from the gnomic *englynion*, and an early dating for it does not imply the same for them. Possibly older still is the rare form *henoeth* for later *heno* in rhyme in VI.1a; this occurs elsewhere in MW only in a part of the *Canu Urien* dated by Jenny Rowland[85] as early as the late eighth to mid ninth century. Rowland reasonably regards VI as being earlier than the Red Book *englynion*, and suggests

---

[84] Ifor Williams, *PKM*, pp. xviii-xix. Williams suggests that it must have been obsolete for a century in order that Cynddelw should not have known of it: this seems excessive. The form is guaranteed by rhyme in an *englyn gwastad* (see below); this type of stanza must therefore have been in use by 1100.

[85] *EWSP*, pp. 388–89.

the tenth or eleventh century as a possible date;[86] the latter is certainly the safer dating. If this were accepted, it would prove the existence of gnomic sequences at this date, and it would be easier to accept an eleventh-century date for at least parts of the others, but the evidence remains tenuous. Apart from the first stanza of this sequence there is no compelling argument against a twelfth-century date for it.

(viii) Conversely, the occurrence of such words of apparently Norman-French derivation as VIII.17a *menestyr*, IV.6a *pastardaeth* or X.7 *amsud* do not prove a late date for the entire poems which contain them, only that the texts continued to be subject to alteration or interpolation in the thirteenth century or, in the case of the Red Book, perhaps even later. In favour of a late date for XII, Jackson cites rhymes between unstressed -*aws* and -*os*, which, as has been noted, are not conclusive, and between -*af* and -*a*, which suggests a fairly late date (see *GMW* §10). Apart from the single form 7e *dielid* there is nothing in this text remotely resembling the language of the Red Book *englynion*.

(c) Metre. The three-line *englynion* in which most of the gnomic poetry is composed are characteristic of the saga poetry relating to Llywarch Hen and others, most of which is earlier, sometimes considerably so, and of some early moral and religious poems as well. The first type, the *englyn penfyr*, consists usually of a first line with between nine and eleven syllables, a second of six syllables and a third of seven syllables. The second and third lines usually rhyme with an internal syllable in the first, for example III.1.[87] The second type, the *englyn milwr*, consists simply of three rhyming lines of seven syllables, for example VII.1.[88] The third type, the *englyn byr crwca*, is rare, and is effectively an inversion of the *englyn penfyr*; here the seven-syllable line precedes that of ten syllables, for example II.11. These stanzas are never used by the poets of the Princes; it is not clear whether this is because the form was already obsolescent in the twelfth century or because it was associated with an unacceptably low style. They are replaced by four-line *englynion* of two main types. The first, the *englyn unodl union*, is essentially an *englyn penfyr* concluded with an additional seven-syllable line, and corresponds to the form used to this day in strict-metre poetry; the second, the *englyn proest*, consists of four equal lines with rhymes ending in the same consonant but with a different vowel.[89] It is commonly assumed, though it cannot be proved, that these types of four-line *englyn* were introduced by the poets of the Princes, or at least in their time; if so,

---

[86] "'Englynion Duad"', 64–65.

[87] Usually the seventh, eighth or ninth. A few other patterns occur, especially in older texts; for a detailed analysis, see *EWSP*, pp. 305–55.

[88] The name *englyn milwr* 'soldier's stanza' may reflect its frequency in saga poetry. The apparent five-line stanza at I.21 is completely anomalous.

[89] There is no certain example of an *englyn proest* in the gnomic corpus, but something similar may lie behind II.8.

it is likely that such stanzas in the gnomic poems are comparatively late, perhaps dating from the late twelfth or early thirteenth century. But only one poem (IV) contains *englynion unodl union*; the four-line stanzas at II.2, 6 and V.1 are of different types, which never found acceptance among the *Gogynfeirdd*,[90] and these cannot be used as criteria for a later date.

As far as the three-line *englynion* are concerned, Jenny Rowland has pointed out a tendency in those sequences which appear, for other reasons, to be earlier for *englynion penfyr* and *milwr* to be used together (with the occasional *byr crwca*) in the sequence; later on there develops a tendency for the sequences to be composed almost entirely in *englynion milwr*.[91] This may reflect a decline of technique over time on the part of the poets. On this basis, it might be argued that the greater the proportion of *englynion penfyr* in a gnomic sequence, the earlier that sequence is likely to be. By that criterion extracts I, III, VIII and the second part of VI would be earlier than the rest, but no absolute dating can be deduced from it, and the ease with which extraneous stanzas can be absorbed into the text greatly undermines the value of the criterion. Interesting, however, is the convergence of evidence for an early date for extract I.

It is probably safe to say that most of the datable features of the gnomic poems in this collection, with the exception of extracts X and XII, fall within the eleventh and twelfth centuries. An eleventh-century date is likely for XI and for the component parts of I, though the date at which the latter was put together in its present form is less clear. The title of X, *Gwarchan Adebon*, suggests a text of high antiquity, and certain lines appear, on the strength of their archaic word-order, to be considerably earlier than anything else printed here; yet the internal evidence is compatible with a twelfth-century date for the poem as it stands. In general the evidence for an eleventh-century origin for the gnomic *englynion* has been somewhat overstated; the date of the manuscripts themselves affords a later limit for the compilation of the existing sequences, but, given that they may have developed at least in some cases by a process of gradual accretion, this provides no evidence as to when the process began. An eleventh-century date for the composition of the individual stanzas, or most of them, would have the advantage of allowing a clear break between the gnomic tradition and the poetry of the *Gogynfeirdd*, who in general composed as if it did not exist. It is not clear, however, that this is how traditions operate: the gnomic stanzas are likely to be the work of an entirely different group of poets, working possibly in a clerical rather than an aristocratic environment, in whose hands the process

---

[90] The first is an *englyn gwastad* (an *englyn milwr* with a fourth rhyming line added); this type antedates the rise of the *Gogynfeirdd*, see note 10 above. The other two are *englynion cyrch*, in which the end of the third line rhymes with the middle of the fourth. This type, with slight adjustment, later enters popular tradition as the *triban* or *pennill telyn*, a favourite vehicle for wit and wisdom.

[91] See Rowland, "'Englynion Duad"', 65, and her discussion in *EWSP*, pp. 317–29.

of accretion or compilation, and perhaps to some extent the composition of new stanzas, could easily have long continued parallel to the activity of the court poets and their successors. The situation in the fourteenth century, when Gruffudd ap Maredudd was continuing to compose in the manner of the grandest of the *Gogynfeirdd* while Dafydd ap Gwilym and Iolo Goch were bringing the newly-developed *cywydd* to perfection, is a warning against too rigidly sequential a view of the development of literary tradition. Conversely, if the gnomic poetry, or some of it, really shows the influence of Victorine thought regarding the macrocosm and the microcosm, a date well on in the twelfth century becomes more plausible. But such a hypothesis, while certainly a consideration in discussing the date of the poems, is altogether too speculative to be a determining factor.

# TEXTS

The simplest of the texts from a linguistic point of view is XII, and the student unfamiliar with mediaeval Welsh is recommended to begin by reading it, while remembering that it is late and untypical of the gnomic corpus as a whole. It is suggested that the Red Book stanzas be approached next, II, IV, V, VII, VIII, III being a convenient order. VI.1–7, which is of comparable difficulty, and IX, with its different style, may follow. By this time the reader should be sufficiently familiar with the general manner of the gnomic poems to confront the linguistic difficulties of I. VI.8–19, X and XI are textually difficult and are probably best left till last.

Expansions of manuscript abbreviations are italicised; emendations and supplements are marked with square brackets [ ], rejected manuscript readings marked with angular brackets < >. Readings regarded as corrupt are marked with obeli † †. For the convenience of the reader the symbol <6> characteristic of the Red Book is replaced with <w>, and infixed pronouns are marked with an apostrophe: so *o'e, ni'm* for MS *oe, nim* etc.

## I. Llym awel

Text from the Black Book of Carmarthen = C (Aberystwyth, National Library of Wales, MS Peniarth 1).

1      Llym awel, llum brin, anhaut caffael clid;
          llicrid rid, reuhid llin;
      ry seiw gur ar vn conin.

2      Ton tra thon, toid tu tir;
      goruchel guaetev rac bron banev bre;
        breit allan or seuir.

3      Oer [guely] lluch rac brythuch gaeaw;
          crin [calaw, caun] truch;
      kedic awel, coed i[m]bluch.

3a guely *Rowland;* lle MS. 3b calaw caun *Rowland;* caun calaw MS. 3c ini bluch

4        Oer gwely pisscaud ygkisscaud     iaen;
                 cul hit, caun barywhaud;
            birr diuedit, guit gvyrhaud.

5        Ottid eiry, guin y cnes;
        nid  a kedwir o'e neges;
        oer  llinneu, eu llyu heb tes.

6        Ottid eiry, guin aren;
        segur yscuid ar iscuit hen;
        ryuaur guint, reuhid dien.

7        Ottid eiry ar warthaw reo;
        gosgupid g[u]int blaen guit tev;
        kadir yscuid ar yscuit glev.

8        Ottid eiry, tohid istrad;
        diuryssint <vy> keduir y cad;
        mi nid aw; anaw ni'm gad

9        Ottid eiry o dv riv;
        karcharaur goruit, cul biv;
        nid annuyd hawdit hetiv.

10       Ottid eiry, guin goror     mynit;
            llum guit llog ar mor;
          meccid llvwyr llauer kyghor.

11       Eurtirn am cirn, cirn am cluir;
        oer llyri<c>, lluchedic auir;
        bir diwedit, blaen gvit gvir.

12       Gvenin igogaur, guan gaur     adar;
           dit diulith [... ... ... ];
         k[a]ssulwin kewin brin, coch gwaur.

12c  kassulwin *Lloyd-Jones;* kyssulwin MS.

13       Guenin igodo, oer agdo     rid;
           reuid rev pan vo;
         ir nep goleith, lleith dyppo.

14       Guenin igkeithiv, gwirtliv     mor;
           crin calaw, caled riv;
         oer divlit <yr> eluit hetiw.

15    Guenin ig clidur rac gulybur    gaeaw;
        glas cunlleit, cev ewur;
      dricweuet llyvrder ar gur.

16    Hir nos, llum ros, lluid riv;
      glas glan, guilan in emriv;
      garv mir; glau a uit hetiw.

17    Sich guint, gulip hint, ki[ua]et[h]lauc   diffrint;
        oer callet, cul hit;
      llyw in awon; hinon uit.

17a kinuetlauc MS; kiuuetlauc *Jackson*.

18    Driccin imynit, awonit    igniw;
        gulichid lliw llaur trewit;
      neud gueilgi gueled &lt;ir&gt; eluit.

19    Nid vid iscolheic; nid vid eleic,  unben;
        ny'th eluir in dit reid;
      och Gindilic, na buost gureic!

20    Kirchid carv crum tal cum    clid;
        briuhid ia, brooet llum;
      ry dieigc glev o lauer trum.

21    &lt;Bronureith, breith bron;
    breith bron bron vreith&gt;
    Briuhid tal glan gan garn carv cul grum cam.
    goruchel awel guaet vann;
    breit guir or seuir allan.

22    Kalan gaeaw, gurim gordugor    blaen gruc;
        goreuynawc ton mor;
      bir dit; deruhid ych kighor.

23    O kiscaud yscuid ac aral    goruit
        a guir deur diarchar,
      tec nos y ffissccau escar.

24    Kintëic guint, [coed creilum];
    crin caun, [llin llaun], caru iscun;
    Pelis enuir, pa tir hun?

24a creilum coed MS: coed creilum *Ifor Williams*. 24b llyn llawn  *Ifor Williams*

25     Kin ottei eiry hid [d]in Aruul     Melin,
           ni'm gunaei artu awirtul;
        towissun<e> lv y Brin Tytul.


26     Can medrit mor ruit y rodwit     a rid
           a riv eiry a diguit,
        Pelis, pan vid kyvarwit?


27     Ni'm guna pryder im Pridein     heno
           kyrchu bro priw †uchei[n]†;
        y ar can kanlin Owein.


28     Kin imtuin ariweu ac yscuid     arnad,
           diffreidad kad Kynuid,
        Pelis, pa tir y'th uaguid?


29     Y gur a rithao Duv o rigaeth     carchar,
           rut y par o penaeth,
        Owein Reged a'm ryvaeth.


30     Can ethiw ruiw in Rodwut Iwerit,
           a teulu, na fouch!
        gwydi met meuil na vynuch!
        *       *       *       *       *       *

35     Gwir igrid, rid rewittor;
        oeruelauc tonn, brith bron mor;
        r[ë]en, rothid duvin kighor.


## II. Eiry mynyd

Text based on the Red Book of Hergest = R (Oxford, Jesus College 111), col. 1028; variants from J (Oxford, Jesus College 20), f. 3b; $D^2$ (Aberystwyth, NLW 4973B).


1      Eiry mynyd, gwynn pob tu;
        kynneuin bran a chanu;
        ny daw da o drachyscu.


2      Eiry mynyd, gwynn keunant;
        rac ruthur gwynt gwyd gwyryant;
        llawer deu a ymgarant
        a phyth ny chyfaruydant.

2d chyfuarfydant R; chyfaruydant J

3       Eiry mynyd, gwynt a'e tawl;
          llydan lloergan, glas tauawl;
          odit dyn dirieit dihawl.

4       Eiry mynyd, hyd escut;
          gnawt ym prydein gynrein drut;
          reit oed deall y alltut.

4c  deall] ddeall D².

5       Eiry mynyd, hyd ar des;
          hwyeit yn llynn, gwynn aches;
          hwyr hen, hawd y ordiwes.

6       Eiry mynyd, hyd ar dro;
          chwerdyt bryt wrth a garo;
          kyt dywetter wrthyf chwedyl,
          mi a atwen veuyl lle y bo.

6d  lle bo J.

7       Eiry mynyd, graennwyn gro;
          pysc yn ryt, clyt y ogo;
          kas vyd a oreilytto.

7a  myny *with* d *written in above line* R

8       Eiry mynyd, hyd ar daraf;
          gnawt gan gynran eiryan araf
          ac ysgynnu o du corof
          a disgynnu bar ar [v]araf

8a  daraf *altered from* daryf R. 8c o tu corff J. 8d varaf *Jackson.*

9       Eiry mynyd, hyd kyngrwn;
          llawer a dywedeis os gwnn;
          anhebic y hafdyd hwn.

9b  dywededeis R dyweis J. 9c  y *om* J

10      Eiry mynyd, hyd hellawt;
          gochwiban gwynt ywch bargawt
          twr; trwm, a wr, yw pechawt.

10a  hyd *above line* R. ellawt J.

11      Eiry mynyd, hyd ar neit;
          gochwiban gwynt ywch gwenbleit     uchel;
          gnawt tawel yn deleit.

12 Eiry mynyd, hyd ym bro;
   gochwiban gwynt ywch blaen to;
   nyt ymgel drwc yn lle y bo.

13 Eiry mynyd, hyd ar draeth;
   collyt hen y fabolaeth;
   drycdrem a wna dyn yn gaeth.

13a hyd] *om* J.

14 Eiry mynyd, hyd yn llwyn;
   purdu bran, buan jyrchwyn;
   iach ryd, ryuedot pa gwyn.

14c pa gwyn] ae kwyn J

15 Eiry mynyd, hyd mywn brwyn;
   oer micned, med ygherwyn;
   gnawt gan bob anauus gwyn.

15b yngwerthryn J

16 Eiry mynyd, brith bronn twr;
   kyrchyt aniueil glydwr;
   gwae wreic a gaffo drycwr!

17 Eiry mynyd, brith bronn kreic;
   krin kalaf, alaf dichleic;
   gwae wr a gaffo drycwreic!

18 Eiry mynyd, hyd yn ffos;
   kysgyt gwenyn yn didos;
   kytuyt lleidyr a hir nos.

18c *copied before* b; *so also* J; *with a sign to indicate transposition* R.

19 Eiry mynyd, kynglhennyd  [yn] auon;
    hwyr [g]wedawc yng kynnyd;
   ny moch dieil meuyl meryd.

19a yngklynnyd J. 19b hwyrwedawc.

20 Eiry mynyd, pysc yn llynn;
   balch hebawc, bacwyawc unbynn;
   nyt ef a geiff pawb a uynn.

20c a geiff *twice* R.

21      Eiry mynyd, coch blaen pyr;
        llidiawc lluossawc ongyr;
        och rac hiraeth vy mrodyr!

21a mynydyd R

22      Eiry mynyd, buan bleid:
        ystlys diffeithwch a dreid;
        gnawt pob anaf ar dieid.

22c    direid J

23      Eiry mynyd, hyd nyt hwyr;
        dygwydyt glaw o awyr;
        megyt tristit lleturyt llwyr.

24      Eiry mynyd, eilion ffraeth;
        gowlychyt tonneu glann traeth;
        keluyd, kelet y aruaeth.

25      Eiry mynyd, hyd mywn glynn;
        gwastat uyd haf, araf llynn;
        baryflwyt rew, glew y erchwynn.

26.     Eiry mynyd, brith bronn gwyd;
        kadarn vy mreich a'm ysgwyd;
        eidunaf na bwyf gannmlwyd.

26b   vymreic *with* h *above line* R

27      Eiry mynyd, llwmm blaen cawn;
        crwm blaen gwrysc, pysc yn eigiawn;
        lle ny bo dysc ny byd dawn.

28      Eiry mynyd, pysc yn ryt;
        kyrchyt carw culgrwm cwm clyt;
        hiraeth am uarw, ny weryt.

28b   kyrch *with* yt *above line* R.

29      Eiry mynyd, hyd yg koet;
        ny cherda detwyd ar droet;
        meckyt llwuyr llawer adoet.

29 *after* 30 J.

30    Eiry mynyd, hyd ym bronn;
      gochwiban gwynt ywch blaen onn;
      trydyd troet y hen y ffonn.

31    Eiry mynyd, hyd ar naw;
      hwyeit yn llynn, gwyn*n* alaw;
      diryeit, ny mynn gwarandaw.

32    Eiry mynyd, coch traed ieir;
      bas dwfyr myn yt leueir;
      chwenneckyt meuyl mawreir.

32c  chwenneckyt] angwhaneccid D². mawrir J.

33    Eiry mynyd, hyd escut;
      odit a'm didawr o'r byt;
      rybud y drwch, ny weryt.

34        Eiry mynyd, gwynn y gnu;
      ys odidawc wyneb ku        o gar
          gyt a mynych athreidu.

34a  gu J.  34 b  wyneb] ne *illegible* R

35        Eiry my[ny]d, gwynn to tei
      bei traethei dauawt a wypei   geudawt
          ny bydei gymydawc neb rei

35b  tauawt J.  35c  gymodawc J.

36    Eiry mynyd; dyd a doeth;
      bit glaf pob trwm; llwm lletnoeth;
      gnawt pob anaf ar an[n]oeth.

36a  ac dooeth R  a doeth J    36b  glas J.

## III. Bidiau

Stanzas 1-18: text based on O version as in R, col. 1030, variants from J, f. 10b
and Aberystwyth, NLW MS 4973B, f. 173 (D²): and from Q version (NLW MS
Peniarth 102 (D¹), London, British Library, Additional MS 31055 (W), and NLW
MS Peniarth 27 (P).) Stanzas 19-21: text based on Q version as in D¹, variants
from W.

1        Bit goch crib keilyawc, bit annyanawl        ei lef
              o wely budugawl;
          llewenyd dyn, duw a'e mawl.

1a  coch J

2      Bit lawen meichyeit wrth ucheneit    gwynt;
            bit tawel yn deleit;
         bit gnawt aflwyd ar diryeit.

2a wrth ucheneit gwynt] gwynt a gyfyd Q. 2b *om.* J; ar ei naid bydd dedwydd Q.

3      Bit guhudyat keissyat; bit gnifiat    gwyd;
            bit gynnwys gan dillat;
         a garo bard, bit hard rodyat.

3a guhudyat] guhuddgar Q. gnifiat] gynifiat Q. 3b bid gynnwys gan ddillad Q; a bit
gynnwys dillat O. 3c gara J; bid garu bardd gan roddiad Q.

4      Bit lew vnben a bit avwy    [y] vryt,
            a bit vleid ar adwy.
         ny cheidw <y> wyneb <ar> ni rodwy.

4a bid lew vnbenn a bit awy vryd Q; bit avwy unbenn a bit lew O. 4b a bid lleiniad yn
ardwy Q. 4c ar *om.* Q.

5      Bit vuan redeint yn ardal    mynyd;
            bit yngheudawt oual;
         bit anniweir anwadal.

6      Bit amlwc marchawc; bit ogelawc    lleidyr;
            twyllyt gwreic goludawc;
         kyueillt bleid bugeil diawc.

7      Bit gywir baglawc; bid rygyngawc    gorwyd;
            bit uab llen yn chwannawc;
         bit anniweir deueiriawc.

7a bid gywir baglawg. bid rygyngawg gorwydd Q; bit amlwc marchawc. bit redegawc
gorwyd O. 7b bid chwannawc mab llen J

8      Bit grwm biw a bit lwyt bleid;
         esgut gorwyd y ar heid;
         gwesgyt gwawn grawn yn y wreid.

9      Bit [drwm] bydar; bit [grwm] keu;
         esgut gorwyd yg kadeu;
         gwesgyt gwawn grawn yn y adneu.

9a bit grwm bydar bit trwm keu O; *corr. Jackson.* 9c *om.* J.

10     Bit haha bydar; bit annwadal    ehut;
            bit ynuyt ymladgar;
         detwyd o'r a'e gwyl a'e kar.

10b bid dirieid (dirieid bid D¹) ymgeingar Q. 10c or] ar P yr D¹.

11          Bit dwfyn llynn; bit lym gwaewawr;
            bit †grancleft† glew wrth awr;
            bit doeth detwyd, duw a'e nawd.

11a lym] lynn R. 11b granclef glew] gwarandeu *above* granclef D²; gwarandeu glau
Q; gwarantlew glew *Jackson*, gwarancleu glew *Lloyd-Jones*; ? *read* grauauc llef glew.
11c nawdd Q; mawr R; mawl *Jackson*.

12          Bit lym eithin; bit e[d]ëin      alltut;
                      chwannawc drut y chwerthin;
                  bit lwm ros; bit tost kenin.

12a Bid llymm eithin a bid eddain alldud Q; bit euein alltut bit disgythrin drut O.
12b chwannawg drud Q; bit chwannawc ynvyt O. 12c *so* J; om. R.

13          Bit wlyb rych; bit uynych mach;
            bit gwyn claf; bit lawen iach;
            bit chwyrn colwyn; bit wenwyn gwrach.

13b *after* 13c Q. gwyn] cwynfan D¹ cwynus P. 13c chwyrn D¹; chwyrnyat OP.

14          Bit diaspat aele<u>; bit †äe†      bydin;
                      [a] besgittor, dyre;
                  bit drut glew a bit rew bre.

14a aeleu O; aele *Jackson*. 14b a] bit O.

15          Bit wenn gwyl<y>an; bit vann tonn;
            bit hyuagyl gwyar ar onn;
            bit lwyt rew; bit lew callonn.

15 *om.* P. 15 a  vann] wann J. 15b ar onn Q: a ronn O. 15c lwyt rew] lwytrew D¹ calet
rew W.

16          Bit las lluarth; bit diwarth      eirchyat;
                      bit reinyat yghyuarth;
                  bit wreic drwc a'e mynych warth.

16 *om.* D¹W. 16a lluarth] buarth J lle buarth P. 16c  wreic drwc ae] ddrwc gwraic oi P.

17          Bit grauangawc iar; bit trydar      gan lew
                      bit ynvyt ymladgar;
                  bit tonn callon gan alar.

17a grauangawc] grauaug J; graviad gann P gogor gan D¹ gregar gan W. 17b bit ynvyt
ymladgar] bit ofal (ofnad P) ar ai car Q. 17c gan] rac Q.

18          Bit wynn twr; bit or[u]n seirch;
            bit hoffder llawer a'e heirch;
            bit lwth chwannawc; bit ryngawc cleirch.

18a orun *Jackson*; orwn O. 18c cleiryach J.

19     Bid gwyrdd gweilgi; bid gorawen[us]     tonn;
           bid cwyn pob galarus;
        bid aflawen hen heintus.

20     Bid chwyrniad colwyn; bid wenwyn     neidr;
           bid nofiaw rhyd wrth beleidr;
        nid gwell yr odwr no'r lleidr.

21     Bid anhygar diriaid; bid ffer     [p]ob eweint;
           bid heneint i dylodedd;
        bid addfwyn yn ancwyn medd.

21a pob] bob D[1]. eweint] efrydh W.

## IV. Gnawt gwynt

Text based on R, col. 1031; variants from J, f.9, additional evidence from D[2].

1     Gnawt gwynt o'r deheu; gnawt atneu     yn llann
           gnawt gwr gwann go deneu;
        gnawt y dyn ofyn chwedleu;
        gnawt y vab ar uaeth uoetheu.

2     Gnawt gwynt o'r dwyrein; gnawt dyn bronrein     balch;
           gnawt mwyalch ym plith drein;
        gnawt rac traha tralleuein;
        gnawt yg gwic kael kic o urein.

3     Gnawt gwynt o'r gocled; gnawt rianed     chwec;
           gnawt gwr tec yg Gwyned;
        gnawt y deyrn arlwy gwled;
        gnawt gwedy llynn lleturyded.

4     Gnawt gwynt o'r mor; gnawt dygyuor     llanw;
           gnawt y uanw uagu hor;
        gnawt y uoch turyaw kylor;
        [. . . . . . . . . . . . . . . . . . .]

5     Gnawt gwynt o'r mynyd; gnawt meryd     y mro;
           gnawt kael to yg gweunyd;
        gnawt ar laeth maeth dyn creuyd;
        gnawt deil a gwyeil a gwyd.

6      Gnawt o bastardaeth grynnwryaeth     ar wyr,
         a gwraged drwc meduaeth,
       a chyni ar wyr <a gorwyr> waethwaeth.

6  *Text from J; stanza erased and illegible in R. According to a note in* D² 'Yma y mae gwag yn y LlC, megis lle dau bennill neu dri', *i.e.* 'there is a gap here in the Red Book, about the space of two or three lines.'

7      Gnawt nyth eryr ym blaen dar,
       ac yg kyfyrdy gwyr llauar;
       golwc vynut ar a gar.

8      Gnawt dyd ac anllwyth yg kynnlleith      gayaf;
         kynreinyon kynrwytyeith;
       gnawt aelwyt diffyd yn diffeith.

D² *has the following stanzas as a separate poem.*

9      Crin calaf a llif yn nant;
       kyfnewit seis ac aryant;
       digu eneit mam geublant.

*A stray stanza from the Llywarch Hen cycle follows in all copies; see Commentary.*

10.         Kyt boet bychan, ys keluyd
      yd adeil adar yg gorwyd     coet;
         kyuoet vyd da a detwyd.

11      Oerwlyb mynyd, oerlas ia;
       ymdiryet y duw, ny'th dwylla;
       nyt edeu hirbwyll hirbla.

### V. Kalan gaeaf

Text based on R, col. 1031; variants from J, f. 10.

1      Kalangaeaf, kalet grawn;
       deil ar gychwyn, llynnwynn llawn;
       y bore gynn no'e vynet,
       gwae a ymdiret y estrawn.

2      Kalangayaf, kein [k]yfrin;
       kyfret awel a dryckin;
       gweith keluyd yw kelu rin.

2a  kyfrin *Jackson*; gyfrin R gyfrein J.

3  Kalangayaf, cul hydot;
   melyn blaen bedu, gwedw hauot;
   gwae a haed meuyl yr bychot.

4  Kalangayaf, crwm blaen gwrysc;
   gnawt o benn dirieit teruysc;
   lle ny bo dawn ny byd dysc.

4b deruysc J

5  Kalangaeaf, [a]garw hin,
   anhebic y gynteuin;
   namwyn duw nyt oes dewin.

5a agarw *Charles-Edwards*; garw MSS.

6  <Kalangaeaf, kein gyfreu adar;
    byrr dyd, ban cogeu;
    trugar daffar duw goreu.>

7  Kalangayaf, kalet cras;
   purdu bran, buan [e]vras;
   am gwymp hen chwerdit gwen gwas.

7b evras *Thomas Jones*; ovras R bras J.

8  Kalangaeaf, cul kerwyt;
   gwae wann pan syrr; byrr vyd byt;
   gwir, gwell hegarwch no phryt.

9  Kalangayaf, llwm godeith;
   aradyr yn rych, ych yg gweith;
   or kant odit kedymdeith.

## VI. Calan Gaeaf a'r Misoedd

Text based on Aberystwyth, NLW MS Peniarth 102 (D¹); variants from London, British Library, Additional MS 31055 (W) and (for stanzas 3, 4 and 19) R, col. 1031.

1  Kalan gauaf yw henoeth;
   cul ewig, elwig rhygoeth;
   daiar ffrwd, <ac> eir[wn]g pob noeth.

1c ac eirvg D¹ or eirut W; eirwng *Rowland*

2      Calan gauaf, \<c\>alaf clyd;
        t[w]n to das, rhyfelfawr rhyd;
        rhybudd i drwch, ni weryd.

2a calaf D¹W; alaf *Rowland*. 2b twn] ton D¹, tew W (*so Rowland*); ryvelawc W.

3      Calan gauaf, cal[et] cras;
        du plu bran, gnawd buan bras;
        am gwymp hen chwerddid gwen gwas.

3a calet] *so* R; calaf D¹W. 3b du plu] purdu R; gnawd *om.* R; bras] ovras R.

4      Calan gauaf, llwm goddaith;
        aradr yn rhych, ych yngwaith;
        odid o'r cant cydymddaith.

4b aradr] erydr W. 4c or kant odid R; cydymddaith] cytymaith W.

5      Calan gauaf, [a]garw nawn;
        llwm*m* blaen gwrysg, pysg yn eigiawn;
        gwae a wnel cam dros yr iawn.

5a agarw *Charles-Edwards*; garw D¹W. 5b blaen] bric W.

6      Calan gauaf, gwlyb rhychau;
        rheieidr naint, braint ar [s]wy[d]dau;
        rhaid \<fydd\> talu gwir dros y ga[u].

6b swyddau] *so Rowland after* swydhau W; gwydau D¹. gwir … gau *from* W; *illegible in* D¹.

7      Calan gauaf, ryn rynaw[d];
        addail rhiw, biw yngwasgawd;
        ni phell waddolir neb tlawd.

7a ren W; rynawt (≡ rynawd) W, *illegible in* D¹. 7b addail] A deil W; rhiw] rew W. c waddolir] ohodhir W.

8      Calan Tachwedd, twym\<n\> ennaint;
        ni nawd difenwir cywraint;
        ni bydd dyvn hun a haint.

8a twymn D¹ twymyn W. 8b nawd d.] hawdh dd. W

9      Calan Ionawr, pesgitawr gorwydd;
              gnawd awel i golofn;
          ni bydd dialwr diofn.

9a pesgitawr] pysc y tawr W. 9b gnawd y gaffe i golofyn W.

10      Calan Chwefrawr, chwerw awel [awr]      blygain;
          [a'e] gofwy, diangawr
        yn nydd dofydd dial mawr.

10a chwerawr W. 10b ae] nis D¹ nyt W. diagawr W.

11      Calan Mawrth, †mygedus ...      ereidr†;
          chwiban [l]lef [e]hedydd;
        †y gelwir kulaethwy hydd†.

11a mygedus] mygydus W. 11b bann D¹, ban W *corrected in another hand to* chwiban;
*so Rowland.* 11c culnaethwy W.

12      Calan Ebrill, cog ar hynt [... ... ...]
          [...] gwenyn yngofag;
        neges pendefig yn rhag.

12b gwenyn yngofag *Rowland*; guouyn yngofag D¹, gwenyn y goval W. 12c rhag]
rat (≡ rhad) W.

13      Calan Mai, egin dyre;
        eilwyd[d]gar kerwyt, esgut gorwydd;
          g[n]o[t]af cyrch gan vore.

13b eilwyddgar *Rowland*; eilwydgar D¹, alwydhgar W. *Text of W ends here.* 13c gnotaf
*Rowland*; guo..af D¹.

14      Calan Mehefin, mochddwyreawg hydd;
          hir y bydd a gerddo;
        calon ni gynnydd, cysgo.

15      Calan Gorphennaf, deon ar gychwyn
          [... ... ... ... ... ...]
        [... ... ... ... ... ... a]m b[r]aw.

15b *nothing legible in MS.* 15c braw] r *illegible.*

16      [Cal]an Awst, cyfnod [... ... ...]   <d>irgig;
          pell vydd dig pob difro;
        arglwydd pawb ar a feddo.

17      Calan Menni, llafurus angad      vore
          [... ...] haul †dygweste†;
        gnawd yw diang glew <o> yng[had].

17c ynghad] o yng D¹.

18      Calan Hyfref, [gwynt ceugant];
        gnawd gwynwyl yn hyddgant;
        mam vechan a ddifanw plant.

18a ceugant gwynt MS; gwynt ceugant *Rowland*.

19      Calan gauaf, llwm blaen gwrysg;
        gnawd o ben diriaid terfysg;
        yn y bo dawn y bydd dysg.

19a llwm] crwm R.  19c lle ny bo dawn ny byd dysg R.

                    [Supplement]

20      Rhagor[awl] gwaneg, gwaeddgreg tonn;
                gwasgarawg ei thudded;
            gwae a gawdd dduw ac nis cred.

20a rhagorawl *Rowland*; rhagor D¹W.

21      Gwyrdd gwaneg, gwaeddgreg gwylan;
        efrifed tonn wrth fronn glann;
        hoedl derfyn dyn, duw a'i rhann.

*21b om.* W.

22      Hyddgant yn niffaith, gorwyddfeith    gorwydd;
            cynhauaf cadwent raith;
        gnawd aelwyd ddiffydd yn ddiffaith.


                VII. Baglawc bydin

Text based on R, col. 1032; additional  evidence from D².

1.      Baglawc bydin, bagwy onn;
        hwyeit yn llynn, graenwynn tonn;
        trech no chant kyssul callon.

1c  kyssul] kyss *illegible* R; cyssul D².

2.      Hir nos, gordyar morua;
        gnawt teruysc ygkymanua;
        ny chytuyd diryeit a da.

3.      Hir nos, gordyar mynyd;
        gochwiban gwynt ywch blaen gwyd;
        ny thwyll drycanyan detwyd.

4.    Marchwyeil bedw briclas
      a dynn uyn troet o wanas;
      nac adef dy rin y was.

5.    Marchwyeil derw mywn llwyn
      a dynn vynn troet o gadwyn;
      nac adef rin y uorwyn.

6.    Marchwyeil derw deilyar.
      a dynn vyn troet o garchar;
      nac adef rin y lauar.

7.    Marchwyeil dryssi a mwyar erni
              a mwyalch [y ar] nyth
          a chelwydawc, ny theu vyth.

7b y ar: ar y R.

8.    Glaw allann, gwlychyt redyn;
      gwynn gro mor goror ewynn;
      tec a gannwyll pwyll y dyn.

9.    Glaw allan y gan glydwr;
      melyn eith[i]n, crin euwr;
      duw reen,  py bereist lyvwr?

9b   eithyn R.

10.   Glaw allan, gwlychyt vyg gwallt;
      cwynuanus gwann, diffwys allt;
      gwelwgan gweilgi, heli hallt.

11.   Glaw allan, gwlychyt eigyawn;
      gochwiban gwynt ywch blaen cawn;
      gwedw pob camp heb y dawn.

## VIII. Gorwynion

Text based on R, col. 1032; variants from J, f. 6b.

1.    Gorwyn blaen onn, hirwynnyon vydant
              pan dyuant ym blaen neint;
          bronnwaly hiraeth y heneint.

1c   bronnwaly J; bron gwala R.  heneint J; heint R.

2.        Gorwyn blaen neint, deweint    hir;
            keinmygir pob kywreint;
        dyly bun pwyth hun y heint.

3.        Gorwyn blaen helic, eilic pysc    yn llynn;
        gochwiban gwynt ywch blaen gwrysc    man;
            trech anyan noc adysc.

3b blaen] *om* J.

4.        Gorwyn blaen eithin a chyfrin    a doeth,
           ac anoeth disgethrin;
        namyn duw nyt oes dewin.

5         Gorwyn blaen meillyon, digallon    llyfwr;
          lludedic eidigyon;
        gnawt ar eidil oualon.

5b eidigyon J; edigion R.

6         Gorwyn blaen kawn, gwythlawn    eidic:
            ys odit a'e digawn;
        gweithret call yw caru yn iawn.

7         Gorwyn blaen mynyded rac anhuned    gayaf;
            crin cawn, trwm callwed;
        rac newyn nyt oes wyled.

7a mynyde *with* d *above line* R.   7b   crin cawn trwm *twice, erased the first time*
R. callwed J; called R.   7c wyled *above line.*

8.        Gorwyn blaen mynyded, hydyr oeruel    gayaf;
            crin cawn, crwybyr ar ued;
        whefris gwall yn alltuded.

9         Gorwyn blaen derw, chwerw bric onn;
        rac hwyeit gwesgerit tonn;
        pybyr pwyll; pell oual y'm kallon.

9b gwesgerit J; gwesgereit R.

10        Gorwyn blaen derw, chwerw bric onn;
        ch[w]ec euwr, chwerthinat tonn;
        ny chel grud kystud kallon.

10b chwec J; chec R.

11      Gorwyn blaen egroes; nyt moes    caledi;
            katwet bawp y eiryoes;
        gwaethaf anaf yw anuoes.

11b   pawb J.

12      Gorwyn blaen banadyl, kynnadyl    i serchawc;
            goruelyn kangeu bacwyawc;
        bas ryt; gnawt hyfryt yn hunawc.

13      Gorwyn blaen auall, amgall    pob dedwyd;
            [whec rewyd] y arall;
        a gwedy karu gadu gwall.

13b wheueryd R, chweferyd J. 13c   garu gadu J.

14      Gorwyn blaen auall, amgall    pob dedwyd;
            hir dyd, meryd mall;
        crwybyr ar wawr, carcharawr dall.

15      Gorwyn blaen coll geir Digoll    bre;
            diaele uyd pob ffoll;
        gweithret cadarn cadw aruoll.

15a  bro J. 15b diale J.

16      Gorwyn blaen corsyd; gnawt meryd    yn drwm
            a ieuanc dysgedyd;
        ny thyrr namwyn ffol y ffyd.

17      Gorwyn blaen elestyr; bit venestyr    pob drut;
            geir teulu yn ysgwn;
        gnawt gan aghywir eir twnn.

18      Gorwyn blaen gruc; gnawt seithuc    ar lwfyr;
            hydyr vyd dwfyr ar dal glan;
        gnawt gan gywir eir kyvan.

18ab  lyfwr ... dwfwr J.

19      Gorwyn blaen brwyn, kymwyn biw;
        redegawc vyn deigyr hediw;
        amgeled am dyn, ny<t y>diw.

19a  biw] lliw J. 19 c  amgeled *written twice, the first deleted* R.

20        Gorwyn blaen redyn, melyn    kadawarth;
              mor vyd diwarth deillon!
           redegawc manawc meibon.

20b diwath *with* r *above line*; diwall J. deillyon J.


21        Gorwyn blae*n* kyrawal; gnawt goual    ar hen,
              a gweny*n* yn ynyal;
           namyn duw nyt oes dial.


22        Gorwyn blaen dar, didar drychin;
           gwenyn yn uchel, geuvel crin;
           gnawt gan rewyd rychwerthin.

22 c  rewyd J.


23        Gorwyn blaen kelli, gogyhyt    ygwyd,
              a deil deri dygwydyt;
           a wyl a gar, gwynn y uyt.


24        Gorwyn blaen derw, †oeruerw  dwfyr†;
              kyrchit biw blaen betuerw;
           gwnelit aeth saeth i syberw.

24 *om* J.


25        Gorwyn blaen kelyn, kalet    [angawr]
              ac ereill [awr] agoret;
           pan gysco pawb ar gylchet,
           ny chwsc duw pan ryd gwaret.

25 *om* J. 25a angawr *Jackson.* 25b eur; awr *Jackson.* 25d garet *with* w *above line* R.


26        Gorwyn blaen helic, hydyr elwic   gorwyd;
              hir dyd deilyedic;
           a garo y gilyd, nys dirmic.

26 *om* J. 26c dir *with* mic *above line* R


27        Gorwyn blaen brwyn, brigawc vyd
           pan danner dan obennyd;
           medwl serchawc, syberw vyd.

27 *om* J.


28        Gorwyn blaen yspydat, hydyr hwylyat    gorwyd;
              gnawt serchawc erlynnyat;
           gwnelit da diwyt gen*n*at.

28a   yspytat (?) J.

29        Gorwyn blaen berwr, bydinawr    gorwyd;
                kein gyfreu koet y lawr;
            chwerdyt bryt wrth a garawr.

29a   bydinawc J.   29 c    cherdit *with* w *above line in a different hand* R. a garawr]
angharawr J.

30        Gorwyn blaen perth, hywerth    gorwyd;
                ys da pwyll gyt a nerth;
            gwnelyt agheluydyt annerth.

31        Gorwyn blaen perthi, kein gyfreu    adar;
                hir dyd, dawn goleu;
            trugar daffar duw goreu.

31a-b adar hir] a drahir J.

32        Gorwyn blaen erwein ac elein   yn llwyn;
                gwychyr gwynt, gwyd nugyein;
            eiryawl ny garawr ny gynghein.

32a   erfein J.   32b nugyein J; migyein R. 32c garawl R.

33        Gorwyn blaen ysgaw, hydyr anaw   unic;
                gnawt y dreissic dreissyaw;
            gwae a dwc daffar o law.

33c   daffa *with* r *above line* R.


## IX. Gossymdeith Llefoet Wynebclawr

Text from R, col. 1055.

(I)
            Golut byt eyt dydaw;
            ket ymgeinmycker ohonaw,
            dychystud aghen dychyfyaw;
            dybyd hinon gwedy glaw.
5           ny nawt kyhafal kyvaethlaw;
            aglew, chwerit creu o'e dinaw;
            pob llyfwr, llemitt<y>or arnaw;
            pob ffer, dyatter heibyaw.
            dychymmyd dedwyd ac anaw;
10          rihyd ac ef duw dywallaw.

(II)

     Golut byt eyt dydo;
     digawn dovyd darparo.
     hydyr gwaed gwanec wrth vro;
     pan elwir chwelit acdo.
15    †dioryuic† dyn ny welo;
     ny didawr, ni dawr cwt vo.
     ny wneyd gwir, ny ein ymro;
     ny chenir [b]wyeit ar ffo.
     bit vleid beidyat a dwyll[o].
20    chwannawc vyd lle[i]n &lt;llwydawc&gt; llaw diuo.

18 mwyeit. 19 dwyll.

(III)

     Golut byt eyt dybyd.
     atwaed chwant atuant riyd.
     dychynneit ieueinc dychynnyd.
     nyt echwen[ic]  clot kelwyd.
25    nyt vn aruaeth kaeth a ryd.
     ys gwac [b]ro ny vo crevyd.
     atuant adaw ny wnehyd.
     llwyt ac annwyt, ny c[h]ymyd.
     ny obwyll o duw, diffyd;
30    ny elwir yn gywreint ny gynnyd.
     keinyathwn, gofrynwn greuyd
     hyt pan y'n bo gan grist grennyd.

24 echwenic *Lloyd-Jones;* ech wenjt R  26 vro.  28 gymyd.

(IV)

     Anghyfaelywr anghyfyrdelit    llann;
          dychystud bron brolit.
35    gwell nac no geu edewit.
     y['w] &lt;g&gt;weithret gwastra gweilit.
     chwec yn anwaws yn odit.
     chwerw dryccor wedy trenghit.
     nyt gnawt escussawt esgwit.
40    ny cheffir da heb [y b]rit.
     pedryfan dwfyn, pedrychwelit.
     a reith, gwell goleith no govit.
     drwc pechawt o'e bell erlit.
     da ynggnif porthi menechtit.
45    duw o nef, gwae drut ny gret it.
     mab Meir, diweir a venhit;

da weith yn gobeith wrthit!
a'th gyrbwyllir ym bron*n*vit.

36 ym.

(V)

Difrys gwanec, †dyffustit† traeth;
50        gosgymonn gwyth gordin.
gwyluein hanes goyewin
pwyll llu a thwyll trwy chwerthin.
bit gynnvidyd [k]ywrenhin;
bit lesc eidyl; bit varw crin.
55 kerennyd fall gall gynnin.
gan rewyd ny phell vyd rin.
dychyffre gwaew gwaetlin.
dychyveruyd trwch a thrin.
enghit a vo llyfeithin.
60 enwir, ef kyll y werin.
namwyn duw nyt oes dewin,
arglwyd gwlatlwyd gwerthevin.

53 gywrenhin

(VI)

Dyvrys gwanec, dygwrthryn    gro;
        gwst eidyl moch detwyn.
65 ry yfant  maon medlyn;
a ordyfyn pawb [a'e] deruyn;
trenghyt, torrit pob denghy[n].
ry brynw[y] nef, nyt ef synn.

66 a'e] oed R.   67 denghyt   68 ry brynw

(VII)

Mor wyt gywrennhin gyrbwyll   o nebawt!
70        gwisgawt coet kein gowyll.
nyt eglur edrych yntywyll.
rac annwyt ny weryt cannwyll.
nyt [d]edwyd nwy diuo pwyll.
kerennyd a dovyd, ny dwyll.

73 edwyd.

(VIII)

75 Nwy diuo pwyll, prif egwa.
a gwnneu edyn, ny wna.
oer gaeafrawt, tlawt morua.
gwell rihyd no ryssedha.

rac drwc ny diwc atneir.
80 llawer mawreir a vethla. 8
keudawt, kyt worymdaa,
o ovrys ny wys kwt a.
ar [ny d]al y drindawt, traha.
mawr duw, mor wyt wrda!

83 ar ny dal *Lloyd-Jones*; arythal R.

(IX)
85 Redeint gorwyd, rwyd pob traeth;
kynnic mynawc marchogaeth.
nyt neb a ued o'e aruaeth;
nyt ef enir pawb yn doeth.
nyt ehovyn bryt yn llong dreith.
90 ny thangnef gwynnawn a godeith. 90
bit vyw gwr heb drycwryaeth.
mynawc kerd ket[r]wyf eillyaeth.
ny byd hyvysgwr neb noeth.
nyt oes reith nat vo pennaeth.
95 breyenhin beidyawt anreith.
dywal, dir vyd ei oleith;
ny nawt eing llyfyrder rac lleith;
enghit glew o'e gyfarweith.
medw [dr]ut, [m]ut pobl anghyfyeith
100 dinas [y] diffyd diffeith.
eiryawl a garawr, hawdweith.
ef molir pawb wrth y weith.
ny char dovyd diobeith.
goreu kyflwyt yn gyweith.

92 ketwyf. 99 mut drut. 100 adiffydd; y d. *Lloyd-Jones*.

(X)
105 Gwaeannwyn, goaflwm tir;
otynt tonnawr gawr ennwir.
diwestyl alaf, dirmygjr.
gwall ar ny mynych welir.
ar a vo diffyd, divennwir    y dra[h]a;
110         kyfa rann ry buchir
bit wastat gwreic ny erchir.
mevyl, ys gnawt o weddawt hir.
ny ry decho, ry dygir.
o hir dinaw dychwynir.
115 a uo marw, ny moch welir.
a vo da gan duw, ys dir.

a vo glew, gochlywir      y glot.
      o vychot godolir.
gwynn y vyt pydiw y rodir.
120    kerennyd duw a hoedyl hir.

109 draa. 111 erchis.


## X. Gwarchan Adebon

Text from the Book of Aneirin (Cardiff: Central Library, MS 2.81), p. 26 (A)

Ny phell gwyd aval o avall.
ny chy[m]yd dy[w]al a di[w]all.
ny byd ehovyn noeth yn ysgall.
pawb pan ry dyngir, yt ball.

2 chymyd] chynnyd.   dywal ... diwall *Ifor Williams;* dyval ... dyvall A

5    A garwn y, ef carei anreith   †gar†;             5
      ny byd[ir] marw dwyweith.
nyt amsud y vud e areith.
ny cheri gyfofni gyvyeith.

6 byd

Em[y]s emwythwas amwyn.
10   amswrn am gorn Kuhelyn.

10 emys *Ifor Williams;* e mis A               10

En adef tangdef collit;   adef led
      buost lew en dyd mit.

Rudvyt keissyessyt keissyadon.
mein uchel, medel e alon.
15   <dy ven ar warchan Adebon.>         15


## XI. Neud Kalan Ionawr

Text from Aberystwyth, National Library of Wales MS Peniarth 182, f.1 (P)

1    Neud Kalan Ionawr, iäenuawr kras;
    neud amdud llynniav, †lliuvawr† gwyrddlas;
    *grandin*[i]*s ymber super terras;*
    neud tremyn *aper inter siluas;*
    periklid *homo per pecunias;*

nid ydyw yn bryd man y mae addas
- a chennym oes bresswyl, pwyllad yn vas -
mor vychod vydd in oes, *mors* ry dadlas.

1c grandinis *Thomas*; grandines P.

\*     \*     \*     \*     \*     \*

6      Neud Kalan Mehevin; mawr Dduw ddymkawn
ar lles dyn erbyn dygw[yl] †i ddawn†.
*segites* ar väes a buches lawn
ac *equus* da i naws a lliaws †dawn†.
gwae ddyn o'i riydd ni weinydd iawn
kan ni wyr ysbayd gerth o derth hyd nawn.
a['i] h[a]edd[wy gan] Dduw ydd erwyll iawn,
ac nis derllyddwy, nis derfyd[d] dawn.

6b dygwy..] dygwyl *Thomas*.   6f ysbayd] *so* P; ysbryd *Thomas*.   6g a heddiw   6h derfyddawn

\*     \*     \*     \*     \*     \*

11      Neud Kalan Tachwedd; awr deuawd a vydd;
neut dygynull Duw da i ddedwydd;
neud ffrwyth yn hely, neud byrr dylif dydd;
neud orffowys llynges, oer tes mynydd.
gwae nis dyvo awr o'i vawr riydd
er edmig perchen pen sywedydd,
kan ni wyr yn y byd pa hyd y bydd:
ai ysbaid hiroes, ai oes vn dydd.

## XII. 'Englynion' y Misoedd

A version (stanzas 1-12): text based on Aberystwyth, National Library of Wales 872D. 267 (W). B version (stanzas 9-12): text based on Aberystwyth, NLW, Llansteffan 117. 84 (Ll$^2$) and Peniarth 155. 142 (P$^5$).

As a full collation would be cumbersome and serve little useful purpose, selected variants only are shown from the following:

Aberystwyth, NLW, Cwrtmawr 2. 1 (Cw$^1$), 6. 84(Cw$^2$), 114. 198 (Cw$^4$), J. Gwenogvryn Evans 1B. 5b, 5a, 4b, 4a (Gw), Heythrop (NLW 21700D) 4a (He), Llansteffan 52. 11 (Ll$^1$), 120. 23b (Ll$^3$), 170. 144 (Ll$^6$), Mostyn 129 (NLW 3037B). 99 (M$^1$), 131 (NLW 3039B). 17 (M$^2$), 145 (NLW 3048D). 662 (M$^3$), 146 (NLW 3049D). 315 (M$^4$), 161 (NLW 3057D). 202 (M$^5$), NLW 16964A. 18a (N$^6$), Peniarth 65. 190 (P$^1$), 84. 192 (P$^2$), 99. 547 (P$^3$), 111. 103 (P$^4$), 198. 325 (P$^6$), 206. 175 (P$^7$), 239. 113 (P$^8$), Sotheby 1. 31 (S).

Bangor, University of Wales Bangor, Mostyn 6. 97 (Bm$^1$), 9. 63a (Bm$^2$).
Cardiff, Central Library 2.4. 159 (C$^4$), 2.617. 172 (H$^1$), 2.619. 66 (H$^2$), 2.623. 47 (H$^3$), 2.627. 18 (H$^4$), 3.4. 263 (C$^2$).

London, British Library Add. 9817. 152 (B[1]), 12230. 214 (B[2]), 14875. 62b (B[4]),
14878. 35 (B[5]), 14885. 97 (B[6]), 14967. 333 (B[10]), 14976. 51 (B[13]), 14982. 2 (B[14]),
14997. 211 (B[15]).
Oxford, Balliol College 353. 36a (O).

Manuscripts dated after 1700 are cited only exceptionally. Where appropriate,
the majority reading of MSS is designated by X.

1        Mis Jonor, myglyd dyffryn;
           blin trulliad, trallawd klerddyn;
           kvl bran, anaml llais gwenyn;
           gwac bvches, diwres odyn;
           gwael gwr anwiw i ofyn;
           gwae a garo'i dri gelyn;
           gwir a ddyvod Kynvelyn:
           gorev kannwyll pwyll i ddyn.

2        Mis Chwefrol, anaml ankwyn;
           llafvrvs pal ac olwyn;
           knawd gwarth o fynych gysswyn;
           gwae heb raid a wnel achwyn;
           tri pheth a vac drygwenwyn:
           kyngor gwraic, mvrn a chynllwyn,
           pen ki ar vore wanwyn;
           gwae a laddodd i vorwyn;
           diwedd dydd da fydd i fwyn.

2a anaml *corrected from* annwyl W. 2d *om.* P1. 2e vac (fag) Ll[2]B[4]Bm[1]Cw[1,4]H[1,4]P[3]; dry
WX. 2i *in* P[1]W *together with Panton 1 and 18 (eighteenth century) only.*

3        Mis Mawrth, mawr rhyfic adar;
           chwerw oerwynt ar ben talar;
           hwy fydd hindda no heiniar;
           hwy pery llid no galar;
           pob byw, arynaig i ysgar;
           pob edn, <a> edwyn i gym*m*ar;
           pob peth a ddaw drwy'r ddaiar
           ond y marw mawr i garchar.

3b ar ben talar] ar dalar W. 3e arynaig *(variously spelt)* B[10,14]Bm[1,2]C[4]Ll[1,3,6] P[5,6,8]; a ryfic
W. 3f a *om. Jackson.*

4        Mis Ebrill, wybraidd gorthir;
           llvddedig ychen, llwm tir;
           gwael hydd, gwarëvs clustir;
           knawd osb er nas gwahoddir;

aml bai pawb lle nis kerir;
gwyn i fyd a fo kowir;
knawd difrawd ar blant enwir;
knawd gwedi traha tranck hir.

4c clustir *(variously spelt)* ] glustir W.   4d osb B[1]Cw[2]H[3]Ll[3]M[4]N[6]P[4,5,8] (o ysb S); gwest
WX. 4e pawb] *om* W. 4g enwir] anwir Bm[1,2]Cw[4]W.


5        Mis Mai, difrodvs geilwad;
         klyd pob klawdd i ddigarad;
         llawen hen diarchenad;
         hyddail koed, hyfryd anllad;
         hawdd kymod lle bo kariad;
         llafar koc a bytheiad;
         nid hwyrach yn y farchnad
         groen yr oen no chroen [d]avad.

5g yn y X, *as correction in* W; mynd ir M[2]P[4] *corrected in* W, yr a ir *(variously spelt)*
B[6,14]Bm[2]C[4]Cw[1,4] M[1,2,3,] S. 5h davad] ddavad W y ddafad X


6        Mis Mehevin, hardd tiredd;
         llyfn mor, llawn marannedd;
         hirgain dydd, heinif gwragedd;
         hylawn praidd, hyffordd mignedd;
         Duw a gar pob tangnevedd,
         Diawl a bair pob kynddrygedd;
         pawb a chwennych anrrydedd;
         pob kadarn, gwan i ddiwedd.

6b llawen B[2,13,14]C[1]Cw[1,2,4]GwH[3,4]M[5]N[6]P[2,6,8]S; llawn WX. marannedd P[5] maranedd
B[2,13,14]Bm[1]H[1]Ll[1]OS; marianedd B[13]W*Jackson*. 6c heinif P[1,4] hainif H[2]; heini WX. 6d
praidd] pridd GwHeW (prydd Cw[1]) trai M[5]. mignedd] mygnedd W.


7        Mis Gorffennaf, hyglvd gwair;
         taer tes, toddedic kessair;
         ni char gwilliad hir gyngrair;
         ni lwydd hil korff anniwair;
         llwyr dielid mefl mowrair;
         llwm ydlan, lledwag kronffair;
         gwir a ddyfod mab maeth Mair:
         Duw a farn, dyn a lefair.

7a hyglvd W *(corr. from* hyglyd); hyglyd X . 7f ydlan] ydlam W


8        Mis Awst, molwynoc morva;
         llon gwenyn, llawn modryda;
         gwell gwaith krymman no bwa;
         amlach das no chwarwyva;

ni lafur, ni weddïa,
nid teilwng iddo i fara;
gwir a ddyfod Sain Brenda:
nid llai kyrchir drwc no da.

8f nid] ni P[1,2,3]W.


[A] 9   Mis Medi, mydr ynGhanon;
addfed oed yd ac aeron;
gwae gan hiraeth fy nghalon;
golwg Duw ar dylodion;
gwaetha gwir gwarthrvdd dynion,
gwaetha da drwy anudon;
traha a threisio'r gwirion
a ddiva yr etifeddion.

A9a mydr] mvdr W. 9c gwae] gwayw W gwaew Ll[3]. 9g threisio'r] threisio B[5,12,13] W. 9h
ddiva] so W, *but with* f *written above*; ddifa X. etifeddion] y tifeddion W


[A] 10   Mis Hydref, hydravl echel;
chwarëvs hydd, chwyrn awel;
knawd ysbeilwynt yn rryfel;
knawd lledrad yn ddiymgel;
gwae ddiriaid ni ddawr pa wnel;
trychni, nid hawdd ei ochel;
angav i bawb sy ddiogel -
amav fydd y dydd y del.

A10c ysbeilwynt B[4,15]Bm[1]Cw[1,2]H[1,4]Ll[2]M[1]N[6]P[7,8] (ysbail wyn H[2]) oerwynt B[15]Ll[3]M[5];
ysbeilwyr WX *Jackson.* 10f nid hawdd B[4]; ni hawdd B[13]H[1]M[1]SW nid rrwydd X.


[A] 11   Mis Tachwedd, tvchan merydd;
bras llydnod, llednoeth koydydd;
awr a ddaw drwy lawenydd,
awr drist drosti a dd[y]fydd.
y da nid eiddo'r kybydd -
yr hael a'i rrydd <a'i> pieifydd
dyn a da'r byd a dderfydd;
da nefol, tragwyddol fydd.

A11d dyfydd M[1] *as correction* Cw[1] ddefydd N[6] (*also* ddybydd *BL Add 15010, eighteenth
century*); dderfydd X. 11f rrydd W rhoddo (rotho) X. ai *om. Jackson.*


[A] 12   Mis Rragfyr, byrddydd hirnos;
brain yn egin, brwyn yn rhos;
tawel gwenyn ac eos;
trin ynghyfedd ddiweddnos;
adail dedwydd yn ddiddos,

adwyth diriaid heb achos;
yr hoydl, er hyd i haros,
a dderfydd yn nydd a nos.

A12d ynghyfedd ddiweddnos] yniwedd kyfeddnos B[6,14]Ll[1,3,6]M[1] *Jackson.*


[B] 9    Mis Menni, maneg planed:
mwynieithus mor a[frif]ed;
knawd gwyr a meirch yn lludded;
knawd aeron ac yd addved.
Mab darogan a aned
a'n dwg o'n dygn gaethiwed.
Gwir a ddyfod sain Bened:
ni chwsg Duw pan ro wared.

B9a maneg P[4] mynnawg P[5] miniog Ll[2]. B9b mwynieithus] mwyn hevthus Ll[2] mwyniheithus P[5]. afrifed] affryfed Ll[2] a threfred P[5]. 9c gwyr a meirch Ll[2]X gwr a merch P[4]. 9e mab darogan P[4]; merch vrenhinawl Ll[2]P[5], merch ddyrogan C[2]. 9f dwg P[4]; duc Ll[2]P[5]X.


[B] 10    Mis Hydref, hydraidd hyddod;
melyn blaen bedw, gweddw havod;
llownfras adar a ffysgod;
lleilai laeth buwch a gavrod;
gwae a haedd mefl er [by]chod;
gwell marw no mynych ddifrod;
triffeth a dawdd pob pechod:
[y]mpryd, gweddi a chardod.

B10b bedw] y bedw Ll[2]. 10c llownfras] llymvyras Ll[2]. 10e haedd] haeddo Ll[2]. bychod] *so William Morris in BL Add. 14873 and (as correction) 14940*; pechod X. 10f ddifrod] ddirvod Ll[2]. 10h ympryd] vmprwd Ll[2] unpryd P[5] vmpryd *as variant* Ll[2].


[B] 11    Mis Tachwedd, moch mehinvawr;
aed bugail, del[e]d kerddawr!
Gwaedlyd llafn, llawn ysgubawr;
llon mor, merllyd pob callawr;
hir nos, heinvs karcharawr;
[parchus pawb a fedd drysawr];
tri dyn nid aml a'i diddawr:
trist, blwng a chybydd angawr.

B11b bugail] bug(g)l Ll[2]. deled] delid P[5] doed Ll[2]. 11c gwaedlyd] gwaedlud P[5]. llafn] lafn Ll[2]. 11d pob] *om.* Ll[2]. 11e karcharawr] i g. Ll[2]. 11f *in eighteenth century MSS; line left blank* P[5] *together with Panton 1; added in an eighteenth-century hand* Ll[3], *om.* X. 11h trist blwng] trist vlwng B[10] tristlwng Ll[2]. angawr] ac a. Ll[2].

[B] 12    Mis Rragfyr, tomlyd archan;
          trwm tir, trym<b>luog huan;
          llwm gwydd, llonydd llywaethan;
          llon keiliog a thylluan
          a'i deuddeng nydd yn hoian
          am eni ysbeiliwr Satan.
          Gwir a ddyvod Ysgolan:
          gwell Duw no<i> drygddarogan.

B12b trymbluog] trymhunog Ll². 12d thylluan] thwyll huan Ll³P⁵. keiliog] keliog Ll².
12e ai deuddeng nydd] ni xii gwydd Ll². hoian] howan Ll². 12f ysbeiliwr] ysbeliwr B¹²Ll².
12h no drygddarogan] noi dd. Ll²  noi ddrwg dd. Ll³P⁵ no drwg dd. B¹²Ll⁶.

# COMMENTARY

### I. Llym awel

This sequence is preserved only in the Black Book of Carmarthen, NLW MS Peniarth 1, now dated about 1250. Because of its composite nature it has been edited in full only by Jenny Rowland in *EWSP*. Stanzas 1–24 and 35, which contain the gnomic and natural elements, are edited by Kenneth Jackson in *EWGP*, pp. 18–20; the remaining stanzas, together with those lines in the others which he regarded as representing the saga element, by Ifor Williams in *CLlH*, pp. 27–29. Jackson's stanza-numbering, as far as it goes, is identical with Rowland's; Williams numbers his stanzas or portions of stanzas sequentially, and his numbering corresponds to Rowland's as follows: 1 = 1, 2–6 = 5–8, 6 = 10, 7 = 13, 8 = 15, 9–10 = 19–20, 11–23 = 22–34, 24 = 35, 25 = 36. Ifor Williams (*Lectures on Early Welsh Poetry*, p. 15) characterized the poem thus: 'like a mountain brook making its way through and under reeds and heather, now in full view, then disappearing for a while, but sure to emerge further on, so there runs a trickle of dialogue right through the 38 stanzas. The theme is cowardice'. Whether there is a single dialogue is uncertain; see the discussion by Jenny Rowland in *EWSP*, pp. 229–40. The text as we have it represents a compilation of saga englynion, of which there are two or (according to opinion) three main sections; the last of these is associated for the most part with the Llywarch Hen cycle, as is one intrusive stanza (19) earlier on, but no such connexion can be demonstrated for the rest. The last section has no gnomic content; the rest has a considerable admixture of gnomic material and, in the first twenty-two stanzas, the best pure nature description in the entire corpus. From 23 on, the saga dialogue on cowardice, some of it itself gnomic, interspersed with the description of a winter scene, is arguably abandoned for another dialogue altogether, whose main connexion with what goes before is that it, too, appears to be set in winter. Rowland, however, regards it as integral. From 30 the sequence continues with the Llywarch Hen material, omitted here as not relevant to the purpose of this anthology, and interrupted only by 35, which appears to belong with the earlier stanzas; this may have originally closed the section now concluded by the possibly intrusive 22, and so is included here. The omitted material may be read in *EWSP*, pp. 456–67, with translation on p. 503. The structure of the text may not be as chaotic as the detailed description suggests: on the possible significance of the conflation of disparate saga elements for the development of gnomic poetry proper, see General Introduction, above.

1a The line comprises three pure nominal sentences (see Language, C 1(a)), the pattern characteristic of gnomic and nature poetry. Note the variation in the rhyming pattern, with the main rhyme in the middle of the line (*brin*). Cf. III.10a, VIII.8a, though the parallel is not exact owing to the presence in these lines of generic or 'Irish' rhyme, where the vowel remains the same but the consonant changes; see on 19.

1b **llicrid, reuhid**: the characteristic old form of the 3 sg. where no preverb precedes.

1c **ry seiw gur**, i.e. because it is frozen so hard. *ry* has here a sense of potentiality; cf. 2c, 20c.

2b **rac bron**: on the analogy of *ger bron* 'before', this should mean something like 'against'. Note the variation in the rhyming pattern, with internal rhyme (*guaetev*, *banev*) but no main rhyme. Cf. VI.9a, VIII.1a, 17a, 18a.

2c **breit**: usually adv. 'scarcely', but here perhaps n. 'wonder, exception' or, as adj., 'exceptional'. **or seuir**: if a verb *gorseuir* (present impersonal of *gorseuyll* 'stand') is assumed, here and in 21e, the initial mutation is unexplained, though the sense 'keep one's footing' is good. *o* 'if' + *ry* of possibility (see Glossary), as in 1c is Jarman's interpretation, following *GBGG*). *yr* (*y* + *ry*) is a possible emendation, and would allow *breit* to be taken in its normal adverbial sense. The position of *allan* 'outside' is unusual; as an adv. of degree 'extremely' it would be unparalleled, but cf. 21e *guir*.

3: Jenny Rowland's emendations are followed in the first two lines.

3a **guely**: so Rowland, following Jackson's suggestion of an otherwise unknown *\*lly* for obscure *lle*: to be preferred because it gives a regular *englyn penfyr*.

3b: the reversal of the order of *caun* and *calaw* normalises the position of the internal rhyme. **caun truch**: nominal sentence with reversal of the usual order; cf. 4b, c below; as often in this poem, in a chiastic pattern with a normal sentence (see Language, C (1) (e), and cf. II.17b, IX.99, XI.1a).

3c **i[m]bluch**, possibly for *ymlwch*, with the likely sense 'stripped bare'. For *blwch* 'bare' cf. Breton *blouc'h* and the name *Blwchfardd*, which (though the phonology is problematic) may be a by-name meaning 'bald *or* tonsured poet'. See Jacobs, 'Sylwadau pellach ar *im bluch*'.

4a **guely**: beside the obvious metaphor, Sims-Williams, *Irish influence*, p.130 n. 23, suggests a pun on *gwely* 'tribal territory'.

4b **baryfhaud**: apparently a verbal adj.; so 4c *gwyrhaud*,' though Isaac, 'The Old-and early Middle-Welsh "future" tense', takes the latter as a future 'shall bend'.

5a **eiry** (modern *eira*) was originally monosyllabic, the final *y* being derived from the soft mutation of *g*, and continues to be scanned as a monosyllable as late as the fourteenth century, for example by Dafydd ap Gwilym. Whatever the pronunciation of this consonantal *y* was, it later became vocalised as -*a*. Here it is disyllabic, as in 6, 9 and perhaps 10, as against 7 and 8. y: this is the definite article according to Jarman, *LlDC* p. 168, but a 3 sg. possessive pronoun (with expected soft mutation not shown) is implied in Rowland's translation, *EWSP* p. 501. The latter interpretation is followed here.

5b **o'e:** = 'to their', ModW *i'w* (see *GMW* §56 N.2).

6b This may mark the beginning of the submerged dialogue on cowardice, or it may be purely gnomic. The dialogue certainly becomes evident in the next stanza.

8 This stanza reappears in 'Claf Abercuawg' (*EWSP* 450. 17), but in a different seasonal context.

8b: the plural verb is anomalous, but, as *vy* (= *hwy*), which should (cf. 25c) be omitted as hypermetric, suggests, the sense may be 'they hasten, the warriors'.

9b **karcharaur**, i.e. in his stable.

9c **annuyd hawdit**, apparently a loose adjectival collocation as predicate in a neg. nominal sentence, 'of the nature of a summer day'. *Hetiv* is the subject.

10 If this is an *englyn penfyr* something appears to have been lost in the first line.

10b **guit** must go with *llog*. *Llog ar mor* by itself does not make good sense in context, since even if ships put to sea in winter, it is not characteristic of winter that they should (cf. XI.11d); it must therefore mean 'masts' (not 'timbers' as Rowland translates) with sails lowered in expectation of storms.

11a **am cluir**: 'around the company' (Rowland), following Jackson's citation of Lloyd-Jones in *EWGP*, p.72, gives the best sense, though this use of *am* is unusual.

12a **igogaur:** = *yng ngogawr*: similarly 13a *igodo*, 18a *igniw*.

12b **diulith**, probably an exceptional sp. for *diwlydd* 'not mild' (which would normally be spelt -*t* in this MS, cf. 14c) , rather than 'without dew'. The line is short by three syllables and lacks rhyme.

12c **k[a]ssulwin**: Lloyd-Jones's suggestion, noted by Jackson and accepted by Rowland; the supposition is that something with *kyssul*- may have been lost in the previous line and that the unintelligible *kyssulwin* arose by haplography.

13b **pan vo** 'whenever it may be' is obscure. Rowland translates 'when it may, i.e. whenever it will'. Is the sense figurative, referring to the indifference of fate?

13c : present subjunctive with future sense, see *GMW* §124(b).

14c **eluit**: normally used without the definite article, whose addition gives an extra syllable; cf. 18c.

15b **cunlleit**. Unknown; 'fresh grass, herbage' (tentatively) *GPC*, 'sofl, calaf' (i.e. 'stubble, stalks') *GBGG*. Jackson emends to *cimleit* for *cyflaith*, 'confection', hence a plant with medicinal qualities. Against the objection that green growth is inappropriate to a winter poem (Rowland) it can be argued that this stanza represents the viewpoint that the weather is not too harsh for a man to go to battle (cf the ref. to cowardice in 15c); but though the stalks of cow-parsley are always hollow, *cev ewur* suggests the dry stalks characteristic of winter. Wmffre, *Language and Place-Names in Wales*, p. 274, note 18, suggests that *cimleit* is for *cunllaith* 'battlefield, destruction' and offers the interpretation 'the battlefield has greened over', the implication presumably being that the campaigning season is long past. It remains doubtful, however, whether greenness of any kind would be thought appropriate to a winter landscape.

15c **dricweued**: the second element is *meuedd* 'property', so 'endowment'.

16b **emriv**. Obscure: 'sea-spray' *GPC*, or *emliw* for *ymliw* 'quarrelling' (Ifor Williams). Jackson suggests a compound of *rhiw* 'slope'; 'embankment' would serve, if such existed at the time of composition.

16c **glau a uit**: (cf 17c *hinon uit*): 'there will be rain': this is probably an instance of the so-called 'abnormal sentence' with *a* as affirmative particle, rather than an emphatic sentence 'rain is what there will be' (see Language, 1(c,d),), but it is not always easy to differentiate between the two, and in these two stanzas, where two speakers are making contradictory assertions, emphasis would not be out of place.

17a **ki[ua]et[h]lauc**: MS *kinuetlauc* (? = *kynfethlawg* 'deceptive') gives no sense. On the basis of *cywaethl* 'argument' (cf. IX.5 *kyvaethlaw* 'quarrel') Jackson translates 'brawling', suggesting that *diffrint* has its etymological sense 'watercourse' (*dyffrynt* < *dwfr* + *hynt*); *GPC* 'disputed', taking up the theme of the need to engage in war. Jackson's interpretation seems the more probable and is followed here. Note the variation in the rhyming pattern. The main rhyme is absent, and the middle and end of the line rhyme instead (*hint, diffrint*). Cf. VII.7a.

18c **gueled**: perhaps in a special sense, 'look, visual impression'. *GPC* (s.v. **gwelaf**) cites *Mae'r graig i'w gweld fel gwenithfaen* 'the rock looks like granite'. If so, *gueilgi gueled* is a loose adjectival collocation 'with the appearance of the sea', with soft mutation of *g* not shown. **eluit**: see on 14c.

19 This stanza appears to have crept in from the Llywarch Hen cycle, perhaps because it fits the theme of cowardice and its reproach. Note the generic or 'Irish' rhyme, where the vowel (here a diphthong) remains the same but the consonant changes (*-eic, -eid, -eic*); for the commoner type with a simple vowel, see 23 (*-al, -ar, -ar*). For a more detailed discussion of such rhymes, see *EWSP*, pp. 333-4.

20 The metre is again irregular here, the first line being too short for an *englyn penfyr* and the third too long.

21a-b 'The speckle-breasted bird (i.e. thrush), speckled is its breast; speckled is the breast of the speckle-breasted bird' is the closest to sense that can be made of this. Its significance in context is entirely obscure, and it does not fit the metrical pattern of the *englynion*. It is tempting to assume an interpolation, but there appears to be no explanation for its presence. The next three lines are metrically difficult, and the whole passage is evidently corrupt.

21e **breit guir**: 'a true wonder' if *breit* is a noun; if it is an adjective, *guir* must be adverbial 'truly'. **or sefir**: cf. on 2c.

22 The saga context of this stanza may suggest a starting-point for sequences such as IV and VIII.

22c **deruhid**: not, as -*d* ≡ /d/ shows, future (for *derfydd*) but 3 sg. imperative (*GMW* §140(b)). Contrast the proverb *byrr dyd ny deruid kyngor*, in Henry Lewis, 'Diarhebion ym Mheniarth 17', no. 124, evidently 'short is the day when no advice comes to fruition'; the sense is not very clear and it is likely that this version is derived from a misconstruction of that represented by the Black Book text.

At this point the saga dialogue on cowardice interspersed with the description of a winter scene is arguably abandoned for another dialogue altogether, whose main connexion with the foregoing is that it appears to be set in winter. Rowland regards it as integral; it is included here so that readers may decide for themselves.

24a The metre here suggests that something has been lost. Ifor Williams (*CLlH*, p. 180) suggests reading *coed creilum* in the first line, then adding *llyn llaun* in the second, thus giving an internal rhyme and restoring an *englyn milwr*; Rowland would rather assume the loss of a further descriptive nominal sentence in the first line, thus giving something like an *englyn penfyr*, but the second line would then still be a syllable short. I have tentatively adopted Williams's transposition.

25a **hid [d]in**: for MS *hid in*. *En* 'chin' is another possible emendation. **Aruul Melin** (= *Arfwl Melyn*): the horse of Pasgen ab Urien Rheged.

25c **towissun**: -*e* in the MS is for the postfixed subject-pronoun *i*; it gives an over-long line and is omitted here, but is of interest as demonstrating the presence of such forms in the spoken language of the 13c; cf 8b. **brin tytul** ≡ *Bryn Tyddwl*. Its location is unknown.

26a **rodwit** 'dyke, rampart': for the defence of the ford?

26b **a riv**: *a* = 'with', i.e. 'despite, notwithstanding'; *riv* probably for *rhyw* 'such' (*GMW* §94), not *rhiw* 'slope'. The sense appears to be 'however much'.

26c **vid**: copula, followed directly by the complement.

27b **priw †uchei[n]†**: Ifor Williams emends to *Nuchein*, supposing a lost place-name. Rowland's suggested emendation *priu uithein* (for *prif wytheint*) 'chief ferocious ones' or 'chief fury' (i.e. hell) may be right.

27c **y ar**: see *GMW* § 223(b), and §223 for the type in general. *y* (OW *dy*, cf. Irish *di*) originally meant 'from', and *y ar* survives in MW with the sense 'off, from off'; confusingly, it was also equated quite early with the simplex *ar*, as here. Contrast III.8b and the emendation at VII.7b. **can**: sc. 'horse'; this adj. is always used of white horses, in preference to the expected *gwyn*. This line, as Williams points out, answers the question in 25c: 'by following …'

28b **Kynuit**: probably a hero of the Old North rather than a place-name, whether Cynwyd in Merioneth or some lost place of the same name now in England.

29b **par, penaeth**: it is not clear why the mutated forms with *b-* are not written. For the construction, emphasizing the adjectival phrase *rud y par* , see *GMW* §39(c). *o* is probably written for original *a*.

29c **ryvaeth** (*maeth* preceded by the preverb *ry*) exemplifies the old t-preterite; see *GMW* §133(b). Historically, instead of *a'm ryvaeth,* one would expect *ry'm maeth* with infixed pronoun; the text here shows the progressive breakdown in Middle Welsh of the old system of preverbs and infixes.

30a **Rhodwut Iwerit**: see 26a on the first element of this obscure place-name, presumably to be located in the Old North. The second element appears to be a personal name; modern *Môr Iwerydd* 'Atlantic Ocean' is of doubtful relevance.

30c An exhortation which in other circumstances could have been used as a precept.

After this stanza the sequence continues with unrelated material connected with the Llywarch cycle, which is omitted as not relevant to the purpose of this anthology, interrupted only by stanza 35, which appears to belong with the earlier material in the sequence; this may have originally closed the series of stanzas now concluded by the possibly intrusive 22, and so is included here.

35b **brith**, i.e. foamy, turbulent?

35c **duwin**, monosyllabic, for *dwfn* 'profound', with *cyngor*; Rowland translates 'wise'. *rëen* is correctly disyllabic, and as an emendation it restores the correct number of syllables. The MS reading implies a misunderstanding, 'let God give us counsel'; *Duw* would be pleonastic after *rëen*, but the error is an easy one.

## II. Eiry mynyd

This series, like IV, V, VII, VIII and part of III, is preserved in the Red Book of Hergest (Jesus College, Oxford, MS 111) of about 1400 (R); all but VII appear also in Jesus College, Oxford MS 20 of the first half of the fifteenth century (J). J is close to R but not a copy of it; there are many later manuscripts, but as these are derived from R they are of only incidental interest and of no value to an editor. The *Eiry mynyd* series is almost entirely in *englynion milwr*. Stanza 19 is the only *englyn penfyr*, stanzas 11, 34 and 35 are *englynion byr crwca*, stanza 6 is an *englyn cyrch* and stanzas 2 and 8 each have four rather than three lines; by Rowland's criterion (see Introduction on 'Date') the sequence may therefore be relatively late. But its text is not homogeneous: stanza 21 appears to belong to a saga and may be older, while the significance of the first-person statements in 6, 26 and 33 is not clear.

The opening phrase *Eiry mynyd* occurs a number of times in another series of *englynion* in the Red Book entitled *Ymatreg* (or *Penyd*) *Llywelyn a Gwrnerth* ('The Penitence of Llywelyn and Gwrnerth'). The content of these is moral and religious, not gnomic, and they are not edited here; for a text, with modern Welsh translation, see Haycock, *BBGCC*, no.32. There is little connexion between the phrase and the subject-matter of these stanzas, and it is clear that *Eiry mynyd* had already become popular as an introductory formula of a quite perfunctory kind. In post-mediaeval manuscripts there are other series of gnomic stanzas of three, six or eight lines beginning with the same formula; these are omitted here as being late and derivative. The entire corpus, including those in the Red Book, is printed in $MA^2$, pp. 358-63. The eight-line stanzas are reminiscent in style of '*Englynion*' *y Misoedd,* printed as extract XII, below.

1a **eiry mynyd**. As all but a few of the instances here demand a disyllabic pronunciation, Kenneth Jackson suggests that the original formula was *eiry ym mynyd*. But note that *eiry* is often disyllabic even in I.

1b **canu**. It is obvious that ravens, crows and rooks cannot sing; they can only croak or caw. We must assume, following Jackson, that the semantic range was wide enough to include the raven's call, unless we take the line figuratively as a rather sarcastic proverb ('many claim talents they do not possess' or 'do as I say, not as I do').

2 The first of three four-line stanzas. The three-line *englyn* is superseded in the poetry of the *Gogynfeirdd* by the four-line type, which appears first in the twelfth century; this may be taken as evidence for the date of those poems in which it occurs. While the addition of the extra line may be no more than an occasional experiment, a twelfth-century date for the Red Book sequences is plausible. All that has happened here is that a fourth line has been added to an *englyn milwr*, giving what is called an *englyn gwastad*, a form avoided, like the *englyn milwr*, by the *Gogynfeirdd*. See Language D 2 (c), and *EWSP*, 330-331, for discussion.

2d **a phyth**: spirant mutation of a new radical form *pyth*, based on the mistaken assumption that *byth* (like some other adverbs) was itself a mutated form.

3c **dirieit**: a recurring and untranslatable concept in these poems. Commonly opposed to *dedwydd* 'happy, blessed', it appears to mean one who is doomed to go wrong even when well-intentioned. The present line may be illustrated by the case of Efnisien in *Branwen* (*PKM* 29, 31-2, 43-4). 'Ill-starred' or 'hapless' are perhaps the nearest English equivalents. For further discussion see Jenny Rowland, *EWSP*, 197-200, though the term may not carry the weight of moral condemnation she supposes. The corresponding maxim in IV.4b makes the same point negatively. It is not clear which is original. **dihawl**, 'without a [legal] claim on him'.

4a **hyd escut**: the nominal sentence with reversed order is unusual but not unparalleled, see Language C 1(c); cf. in this poem 9a, 10a, 33a, where it may be an extension of the 'hanging' construction seen in 23a *hyd nyt hwyr* 'the stag, it is not slow'.

4c **oed**, modal (*GMW* §120(f)), combining, somewhat illogically, the senses 'would be better' and 'is necessary'. **deall**: normally 'understanding'. Jackson translates 'discretion'; something like 'savoir-faire' is presumably intended.

5a **ar des.** Compare 6a, 8a, 11a, 31a, V.1b, VI.15a for the idiomatic use here of the preposition *ar* in an adverbial phrase denoting physical activity or mental state; see *GMW* § 204 (second and last paragraphs) and *GPC* (2nd ed.) s.v. **ar** 8 (*d*) for some approximate parallels. The idiom requires further investigation. *Ar des* may mean 'frisky' or even 'in rut', though a figurative sense for *tes* 'heat' is not otherwise recorded so early.

6 A different type of four-line stanza (*englyn cyrch*) with the penultimate line giving an internal rhyme in the last.

6d **lle y bo**: *y* is probably not to be counted as a syllable.

7a **graennwynn**, Probably 'wondrously white' (*graen* 'awe-inspiring'), but possibly 'white-capped' (cf. Middle Irish *gráin* 'point, ?top'); used of a wave in VII.1a: here referring to the swirling foam of an incoming wave?

7b **i ogo**, i.e. its lair among the stones. Jackson's translation of *y* as 'in' cannot be sustained, since this form is used only with infixed pronouns; see *GMW* §222.

8 The stanza appears corrupt. As Jackson observes, *corof* (≡ *corf*) gives only *proest* (consonantal rhyme) with the other lines. But a correct *englyn proest* should have a different vowel in each line. As a minimal correction to avoid the repetition of *araf* (≡ *arf*), I print Jackson's suggestion of *varaf* in the fourth line, in the figurative sense of 'honour' (cf. *mefl ar fy marf*, 'shame on my beard' implying an insult to a man's virility) and translate 'for anger to descend on insulted honour'.

9b **os gwnn**: literally 'if I know (it)'; cf. ModW *ys gwn*, idiomatic for 'I wonder'. The phrase seems to express varying degrees of perhaps affected tentativeness in stating an opinion. The original sense may have been 'if I am right', then 'if I am not mistaken' or 'I dare say' and, with deliberate understatement, 'to be sure', as, apparently, here. The significance of this line, which is not gnomic, is quite obscure. The following line, with its specific reference, suggests a saga poem (cf. I. 8c), as does the vocative in 10c below. For an even more striking case, see 21c.

10a **hellawt**: *-ll* here is a genuine doubled *l*, not the standard voiceless *-ll*; see Jackson's note. The doubled *l* derives from earlier *l* + mutated *g*; see on I.5a.

10c **twr**: Jackson scans the stanza as an *englyn byr crwca*, and translates 'tower', with internal rhyme (long vowel) on *a wr*. This gives good sense and metre. But one could take *twr* as 'heap', thus 'burden' (short vowel), qualified by *trwm*, keeping the stanza as an *englyn milwr*. The next stanza is indisputably an *englyn byr crwca*.

13c **drycdrem**. Either 'an ugly face' (Jackson) or, better, 'poor sight'.

14b **purdu**: = V.7b as against *du plu* in VI.3b; 'very black' because it stands out against the snow? Perhaps a sophistication.

14c **iach ryd**: taken by Jackson as a loose compound 'healthy and free' in a hanging construction; but perhaps fig., in a nominal sentence, 'the free man is well off'. For *pa* 'why', followed by soft mutation, see *GMW* §83 N.2, and cf. VII.9c *py*.

18c **kytvyt**: *t* written for *dd*, suggesting an exemplar in the spelling system of I. As the line stands it is a syllable short.

19a **kynglhennyd**: the name occurs for 'liverwort' of the genus *Jungermannia* (see Davies, *Welsh Botanology*, p. 179), some species of which grow on stones under water, though so inconspicuous a plant seems hardly to merit such attention. The name could conceivably have been used earlier for 'water-weed' in a more general sense.

19b **hwyr [g]wedawc yng kynnyd**: *hwyrwedawg yng kynnyd* 'slow in succeeding' MS. The significance of this is not clear, though out of context it makes adequate sense. Jackson suggests 'the slow succeeds', but in that case the syntax, with nasal mutation of the predicate, is unusual, and comparable compounds of *hwyr* usually carry a derogatory sense, which fits awkwardly with the translation. A nominal sentence might be expected here, in which case one could emend to *hwyr gwedawc...* 'a man under subjection is slow to prosper'.

20c **ef a geiff**: for *ef a* as particle preceded by a neg., see *GMW* §191.

21c **vy mrodyr**, i.e. 'for my brothers'. Richard Sharpe, however, in his 2007 University of Wales O'Donnell lecture, takes this as a vocative; cf. 10c *a wr*.

22 The second line, unusually, extends the description of the wolf in the first line.

23a **hyd nyt hwyr**: here the subject is brought to the head of the sentence and is followed by the standard construction with *nyt*, effectively the negative form of the copula; the same can be done with the strong assertive *neut*. This 'hanging' construction (cf French 'L'État, c'est moi') may have been extended to affirmative nominal sentences, where the copula is not expressed.

23b The absolute form would not strictly be expected after the preverb *dy*, but clearly this was ceasing to be thought of as a preverb at all. Cf. IX.49.

24a **eilion ffraeth**. see on 4a above, and cf. I. 3b.

25b **uyd haf**. The reading is suspect. The reference to summer may be a gnomic statement, not a topical observation, but still comes in awkwardly, and the consuetudinal verb is untypical. Cf. V.6.

25c **glew y erchwynn**. Jackson's 'the brave is on the exposed side' is unacceptable; see on 7b. Since *erchwynn* can have the sense 'defender', *i* could be omitted. This leaves the line a syllable short, unless we read *aglew* (with the same sense) as in IX.6, but cf. 18c.

26. This is another stanza reminiscent of the saga material in I.

27b Cf. VI.5b.

29b i.e. the man favoured by God is prosperous in the world.

29c: cf I. 10c.

31c: 'the *diriaid* will not listen (to advice)', in a 'hanging' construction, see Language C 3. **ny mynn**: the radical (or the spirant mutation where that is possible) is historically correct in a principal clause, the soft mutation being used in rel. clauses, see *GMW* §65 N.1. The distinction is not always observed in the gnomic *englynion* (contrast 33c *ny weryt*, VIII.32c *ny gynghein* if that is the correct reading), but it is appropriate that it should be in this case, since with soft mutation the line would be a nominal sentence with a different emphasis: '*diriaid* is he who will not listen'.

32b A nature-gnome capable of being taken as a proverb warning against talking too much; cf VII. 4-7. As it stands there is a syllable lacking, since *dwfyr* is monosyllabic; the D reading *y dwfr* would restore it, but it has the look of an emendation.

32c: another short line, cf. 18c. 25a; but D reads *angwhaneccid* (with the same sense); this appears also in Davies's list of proverbs, and is perhaps original.

33b Another intrusive personal reference.

33c **trwch**: the sense is related to that of *diriaid* (see on 3b), but in context appears to carry a greater sense of moral depravity and less of a man doomed to trouble even despite his best intentions.

34b **ys odidawc**: a variant, with the old copula *ys*, on the more usual *odid*. The stanza scans as an *englyn byr crwca* with a short second line.

35 Note the generic or 'Irish' rhyme (see *EWSP*, pp. 333-4) between *geudawt* and *gymydawc*.

## III Bidiau

This series is represented in one redaction, which I call O, in the Red Book of Hergest (R) and in Jesus College, Oxford MS 20 (J), and in another redaction, which I call Q, in the hand of Dr John Davies, Mallwyd in NLW MS Peniarth 102 (D¹), in the hand of Thomas Wiliems in BL Add MS 31055 (W), and a third, somewhat deviant, text, perhaps in the hand of Gutyn Owain, in NLW MS Peniarth 27 (P). Copies of both redactions are preserved, again in the hand of Dr Davies, in NLW MS 4973B, where the O version (D²) is a transcript of what was probably a copy of the Red Book and the Q version is virtually identical with Peniarth 102. In W and D¹ the stanzas appear in a sequence entitled *Englynion Duad*. For a detailed account of these see Jenny Rowland, "Englynion Duad". Dr Rowland did not edit these stanzas, since they had already been edited by Jackson in *EWGP*, but see below under VI. The complicated textual tradition of this series points to an extended period of oral variation. There is a considerable degree of overlap between the two versions, but each contains some stanzas not present in the other, which serves to remind us of the fluidity of the gnomic tradition and the likelihood that some stanzas and many variant versions may have been lost from those series preserved only in the Red Book. The stanzas common to both do not appear in the same order. Jackson edited the two versions separately under the titles *Bidiau* I and II, but the common stanzas are here edited together in the order and orthography in which they appear in the Red Book, with the remainder added as a supplement.

1a **bit**: see above, on 'Language', C.1(d). The exact sense varies from stanza to stanza, and has to be inferred from the context. The validity of Jackson's distinction between 'is by nature' and 'must be' is not clear, and his claim that Old English *sceal* always has the latter force is an erroneous generalisation. Elements of both these senses are present in different cases, and sometimes even a prescriptive element 'let … be' (so 4a, 4b, 6a, 7a, ?11b, 15c, ?16a, 16b, 17a, ?21c). The syntax of *bit* is as follows: (i) *bit* + predicate + subject; (ii) *bit* + subject + *yn* + predicate or *bit* + subject + prepositional phrase; exceptionally (iii) subject (in 3a a noun phrase) + *bit* + predicate, in the 'hanging' construction. *Bit* is normally followed by the soft mutation, but this cannot be shown in the case of *d* in the Red Book orthography, and is not consistently shown in the later MSS of the Q group; see stanzas 19-21 below. For its apparent failure in the case of *t*, see on 2b below.

2 = Q 10. 2a: i.e. because it shakes the acorns from the trees; so Jackson, citing William Owen (Pughe).

2b **Bit tawel**: for *bit dawel*; see *GMW* §17(a)(1); so also 9a *trwm*, 12c *tost*. Cf II.11c, with substitution of *bit* for *gnawt*. It is hard to say which version, if either, is original; the frequency of *englynion penfyr* in this series may suggest that it is in general somewhat older (as implied by Rowland, "Englynion Duad", 65), but that is no guarantee of the originality of the formula with *bid*.

2c **diryeit**: see on II.3b.

3 = Q 11.

3a **cnifiat**, beside *cynifiad* in Q. Both mean 'fighter, truculent'. The O reading may be preferable since it brings the line down to the usual ten syllables, but the radical form is *gnifiad*, and in order to account for that as a mutated form we must assume an alternative form with *c-* under the influence of *cynifiad*.

3b: following Q; cf. the parable of the wedding-feast, Matt. xxii: 11-14. Jackson translates Q as 'clothes are well-fitting', which seems trivial.

3c **bit** has the force of a precept here, in an expression of moralised self-interest.

4 = Q 13. The variants in this stanza suggest a degree of oral corruption, of a kind that occurs elsewhere in *englynion penfyr*, where the metre may have been imperfectly understood.

4a **gavwy:** *gawy* Q is an equally valid form. The transposed predicates in O disrupt the rhyme, and *vryt* (better *y vryt*) is desirable to provide the *gair cyrch*. **Lew** could be mutation of *glew* 'brave' or of *llew* 'lion'. The animal imagery of *bleid* might be thought to favour the latter. But there is no sign of the wolf in Q's second line, where we read *a bid lleiniad yn ardwy* 'let a spearman be a defender'; this again has an extra syllable, and *yn* could be dropped, giving 'let a defender be a spearman'.

4c: nine syllables make O's line excessively long. Q omits the pronoun *ar* (see *GMW* §75), and the possessive *y* is unnecessary.

5a **redeint**: '? (young) deer', GPC, perhaps better than Jackson's 'coursers'. Cf IX. 85, but there it is apparently a different word altogether.

6 = Q 4. 6b Is there a hint here of the *fabliau* motif of the rich old man, his young wife and her young lover? The third line suggests the same figuratively. But this would be unusual in a tradition which seems largely impervious to foreign influences.

7 = Q 3. 7a **bit gywir baglawc**: from Q, where O merely repeats the opening phrase of 6a in a series in which otherwise only the first word is repeated: this suggests carelessness. **rygyngawc:** 'ambling', from Q, appropriate to a church dignitary but not to a mounted soldier, hence the alteration to *redegawc* 'swift' in O.

7b **mab llen**, perhaps a calque on Irish *mac léinn* 'clerical student', and with similar sense. *Chwannawc* may mean 'eager' or 'greedy' according to the original milieu of the stanza: clerical in the former case, secular, with anti-clerical bias, in the latter.

8a **crwm**: i.e. with heads lowered to graze?

8b **y ar**, see *GMW* § 223(b); but no sense given there quite covers this. Translate 'fresh from', and cf. 'full of beans' in English.

8c: apparently figurative. Jackson's explanation 'even a light thing … can be burdensome to the young or weak' has not been improved on.

9a **trwm … grwm**: Jackson (Addenda) proposes this transposition, following Thomas Jones. 'A hollow thing is concave', though an odd observation, is not nonsensical; but *crwm* means 'convex', not 'concave'. Can *ceu*, like its derivative *ceudod*, mean 'belly'? It is used by Dafydd ap Gwilym (*GDG* 109.20) of the cavity of a pair of bellows.

9c **adneu**: see on IV.1a. If the sense is 'store' one might take *gwawn* as 'cobweb', giving a proverb on the dangers of hoarding; but to keep a store of grain is surely sound economy. If 'place of burial' the reference would be to sowing, and the point of the line would be closer to that proposed by Jackson for 8c. Note the spelling <d> rather than <t> (as expected and as in IV.1a), a possible relic of an exemplar in Black Book orthography

10 = Q 2. 10a **haha**: Jackson (Addenda) cites Henry Lewis's suggestion that this expresses 'a request for a repetition of what has been said': so 'the deaf man keeps saying "Eh? Eh?" '. For the variation in the rhyming pattern, see I.1a.

10b: this and the Q variants *bid dirieid ymgeingar* 'the quarrelsome man is *diriaid*" or *dirieid bid ymgeingar* 'the *diriaid*, he is by nature quarrelsome' (see on II.3c) appear a genuine case of oral variation, and it is inappropriate to speculate on priority.

10c  The syntax is difficult. Jackson (reading *yr* for *or* as in D¹) translates 'happy is he on whom looks one who loves him', which would seem to require emendation of *ae gwyl* to *a wyl*. Emendation can be avoided by taking *ae gwyl* as incorporating an infixed third person pronoun with proleptic force (*GMW* §60) and translating 'happy is he who looks on the one who loves him'. On the use of *o* in a pure nominal sentence, see *GMW* §§39(c), 231 N.3. Perhaps better, however, is the suggestion of Dr Rhian Andrews (private communication) that *dedwyt* stands in a 'hanging' construction (see Language C.3, above), giving the translation 'the fortunate man, [all] of those who see him love him'. See *GMW* §75 for this use of *o'r a*; it is most commonly used after a superlative adjective or a pronominal such as *pawb* 'all', but it is not unreasonable to suppose that the latter could be understood here.

11 = Q 9.

11b †**granclef**†: unknown, and does not look much like a MW word. Since *bit* is normally followed by soft mutation, whatever is intended might be expected to begin with *c*. Jackson proposes, on the basis of the variants, *gwarantlew* 'a dependable lion'; this is palaeographically plausible and supplies the necessary extra syllable, but seems an unlikely compound; no other such compound with *gwarant* 'surety' is recorded. Equally doubtful is *gwarancleu* 'easy to find' suggested in *GBGG* on the assumption of an otherwise unknown *gwaranc* 'acquisition, discovery, reception' + *clau*, still usual in South Wales for 'quick, ready'. Some word meaning 'reliable' or (taking *lef* as *llef* 'shout') 'loud' would give good sense. A possible emendation is *bit grauawc llef glew* 'raucous is the shout of the hero', though *crauawc* (modern *crafog*) is not otherwise recorded before 1800. See Jacobs, 'A Jacksonian Emendation Revisited'.

11c **nawd**: from Q. Jackson emends the unintelligible O reading *mawr* to *mawl*, assuming 'an alteration by a scribe who did not understand "Irish" rhyme'. On the latter, see *EWSP*, 333-4, where it is shown that *nawdd* would rhyme as well. A scribe might have favoured *mawl* as a more acceptable rhyme. If it is correct, it is better translated 'will honour' or 'will commend' than Jackson's 'praises'.

12 = Q 14, in part.

12a: based on the Q reading. **edëin**: for *eddain* Q; seemingly the same word as *euein* O, and, as the more usual form, preferable. The word is trisyllabic and thus rhymes with the main rhyme. There is nothing much to choose between the O reading *bit euein alltut bit disgythrin drut* and Q's related *bid llymm eithin a bid eddain alltud* in themselves. Jackson regards the Q version as more authentic, as including an additional gnome; that could be a sophistication, but Q is clearly superior in 12b, the omission of *bit* and the substitution of *drut* 'rash' for *ynuyt* 'foolish' reduces the line to its proper length, and if we read *drut* in this line it cannot be right in 12a. The omission of 12c in R confirms some degree of corruption there, but the rare *disgythrin* 'fierce' points to genuine oral variation here.

13 = Q 6.

13a **bit uynych mach**: the sense is clear, but the point is not. *Mach* is one who acted as guarantor to one or other party to a legal contract, by undertaking either to enforce the fulfilment of that party's obligation or to fulfil it himself in the event of his defaulting; see Charles-Edwards, 'A Note on Terminology'.

13c **chwyrn**: so Q. O expands to the synonymous *chwyrnyat*, giving an excessively long line which resembles the first line of an *englyn penfyr*; and indeed such a line occurs in one of the stanzas peculiar to Q, see below. This suggests a confusion of two distinct stanzas in the process of memorial transmission. The line is still a syllable too long; if the second *bit* were omitted, the second half of the line would be grammatically acceptable as a pure nominal sentence (cf. 18c), but the repeated *bit* may be an element of style capable of overriding strict metrical criteria.

14 This stanza appears corrupt, but there is no Q version to correct it.

14a **diaspat**: normally a noun, here perhaps adj. 'vociferous': cf. 13b *cwyn*, 14c *rew*, XII.1b *trallawd*. **aele[u]**: Jackson's emendation, to give the internal rhyme usual in this series. †äe†: unknown. *GBGG* recommends emendation to *aele*, ?'given to complaint', but that excludes Jackson's emendation, and it is not clear that there are two semantically distinct words here.

14b [**a**] **besgittor**: *pesgittor* is normally a verb (an old passive, see *GMW* §131(a)), which makes no sense after *bit*. The obvious emendation printed here breaks the pattern of the series by which each line begins *bit*, but this is not unknown: cf 1, 6, 8, 9. *Pesgi* and *dyre* are commonly used of animals (cf VI. 9a, but contrast VI.13a): translate 'the well-fed beast is skittish'.

14c **bit rew bre**: *sc.* when the low ground is free of it.

15 = Q 12. 15b **ar onn**: the Q reading, against *a ron* O. *Rhôn*, like *onn*, means 'spear', but gives a false rhyme with *tonn*.

16 = Q 15.

16a **lluarth**: 'corrected' to *lle buarth* 'site of milking-enclosure or sheepfold' in Q.

16b 'the suppliant is shameless' Jackson, but *gwarth* is a public disgrace rather than a private response, and thus *diwarth* is more commonly used in a positive sense. The maxim might be taken as prescriptive 'let a suppliant be without reproach' or 'let a suppliant incur no shame for asking'; cf VII.20b.

16b **reinyat**: probably from *rhan* 'portion' so 'one who distributes; generous man' (*GPC*). **yghyuarth**: literally 'at bay'. Does this mean 'a lord under assault from his enemies should still be generous'?

17 = Q 1.

17a **trydar**: better 'battle', so 'martial spirit', than 'clamour' (Jackson), a usage otherwise confined to the chatter of birds or of fools.

17b **ymladgar**: presumably the subject.

17c: a general observation about the effects of bereavement, as *bit* shows, not a personal statement.

18a **gwynn**: i.e. lime-washed. **gor[u]n**: 'noisy', for unknown *gorwn*; so Jackson, who translates 'rattling'; better 'resonant', *sc.* when struck. Another of his suggestions, *gwrwm* 'dark blue', a favourite epithet for armour in the *Gododdin*, is unfortunately a monosyllable.

18b: obscure. Jackson translates, 'a favourite thing, many ask for it', which makes sense but does not explain *bit*. Can it refer to the armour of the previous line?

18c **ryngawc**: for the sense 'interfering' (derived from *rhwng* 'between') see *GPC* s.v. *rhyngog*. The line is already too long; Jackson's emendation to *rhygyngog* 'ambling, unsteady' adds an extra syllable. Omission of the second *bit* would give a standard line; cf. 13c.

19 = Q 5; this and the two following stanzas are in Q only.

19b **cwyn**: for the adjectival use, cf. 13b. A variant version is preserved among the proverbs in NLW MS Peniarth 17 (see on I.22c above), no. 196 *bytrisd* (for *bid trist*) *pob galarus*.

20 = Q 7.

20a. See on 13: this stanza is clearly part of the tradition from which O derives, since the first line has influenced 13c in O but not in Q. Note the variation in the rhyming pattern. The main rhyme is at the end of the line, and there is internal rhyme between the fifth and the eighth syllables (*colwyn, wenwyn*); cf. VIII.12a.

20b **nofiaw**: normally 'swim'; here a matter of wading rather than vaulting over the water.

20c **odwr**: not 'adulterer' (Jackson) but 'receiver (of stolen goods)'.

21 = Q 8.

21a **diriaid**: see on II.3c. **ffer**: from Lat. FERVS. At IX.8 it appears to have connotations of dangerous unpredictability; here perhaps 'wild' is the best rendering. **eweint**: the connotations are of youth, liveliness and lustfulness.

21b **bid**: here almost 'leads to' (Jackson).

21c **bid**: most probably prescriptive, 'let (a man) be', as if an impersonal imperative.


## IV. Gnawt gwynt

This series is preserved in R and J (see on II). Of the first five stanzas beginning *gnawt gwynt*, four are *englynion unodl union*, and this suggests, according to Rowland's metrical criterion, that at least this section of the series is one of the latest parts of the corpus. Three more stanzas beginning simply *gnawt* follow; the first of these looks very late, since not only is *pastardaeth* a Norman-French word but the concept itself is unknown to native jurisprudence. The series is evidently a loose compilation from a number of sources: note that the *cymeriad* with *gnawt* fails after stanza 8, and after 9 follows a saga stanza interpolated from the Llywarch Hen cycle; see *EWSP*, p.417, 14, where it plainly fits the context better.

1a **atneu** 'place of burial' with **llann** 'churchyard' gives good if rather trivial sense. But if *llann* is taken to refer to the church itself, the alternative sense 'deposit, treasury' is possible: a church, especially if it had a substantial stone tower, was an obvious place to deposit precious objects or documents for safety. Jackson favours this interpretation, citing Lewis, *HGC*, p.190, who identifies *Llann adneu* in a poem to St David by Gwynfardd Brycheiniog (*HGC*, no. xviii) with *Depositi Monasterium* in Rhygyfarch's Life of the saint. The poem has more recently been edited by Morfydd E. Owen in *Gwaith Llywelyn Fardd I ac Eraill*, ed. Kathleen Anne Bramley et al., CBT II (Cardiff, UWP, 1994), pp. 441-92.

2d **gwic**: normally 'wood, forest'; this gives a line which may be factually true but seems somewhat pointless. Jackson, following Loth, suggests that this is a different word, cognate with Irish *fich* 'battle' (better 'feud'); this gives a pointed comment on the consequences of civil strife, and is probably to be preferred. **o vrein**: on the idiomatic use of *o* with the subject of a preceding verbal noun, see *GMW* §181(a).

3d The observation is notable for its realism, given the heroic tradition whereby a generous supply of drink is seen as a stimulus to martial valour.

4d In a sequence of four-line stanzas (*englynion unodl union*) it is likely that a line has been lost here.

5a **y mro** i.e. at home rather than on campaign?

6 This stanza has been deleted from the Red Book and is illegible there, as was already noted in the seventeenth century by John Davies, Mallwyd in his copy in NLW MS 4973B, f. 173v. I have suggested that it may be a late addition to the sequence, referring in the third line to the calamitous end of the principality of Gwynedd in 1282 with the death of Llywelyn the Last, whose father Gruffudd ap Llywelyn was illegitimate. See Jacobs, 'Animadversions on Bastardy'.

6a **pastardaeth**: the condemnation is unexpectedly severe, given that Welsh law and custom attached no stigma to the condition (see Jenkins, 'Property Interests in the Classical Welsh Law of Women'). **grynnwryaeth**: evidently 'paltriness, mean-spiritedness', related to *crwn* 'round, ? small; the same semantic development is perhaps to be seen in XII.7f *kronffair* '? petty fair'.

6c: the excessive length of this line and its rhythmical feebleness suggest that two original lines have been run together here; but this and the next two stanzas make no reference to the wind and may originally come from a different sequence in three-line stanzas. The final line could be reduced to standard length by deleting the reference to great-grandsons, which may well be the addition of an over-enthusiastic copyist.

7a. The association of an eagle and an oak-tree recalls the story of Lleu Llaw Gyffes in the Fourth Branch of the Mabinogi.

7c **golwc vynut**: the reverse order is to be expected, cf. 8b, and on I.3b.

8a **anllwyth** 'flood', *GPC*. Jackson's suggested emendation to *a tanllwyth* 'with a blazing fire' is attractive, but, as he points out, founders on the lack of spirant mutation, which should be written at this time. **kynlleith**, etymologically 'slaughter', according to *GPC*, here 'ravages' (cf. on I.15b), but Jackson associates it with the better-attested adj. of the same form meaning 'soft, tender' and translates 'in a mild winter'; this would give a superior sense.

8b **kynrwytyeith**: *GPC* suggests that this may be an error for *kyurwytyeith* (ModW *cyfrwyddiaith*, though with the same sense 'loquacious'. Note the use of *t* instead of *d* (≡ /ð/)) suggesting an exemplar in the Black Book orthography (see above, Language, A.4(b)).

8c: cf. the same line in VI 22c.

9. This and the following stanzas appear not to belong to the sequence. Dr John Davies transcribes them as a separate poem. Between 9 and 10 follows this stray stanza: *Y deilen a dreuyt gwynt | gwae hi oe thynget | hen hi eleni y ganet* 'the leaf that the wind worries, alas for its fate: it is old, this year it was born'. This is well known from its appearance in 'Cân yr Henwr' in the Llywarch Hen cycle (see *EWSP*, 415-8, stanza 14) *Y deilen honn neus kenniret gwynt | gwae hi oe thynghet | hi hen eleni y ganet*. Note (1) that that stanza is a correct *englyn penfyr*, where the present version has a defective first line; (2) that *honn* gives the stanza a particular reference within the time-scale of the saga, whereas its absence gives the present stanza an appropriate gnomic quality; (3) that in the last line the present version places the predicate first, which is not strictly necessary where the subject is a personal pronoun (*GMW* §145 N.3) but gives an additional internal rhyme; it could represent the correct reading, but may be some redactor's attempt at improvement.

10a **bychan**, 'a small thing', i.e. the nest (understood), not the bird; this obviates Jackson's objection to *yd* on the grounds that *bychan* should be plural in agreement with *adar*. This preserves the scansion of the whole as an *englyn byr crwca*. Translate: 'though it be a small thing, skilfully do the birds build…'

10c **kyuoet**, lit. 'of the same age', as tr. by Jackson, but a secondary sense 'companion' is well attested and perhaps more likely.

11b **ymdiriet:** verbal noun (effective subject of the verb in a 'hanging' construction), not an imperative.

11c **edeu:** 3 sg. pres. ind. of *adaw* 'promise'; figuratively 'gives expectation of'? Is there a confusion with *gadael* 'allow (3 sg. pres. ind. *gedy*)? Either way, *pace* Jackson, *hirbla* is probably the subject.


## V. Kalan gaeaf

This series is preserved in R and J (see on II). In a sequence of *englynion milwr*, it contains one four-line *englyn cyrch*, and this may suggest a relatively late date. There is no need to take it, with Jackson (*ECNP*, pp. 159-60), as evidence for the influence of a tradition of seasonal verse in which the passing of summer was lamented, but such an origin cannot be conclusively disproved. Stanza 6 is interpolated from a series set in summer, cf. VIII.31, as the reference to bird-song makes clear; it has been half-heartedly assimilated to the context by altering *hir dydd* to *byr dydd*. Some of the stanzas reappear in the next extract.

1 *Englyn cyrch*: see Language, D, note 17.

1a **Kalangaeaf**, the first day of winter, 1 November.

1b: for the inverted word-order in a pure nominal sentence, cf. I. 3b, II.17b; but note that in this case there is no preceding sentence with normal order to provide a chiastic pattern.

2a **kein [k]yfrin**. Note the etymological sense of *cyfrin,* now merely 'secret': Jackson translates 'a secret shared'. The lenited *gyfrin* of the MSS is not appropriate in a nominal sentence; Jackson suggests, reasonably, that it anticipates 6a *kein gyfreu.*

2b **kyfret**: equative formed on a verbal stem 'as swift-(running)'

2c **gweith keluyt**: better 'the work of a skilful man' (Jackson) than 'a skilful action'.

3b **gwedw hauot**: because it was abandoned for the permanent pasture on lower ground (*hendref*) from this day. Cf. XII[B]. 10c.

3c: cf. XII[B].10e. Shameful conduct for the sake of trivial gain is foolish as well as dishonourable. Note that the lines shared with XII[B] belong there to October, not November.

4. Essentially = VI.19.

4a **gwrysc**: 'herbage', rather than 'branches' (Jackson on IV.4a); used to this day for 'haulm', the green growth of potatoes or the like.

4b **dirieit**, see on II.3b.

5a. The line as it stands is a syllable short. It can easily be restored, as Professor Charles-Edwards suggests, by reading the synonymous *agarw*; see on VI.5a.

6. This stanza comes from a summer sequence (see, e.g. the almost identical stanza VIII. 31) and has been only partly assimilated to the winter setting; the uncorrected reference to cuckoos makes nonsense. For a similar incongruity, cf II. 25b. But if Jackson is correct, the stanza was present in the sequence from an early date, since it appears to have influenced the reading in 2a; it is therefore printed here.

6a **kein gyfreu**: loose adjectival collocation as predicate in a pure nominal sentence.

6c: Jackson takes *goreu* as predicate, but *trugar* is the more natural one: tr. 'merciful is the providence of the most gracious God'.

7: cf. VI. 3.

7a **kalet cras**: against taking *kalet* as a spelling for *calledd* 'pasture' is Jackson's objection that November is not a parched season. Best, then, to take *cras* as a noun 'dried herbage'.

7b: cf. II. 14b, but the point has less force in this context. [e]**vras**: Thomas Jones's suggestion for MS *ovras*, unexplained mutation of *govras* 'stout'.

8c **gwir**: Jackson suggests reasonably that this is equivalent to *ys gwir* 'it is true'; cf. XII.1g, though there *gwir* could be taken as a noun 'truth'. **hegarwch**: the spelling (*e* for *y*) is archaic, but too much weight should not be placed on it.

9: cf. VI. 4, where in the last line, perhaps preferably, *odit* stands first.

9a **godeith**: usually 'burnt ground', but in a winter stanza must mean 'ground for burning', since the burning of the mountain took place in March and April, so as to provide tender growth for the beasts when they were moved back to the *hafod* (see IV.3b) for the summer.

9c **kedymeith**: the sense must be that, though there may be no lack of company, a companion worthy of the name is hard to find. Note *e* for *y*, and cf. 8c.

### VI. Calan Gaeaf a'r Misoedd

A second sequence of 'Calan Gaeaf' stanzas is preserved in the sequence entitled *Englynion Duad*, on which see above on II. The present sequence overlaps at some points with that in the Red Book, but it is extended with eleven stanzas referring in order to all but one of the months of the year, and for this reason the whole sequence is edited separately here. The text, especially the portion dealing with the months, is not well preserved, and presents many difficulties of interpretation. It may be somewhat older than the Red Book version. The sequence has been edited by the present author in 'Englynion Calan Gaeaf a'r Misoedd'. It was previously edited with introduction and commentary by Jenny Rowland in "'Englynion Duad'", together with three other sequences which are preceptual or moral rather than gnomic and do not contain the characteristic combination of gnomic and nature poetry; these are accordingly not edited here, with the exception of three stray stanzas which do fit the pattern and are added as a supplement at the end of this section. Two other poems survive based on the months of the year: the fragment in NLW MS Peniarth 82 (see XI, below) and the later and better-known *'Englynion' y Misoedd* (see XII, below), but there is little if any connexion between this text and the others.

1a **henoeth**: an old form suggesting an early date, perhaps late 11th century. The specific detail suggests a 'saga poem'.

1c **ac eirvg**: obscure and possibly corrupt. Among Rowland's suggestions is that this contains a supposed verb *eirwng* 'deserve' (see *GBGG* s.v.), presumably in the 3 sg. As *eirvg* is a possible spelling for this word in the Black Book orthography (see Language, A. 2(d)(iii), 4(a)(ii)) this is not strictly an emendation, but *ac* gives an extra syllable and, as it contributes nothing, should probably be deleted. The sense appears to be that all the poor are entitled to charity, whatever their moral condition.

2a **alaf**: Rowland's emendation for *calaf*; cf. *EWSP* 451, 23a.

2b **twn**: for MS *ton*, ? anticipating *to*.

2c: = II.33c, q.v. on *trwch*.

3: essentially = V.7.

3a **kalet**: the Red Book reading against *calaf* in this text. 'Reeds are parched' does not give good sense for November; for interpretation, see on V .7a.

3b **du plu**: contrast *purdu* II. 14b (see note), but cf. V.7b. **bras**: perh. a substitution for the difficult *evras* (MS *ovras*) of the Red Book, with the metre filled up with *gnawt*.

4: essentially = V.9. It is doubtful whether this stanza really belongs in a *Calan gaeaf* series at all, since ploughing was usually done in spring: cf. the poem from the Black Book of Carmarthen cited at *EWSP* 203 *kintevin keinhav amsser | dyar adar glas callet | ereidr in rich ich iguet* 'early summer, fairest season; loud are the birds, green is the foliage; ploughs are in the furrow, the ox yoked'. Autumn ploughing is not inconceivable in mediaeval Wales, but November is very late for it.

4a **goddaith**: see on V.9a.

4c **odid or cant**: the word order is preferable to that of the Red Book version.

5a **[a]garw**: the emendation (proposed by Professor Charles-Edwards) needed to restore the metre. *Garw* later came to be pronounced (though not, correctly, scanned) as a disyllable; cf. II.1a, on *eiry*.

5b: cf. II.27b. There is little to choose between *llwmm* here and *crwm* there.

5c: i.e. 'the end does not justify the means'; cf. XII. A 9f.

6b **braint ar swyddau**: Rowland's reading for unintelligible *gwyddau*, on the strength of B. The sense is 'there is permission to frequent the courts'. Thomas Charles-Edwards observes that the two periods of 'open law' ran from November and May (strictly from the tenth of each month) to the end of February and July respectively; during these periods suits might be brought relating to land, but not at other times, when ploughing and sowing or harvest were in progress.

7a **ryn rynawd**: cf I.13b. This apparently trivial statement is curiously reminiscent of that in the Old English *Maxims* I, 71, (in *The Exeter Book*, ed. Krapp and Dobbie, p. 159) *forst sceal freosan* 'it is the nature of frost to freeze'. Here, however, it is best taken as a seasonal statement appropriate to *Kalan Gaeaf* 'the frost will freeze'. An alternative is to take *rynawd* as a noun 'space of time', here used adverbially: 'cold for a while'; see *GPC* s.v. rhynnawdd, rhynnawd.

9a For the variation in the rhyming pattern see I.2b.

9b **i golofn**: of obscure significance; perhaps figurative, of the temptations incident to material or spiritual advancement.

9c: probably 'a fearless man is not a good avenger' (i.e. caution is needed). But 'an avenger will not be without fear' (Rowland) is not impossible.

10 Uncertain. The emended text assumes a reference to the penitential disciplines of Ash Wednesday, traditionally performed early in the morning (*plygain*).

10b [a'e] gofwy: '(for) the one who frequents it'. diangawr, sc. from the pains of hell: an archaic future impersonal form.

11a   Not much sense can be made of the line as it stands. Rowland suggests emending to *Calan mawrth, mygedus dydd; ereidr yn rych* '... the day (morning) is misty; ploughs are in the furrow', which gives good sense.

11c: perhaps 'the stag is *or* shall be called Culaethwy', a suggestion by Dafydd Glyn Jones (private communication), with reference to the story of Gwydion and Gilfaethwy in *Math uab Mathonwy* (*PKM* 75); compare, in the same tale, *PKM* 91.17 *ac ef a elwir etwa y dylluan yn Blodeuwed* 'and to this day the owl is called Blodeuwedd'.

12 Three syllables are lost from the first line and perhaps one from the second.

12b yngofag: possibly 'breeding, multiplying'.

13a egin dyre, cf. I.3b.

13b eilwydgar: in the summer (though perhaps not usually as early as May) stags move as a group to the high ground away from the hinds.

15b ar gychwyn: perhaps homeward bound after a spring campaign. Most of the stanza is lost. It is possible to reconstruct the last line as *gnawt y chweir colled am fraw*, 'usual is for loss to befall on account of fear', on the basis of a proverb recorded in MS Peniarth 17 and in the Red Book of Hergest; but that is a mere guess.

16a irgig: 'fresh meat', for unintelligible *dirgig*. This appears to refer to the practice of killing the wether lambs towards the end of the summer. Something is lost before this word, perhaps a verbal noun with the sense 'serving' or 'eating'.

17b †dygweste†: unknown. Possibly for *dydd gwastad* 'the day is even', ? with reference to the equinox. An adjectival predicate presumably preceded *haul*, perhaps with the sense 'still warm' or 'moderate'.

19 Essentially = V.4; see note for comment.

Two of the three stanzas which follow belong to the second and one to the fourth series of *Englynion Duad*, which are not in general gnomic. They are included here for convenience.

20a For the variation in the rhyming pattern, cf. 9a. But note that *gwaneg, gwaeddgreg* give generic or 'Irish rhyme (see on I.19) with the main rhyme.

21c hoedl derfyn: 'life's limit'; this type of compound, with the determining element placed first with soft mutation of the second element, is rare in the gnomic poetry, though common in the work both of the *Gogynfeirdd* and of the *cywyddwyr*.

**22a, c diffaith**: the repetition of the same word in a single stanza is unusual, but may be explained by the difference in sense, 'wilderness' as against 'waste, deserted'.

**22b raith**: the sense 'violence' is postulated on the basis of the Irish cognate *recht* 'sudden attack, rage'. But Rowland's emendation to *anraith* 'plunder' may be preferred, though it leaves the line a syllable too long.

**22c yn** should probably be omitted for the sake of the metre.

### VII. Baglawc bydin

This, unlike the other Red Book sequences, does not appear in J. It appears to be a composite piece, made up of the detritus of a number of separate sequences, of which at least two seem to have been saga poems. These are represented by 4-7, which suggest a story of someone imprisoned as a result of an indiscreet revelation, and 8-11, which belong to a discussion of cowardice much like the earlier part of I, 'Llym awel'. But it differs from the latter in that all the stanzas contain nature-poetry, most containing gnomic matter as well, and this explains its position in the manuscript in the middle of a series of unequivocally gnomic poems.

**1a baglawc bydin.** Not so much a gnomic statement 'a host is serried' *or* 'is armed with spears *or* staves' as a seasonal description going with *bagwy onn.* Spring or early summer was the season for campaigning: cf. 'Claf Abercuawg' 17 *Kynnteuin, kein pob amat. Pan vryssyant ketwyr i gat Mi nyt af: anaf ny'm gat* 'Early summer, every growing thing is beautiful. When warriors hasten to battle, I do not go; my wound does not let me'. Cf. the dialogue in I.7-22.

**1b graenwynn**: see on II. 7a.

**2c diryeit**: see on II.3c.

**3b gochwiban.** Noun, according to *GPC*, but better understood as adj..

**4a marchwyeil.** *March* = 'stallion'; in plant-names it implies coarse or vigorous growth, like 'horse' in English 'horseradish', 'horsemint' and so on, hence, in combination with *gwiail*, 'strong saplings'.

**4b gwanas** 'peg', here the fastening to which a chain is attached. *A'i draed yn rhydd* is a common idiom for freedom of action; the line is figurative, in that the freshness of early summer turns the prisoner's thoughts to freedom. Compare the woodland imagery of Dafydd ap Gwilym.

**4c gwas** 'young man' or 'manservant'; it is not clear which is meant. *Morwyn* in the next stanza is ambiguous in the same way.

6b **carchar**, normally 'prison', but has also the sense 'fetters', and this fits better with the previous two stanzas.

7 The significance of this stanza is obscure. From its form one might expect a triad expanding on the *llafar* 'chatterbox' of 6, but the relevance of the brambles laden with berries is not clear. Is the bush noisy with the buzzing of flies?

7a **erni**: the feminine form referring to a collective noun is hard to explain, as Jackson observes. *Arnu*, the old 3 pl. form, would restore the syntax, but at the expense of the internal rhyme. For the variation in the rhyming pattern, cf. I.17a.

7b [**y ar**] **nyth**: 'off the nest', a necessary emendation (see *GMW* §223(b), cf. III.8b and contrast I.27c) for MS *ar y nyth* 'on its nest', which makes no sense since a bird on the nest is necessarily silent. But a blackbird driven from its nest would indeed utter a loud alarm-call.

8b **goror ewyn**: loose adjectival collocation, 'edged with foam'.

8c **tec a gannwyll**, 'an excellent candle';  see *GMW* §39(c), for the idiom. *a* originally = 'of'; it comes to be replaced by *o,* already in I.29b and regularly in later Welsh.

9a **y gan**: 'out of', see *GMW* §223(c).

9c **llyvwr**: the etymologically correct disyllabic form, later *llwfyr, llwfr;* cf. I.10c. Unless *rëen* (see on I.35c) has been contracted to a monosyllable (first recorded about 1195), there is therefore an extra syllable here;  that is not unparalleled, but *Duw* may be a gloss. This last line betrays the origin of the sequence in a 'saga poem', which evidently had much in common with the first section of I.

10a **heli hallt**, cf. I. 3b. *Heli*, like *hallt*, is etymologically connected with *halen* 'salt', but the semantic emphasis may by this stage have shifted to the idea 'sea water', so that the statement may not be quite as pointless as 'salt water is salty'.

## VIII. Gorwynion

This series is preserved in R and J (see on II). It is for the most part concerned with summer, but contrast stanzas 7 and 8. It is interesting that in these *gorwyn* may have its etymological sense 'very white', whereas elsewhere it seems, as Jackson argues, to have the more general sense 'delightful'. It is possible that the two winter stanzas belong to another series altogether, which may have arisen from a misunderstanding of *gorwyn*, while 2 appears to have drifted in from a saga sequence; see notes to the lines. If the preponderance of *englynion penfyr* is of any significance, this series may be relatively early, but note that 25 is an *englyn unodl union* and may be later. In addition, this sequence appears to have more irregular lines than the others in the Red Book.

1a. For the variation in the rhyming pattern, cf. I.2b.

1c **bronnwaly hiraeth y heneint**: J's reading; Jackson prints the R reading *bron gwala hiraeth i heint*. *gwaly* in J represents the original monosyllabic pronunciation (as in *eiry*; see on I.5a). R has the more modern form in -*a*, but conversely the failure there to show the mutation expected in the second element of a compound is explained by Jackson as evidence of an early copy. *heint* for *heneint* may well be an alteration designed to accommodate disyllabic *gwala*. Jackson translates the R line as 'a heart full of longing leads to sickness', citing III. 21b in support of *i* for 'leads to'; possible too is 'regret fills the heart for sickness', i.e. 'for the sick man', a statement exemplified by the whole of 'Claf Abercuawg'. But *gwaly* should mean 'enough', and the J reading with *heneint* yields a bitter understatement perhaps more effective than either translation: 'regret is a heart's sufficiency for old age'.

2 A similar stanza occurs in 'Claf Abercuawg' (*EWSP*, p. 449, stanza 12) of which Rowland takes this to be an 'unskilful modification' which may nevertheless have influenced the transmission of the original stanza. That stanza rhymes on *heneint*, and the line fits the situation of the prematurely aged speaker. The last line here is intelligible, but its point is not clear, and unless *dyly*, the second *y* of which is historically a mutated *g*, as in *eiry* (see on I.5a), is disyllabic (as it is in the poetry of the *Gogynfeirdd*), it is a syllable short. As it is followed by *y heint*, *dyly* must mean 'owes' rather than 'is entitled to'.

3 The metre is confused. The stanza starts as if an *englyn penfyr*, but continues as if an *englyn byr crwca*. But since it makes good sense, it is left unemended.

4a **a doeth**, 'with a wise man'; cf. V. 2a. Note the implied equivalence between natural description and moral reflection.

4b: the contrast with 4a suggests that Jackson is right to take *anoeth* as subject, cf. I.3b, 4c: cf. IX. 61.

6a **eidic**: the next line suggests 'greedy, rapacious' rather than 'jealous', and the same translation may be correct in 5b.

6c **call** must be 'wise man', since *gweithred* is feminine. **caru yn iawn**, i.e. the Creator rather than the creature. But John Davies's *iawn* 'righteousness' represents an intelligent correction.

7a **anhuned** 'sleeplessness', here apparently figurative, 'turbulence'. Jackson takes this phrase as explaining *crin cawn*; on the other hand the mountain-tops are literally *gorwyn* after snow, as well as being 'beautiful' in the generalised sense.

7b **cawn**: *calaf* would provide both the required six syllables and a rhyme on *gayaf*, here and in the next stanza, but *cawn*, if an error, is unexplained. **callwed** is the J reading; *called* R 'green growth' makes no sense.

7c **wyled** : the soft mutation is normal after *oes* in MW (*GMW* §21(a)).

8a **oerfel**: for the variation in the rhyming pattern, cf. VI.20a, on the assumption that *oeruel* gives generic or 'Irish' rhyme (see on I. 19) with the main rhyme.

8c **whefris**. Jackson translates as a verb 'befalls', but does not identify the verb or the form. *GPC* and *GBGG* take it as an adj., perhaps 'rough'. The sense appears to be 'an error made in exile is grave *or* perilous'. For the spelling, cf. 13 *wheueryd*. <wh> for <chw> is characteristic of South and Mid Wales, where it survives as a pronunciation to this day. It is not, however, common in the Red Book, even though that is a Southern manuscript (see Huws, *Medieval Welsh Manuscripts*, p. 80); these forms may therefore be evidence of the separate transmission of the *Gorwynion* sequence.

9c **pell**, 'long-standing', not 'far'. **ym**: 'in my', see *GMW* §222. Another line suggesting an origin in 'saga poetry'; cf. II. 21c, and see on following stanza. The line as it stands has two extra syllables.

10c A very similar line occurs in 'Claf Abercuawg' (*EWSP* 450, 19c).

11a **caledi** 'hardship' Jackson, the commonest sense, but better perhaps 'miserliness (is not good manners)', a common observation in poetry of this type. Cf. 25a.

12a For the variation in the rhyming pattern, cf. I.1a. But the second and third lines are still over-long, the second by two syllables and the third by one.

12a Jackson sees here an early example of the 'house of leaves' motif so favoured by Dafydd ap Gwilym and his followers as a meeting-place for lovers.

12c i.e. a good-natured man sleeps easy.

13b **whe[c rew]yd**: MS *wheueryd* is not in any dictionary, and Jackson offers no translation. 13c suggests some reference to illicit love; good sense can be restored by emending to *whec rewyd i arall*: either 'wantonness is sweet to the other', *sc.* the *diriaid* (see on VI. 3c) who is far from prudent (*amgall*), or 'wantonness is sweet to another', more agreeable, that is, to the seducer than to the seduced. Contrast *rewyd* 'lustful' as adj. used substantivally in 22c. The manuscript reading may be the product of mishearing; it appears that whoever was responsible did not understand the text. On the spelling, see on 8c.

14b **merydd mall**: 'the dullard is depraved', Jackson, assuming chiasmus (see Language C 1(e)); but 'the degenerate man is sluggish' is equally possible.

14c **carcharwr**: predicate, in a figurative sense.

15a **Digoll bre**: now Mynydd Hir or Long Mountain, south of Welshpool. The topographical reference suggests that the line may belong to a 'saga poem'. Digoll is indeed celebrated in another such poem in the Red Book as the site of one of the battles of Cadwallon ap Cadfan; see *EWSP*, pp. 446, 495, 614. It is mentioned in a different context as *Kevyn* (i.e. *Cefn*) *Digoll* in *Breudwyt Ronabwy*, ed. Richards, p. 9.9. The evidence is summarised by Rachel Bromwich in *TYP³*, pp. 192-3.

15b **ffoll**, from Lat. FOLLIS 'bag, football', so, through the idea of inflation, 'coxcomb, pompous ass'; unrelated to *ffôl* 'foolish', despite the semantic convergence.

15c **cadarn**: cf 6c for the significance of the unlenited form.

17a **venestyr**: Jackson explains 'the reckless are their own cupbearers, i.e. continually pour out wine for themselves'; is this 'wine' figurative? If *menestyr* is a Norman-French borrowing it confirms a date for the stanza well on in the twelfth century; but see Jarman, *Gododdin*, p.156, on 1113.

18b i.e. the stream runs fastest on the outside of a bend where it is eroding the bank. *Tal glan* is the portion of the bank which stands proud.

19c **ni diw** 'does not avail', from a supposed verb *diuod*; *nid ydiw* MSS. Almost exactly the same line occurs in the Heledd sequence: *EWSP* 431, 15c *amgeled am vn ni diw*; *nyt ydiw* with its extra syllable is clearly an alteration of an obscure expression. The whole stanza appears to belong to a 'saga poem'.

20 For the variation in the rhyming pattern, cf. 1a.

20b **diwarth**: either because they do not see things which would scandalize them (Jackson) or because they lack the opportunity to incur reproach; either way this is a rather cynical observation, and may have the force of a proverb.

21a: the line as it stands is a syllable too long.

21b The significance of this is not clear. Singular *gwenynen* would give the expected rhyme on *hen*, but also an extra syllable. Is the image one of a solitary bee at the end of the summer?

22a Note that this and the following line have eight syllables, not the usual seven.

22b **geuvel**: presumably the name of some plant. The elements look like *geu* 'false' and *mêl* 'honey'. The species may be ragwort, whose honey is unpalatable and now known to be slightly poisonous; see Jacobs, 'Geufel'.

23b **a** anticipates *a* at the beginning of 23c and makes the line too long, but see on 25. 23b probably shows the 'hanging' construction, rather than being an instance of archaic word-order; see Language C 2(a), 3.

24a The line is very short for an *englyn penfyr*, as the *gair cyrch* (the syllable or syllables at the end of the line following the main rhyme) and the two following lines suggest the stanza to be, since -*w* does not count in scansion and *dwfr* is a monosyllable. What has been lost, however, is not clear; possibly a trisyllabic predicate for *oeruerw dwfyr* taken not, with Jackson, as a nominal sentence 'cold and bubbling is the water' but as a noun phrase 'the cold bubbling of the water'. The latter would then have been described by whatever has been lost. But emendation on metrical grounds is risky, given the many irregularities in this sequence.

25 This stanza could be read as an *englyn gwastad* (see on II.2), but little sense can be made of the first line, where a reference to niggardliness seems to be needed. It is taken by Jackson to be an *englyn union unodl* lacking its *gair cyrch*, which should carry the sense 'miser'. His supplement *angawr*, with that sense, is plausible and accepted here, as is his further suggestion, which he does not allow into his text, of *awr agoret* (equivalent to *eur agoret*), which would give the expected internal rhyme. The heptasyllabic second line is, however, irregular, and *ac* should perhaps be omitted, though this sequence seems to favour it, cf. 4b, 16b, 21b, 23b.

25d, cf. XII.9[B]h.

26b **hir dydd**: translate, following Jackson, 'long is the day of the serf *or* prisoner', taking the two words separately rather than together as a compound adj., 'whose days are long', with *deilyedig* as subject.

26c **y gilyd**, 'each other' in Modern Welsh, but better here 'his friend *or* fellow', like Irish *céile*.

27a,c: the repeated rhyme on *vyd* is suspicious and suggests corruption. *brigawc hyd* 'the stag is branchy-headed' is at first sight an attractive emendation, but leaves the second line making no sense.

28c **gwnelit**, subjunctive stem with indicative termination; see Jackson's note and *GMW* §129(d)1.

29a **bydinawr**: not in dictionaries; ? 'companion of armies'.

29b **kein gyfreu**, cf V. 6a, and 31a below.

30b The need for *sapientia et fortitudo* (wisdom and bravery) is a mediaeval commonplace.

30c: either of the nouns could be the subject. In favour of *gwnelyt* is the form in 28c, but here there is an extra syllable, and *gwneyt*, with the same sense, is possible.

31c See on V.6b. This presumably represents the original stanza, clumsily adapted there.

32b **nugyein**. J's reading as preferred by Jackson (*migyein* R is unknown). *-ein* appears to be an old 3 pl. ending (*GMW* §130 (b)(1)); if so, the syntax is archaic (see Language C (2)(a)), and the *-e-* is problematic.

32c: cf. on 29c. **ny gyghein**: 3 sg. pr. ind. not of *cynghanu* but of *cyngenni*. The spirant mutation might be expected here; is *g-* a scribal error under the influence of *garawr* (see *GMW* §65 N.1)?

33c **o law**: 'from the hand' (Jackson): if so, 'one who has to receive alms'. But *dwyn* in the sense 'receive' (as opposed to 'take (away)', usually without consent) is unusual; if *dwc* implies seizing something, *llaw* 'humble, poor' might fit better.

## IX. Gossymdeith Llefoet Wynebclawr

This and the following poem appear to belong to a somewhat different tradition. They are not composed in *englynion*, and have little in common with the saga tradition; both, on the other hand, contain gnomic material. *Gossymdeith Llefoet Wynebclawr* has some connexion with the moral and cosmological poetry in the Book of Taliesin, and indeed stands in the Red Book between a number of pieces in that tradition and a collection of proverbs not primarily in verse, though some of them scan and appear to be drawn either from the saga *englynion* or from the gnomic poems edited above. The poem is edited by the present author as "'Gossymdeith Llefoet Wynebclawr'". *Gossymdeith* appears to mean 'sustenance', and to have here the sense of the moral provision needed to sustain the individual through life's pilgrimage. *Llefoed* is named as a poet by Gwilym Ddu o Arfon (c. 1280-1320) and perhaps by Dafydd Benfras (c. 1220-60); since he is mentioned in the company of Taliesin, Myrddin and Cynddelw he was evidently regarded as a poet of high distinction, though that may seem exaggerated on the strength of this, the only poem attributed to him. *Wynebclawr* or *wynebglawr* 'flat-faced' is commonly taken as a synonym for 'leper', and there is some reason to think that the character may have become associated at some stage with the leper whose healing is narrated in the life of St David; if so, this would be a striking example of the tendency to represent early mediaeval Welsh poetry as being much earlier than it actually is, as with the attribution to Aneirin of *'Englynion' y Misoedd*. It is possible that the gift of wisdom and poetry was associated, as in the case of Homer's blindness, with physical affliction, for which it could be seen as divine compensation.

1 **eyt**: 3 sg. pr. ind. of *mynet*, from the stem *a-* + the absolute termination *-yt*; see *GMW* §129(d)2.

6 **aglew** stands by itself in a 'hanging' construction, as do *llyfwr* and *ffer* in the parallel statements in 7 and 8. **dinaw**: 'drive, push' is the sense here, figuratively 'provoke'.

7 **llemittor arnaw**: here in the sense 'he is attacked'.

8 **ffer**: cf III.21a. Here a wild and violent man who, unlike the brave man or the coward, whose reactions are at least predictable, is best avoided altogether.

10: difficult. Either 'God shares glory with him', or, taking *ac* as an error for the copula *ys* (see *GMW* § 146) 'glory - it is God who distributes it'.

12 **digawn**: either a pronoun, with its modern sense 'enough': 'the Lord will provide a sufficiency' (for subjunctive with future sense, see *GMW* §124(b)), or the same verb as in *dichon* 'can': 'what the Lord can do, let him provide'; for the variation of consonant in a rel. clause, which is a relic of an older pattern, see *GMW* § 65 N.1.

13: in a stanza which appears largely concerned with the Last Judgment, this apparent nature-gnome may be figurative.

14 **acdo**: *sc.* between God and human understanding, or between heaven and earth?

15 **dioryuic**: unknown. *Diorfyg*, from *gorfyg*,  ? 'urge', is possible; if so, 'stubborn'.

16 **ny didawr**: rel. clause; cf 17, 29.

18 **ar ffo**: ? *sc.* from judgment, when nothing is to be gained by reciting Scripture.

19 **bleid**: perhaps in the figurative sense 'outcast, outlaw', as in Old English and Old Norse.

20 **llaw divo**: epithet for the avenging angel? The additional epithet *llwydawc* leaves the line far too long, and is the only word that can be spared; it appears to be a sophistication.

22 **atwaed**: ? comparing worldly desire to noise that fills the ears of the soul.

25 **vn aruaeth**: adjectival collocation 'at one in their purpose'.

27 **ny wnehyd**, 2 sing.; see *GMW* §128(b).

28 **annwyt**: better 'enthusiasm, passion' than 'cold', in a stanza which seems much concerned with the ultimately futile exertions of young men.

29 The predicate here follows the subject, which is a rel. clause.

36 **y'w**: ≡ *i'w* 'in his'; see on VI.9c. **gwastra**: the interpretation of the line depends on this word, whose meaning is not certain:  the context of another instance may suggest 'fierce', but *GPC* proposes '? base, vain'. Thus here,  either 'the man without anxiety is fierce in action' or 'the reckless man is good for nothing in what he does'; the second fits the general drift of the stanza better.

38 **dryccor**: *drwc* + a second element *cor* easiest taken as a loan-word from Irish, where it can mean 'agreement'. For the phonology ($g + g > c + c$) see *GMW* §17.

41 'Four-cornered is the world, four-sided'. The irruption of this scrap of Taliesinic cosmology into a straightforward series of precepts is puzzling.

42 **a reith**: *a* for 'in face of' is doubtful; *am* 'concerning' might be read. *Reith* normally means 'law', but, as I have argued elsewhere (*SC* 36 (2002), 87), it could be a rare word meaning 'violence'. *Goleith* has been translated 'retreat' or 'death'; if the former, either sense of *reith*  would serve; if the second, only 'violence'.

46 **mab Meir**: probably an apostrophe.

47 **yn**: probably = possessive *ein*; better sense would come of taking it as *in* (*inni*), but mutation would be expected after that.

48 **a'th grybwyllir**: see *GMW* §192.

49 **dyffustit**: see on II.23b.

51-2 **goyewin, pwyll**: the coincidence of two words resembling the names of characters in the *Four Branches* (Goewin, Pwyll) cannot be passed over, but little sense can be made of the lines by pursuing it. It is perhaps safer to translate 'a brave man's speech should be quiet; a host [of men] is deliberate in deceiving while laughing', but the passage is obscure.

55: uncertain. If *gynnin* is equivalent to *gynt* (Lat. GENTES), 'pagans', 'Scandinavians', the line may be taken as a nominal sentence with a complex predicate, *kerennyd fall* 'false truce' compounded with *call* 'clever', with the mutation normal in the circumstances; such collocations are not generally typical of gnomic poetry. 'Skilled at faking a truce' might be a fair translation.

58 **trwch**: see on VI. 2c.

60 **kyll**: i.e. causes their destruction.

64 **detwyn**: either an adj. or a verb, with the sense of 'returning'. The adverb *moch* 'quickly' can be prefixed to either; this is preferable to taking the line as a maxim about *moch* 'pigs'.

65 **ry**: with potential sense, cf. I.3c. The unstated suggestion is 'but they must still die'.

66 **a ordyfyn**: cf 48. The use of *a* as an affirmative particle without an infixed pronoun is, however, exceptional, but the metre requires it. **o'e**: = modern *i'w* 'to his', the simplest correction for MS *oed*. But it is not clear which preposition, if any, should follow this verb; *a'e* is perhaps preferable.

68 **nid ef synn**: see *GMW* §191 for the double particle. The probable sense of the verb is 'be put to confusion'; cf. Psalm xxxi:1.

69 The line is easiest taken as an address to God. **kywrennhin gyrbwyll**: a loose adjectival collocation with its second element a verbal noun governing the person addressed. 'Mighty by being named, invoked' is the approximate sense; cf. Psalm viii: 1.

70 **gwisgawt**: on this form, with future sense, see *GMW* §129 (d)(3). A figurative sense seems likely here. Professor Charles-Edwards suggests an image of new life after the winter of this world, or there may be a reference to the parable of the fig-tree in Matt. xxiv:32, with its suggestion of the impending end of the world.

72 Not so much a reference to the feeble heat of a candle, probably, as to the inadequacy of prayers for the dead.

73 **[d]edwyd**: Professor Charles-Edwards's suggestion for MS *edwyd* ≡ *edfydd*, 3 sg. of *adfod* 'perish', with which the neg. would make no sense, necessitating the more substantial emendation to *neud*.

74 **ny dwyll**: the soft mutation suggests a rel. clause, see *GMW* §65 N.1, in which case the line is in apposition to *pwyll* in the preceding line.

75 Note the stanza-linking (*cymeriad*) with *pwyll*; this is the only such instance in the text. **nwy**: = *ni* + 3 sing. infixed pronoun, see *GMW* §58 N.; for its use with indirect object, §61. **prif egwa**: loose adjectival collocation. *Egwa* appears to mean 'speech, talk'; 'prominent in talk' must in context mean something like 'blatherer, chatterbox'. In both this and the next line a rel. clause constitutes the subject in a 'hanging' construction.

76 **cwnneu**: phonologically odd in a native word, and probably for *cynneu* 'kindle" (so *GBGG*), figuratively 'begin'. **edyn**: since a disyllable is needed, this cannot be for *edn* 'bird'. It is probably a variant of *adyn* 'wretch, reprobate'.

77 **morua**: commonly 'coastal marsh', but perhaps here referring to grazing land by the sea which is damaged by winter storms.

78 **rihyd**: cf. 10; here too eternal glory is meant.

79-80 Two further warnings against impetuous speech; cf. 75; for the second, XII. 7e.

83 **ar [ny d]al**: Lloyd-Jones's correction for unintelligible *arythal*: on *ar*, see *GMW* §75. *talu* here = 'make amends'.

85-104 This section is linked by a combination of proest and rhyme, as follows: 85-6 rhyme (*-aeth*), 87-8 proest (*-aeth/oeth*), 89-90 rhyme (*-eith*), 91-2 rhyme (*-aeth*), 93-4 proest (*-oeth/aeth*), 95-104 rhyme (*-eith*). A similar combination is found in early twelfth-century court poetry: *Gwaith Meilyr Brydydd a'i Ddisgynyddion*, ed. J. E. Caerwyn Williams et al., CBT I (Cardiff, 1994), nos. 1. 35-49, 2.31-50.

85 **rwyd pob traeth**: 'on' must be understood, assuming a 'hanging' construction with *redeint gorwyd* as subject.

87 **nyt neb**: 'it is not anyone': the sense may be 'there is no one', but in that case *nyt oes* would be expected. 'It is not everyone' would be a more satisfactory sense, if that were possible.

88 **nyt ef**; for the double preverb, see *GMW* §191.

89 **treith**: if this is a plural form of *traeth*, the sense may be 'between two shores', i.e. in danger of being wrecked.

91 **bit**: here with a clear prescriptive sense; see on III.1a.

92 **ketrwyf** 'living on gifts': suggested in *GBGG* for unintelligible *ketwyf*. Followed by *eillyaeth*, it is equivalent to 'dependent'. The line is a thinly veiled plea for patronage.

94 **nat vo**: apparently with implied conjunction 'where/when there is no [lord]'.

95 The sense may be generalising or prescriptive, 'a king is *or* let a king be fearless in plundering', as if with *bit*.

96 See Language C (3) for the syntax.

99 **[d]rut [m]ut**: the words appear to be transposed in the MS. The emendation is necessary to give good sense. See on I.3b.

106 **otynt**: commonly of snow (*od*), cf I.5 etc; here with extended reference. The plural verb is archaic. **gawr ennwir**: loose adjectival collocation 'with terrible roar'.

107 **diwestyl**: probably an old spelling for *diwystl*; in a loose adjectival collocation used substantivally 'he who has no legal title to his property'.

110 **rann**: i.e. his full debt. This should probably be taken as the old construction with subject preceding verb (see Language C (2)(a), but a nominal sentence with *kyfa* as predicate and *ry buchir* as a relative clause is conceivable.

112 **gweddawt**: for *gwedd[w]dawd*, with non-syllabic *w* not represented in writing.

113 **rydygir**: euphemistic for death in battle.

116 **ys dir**: an instance of the old copula (cf. Irish *is*), commonly omitted in a nominal sentence, here necessary because of the 'hanging' construction (see Language C.3).

118 **o**: with the sense of change from one situation to another.

119 **pydiw**: see *GMW* §84(a).


## X. Gwarchan Adebon

This poem is preserved as the second of four relatively short poems copied in the Book of Aneirin at the end of the *Gododdin*, apparently by way of a supplement to it. It was previously edited by Ifor Williams, *CA*, pp. 52, 358-62; for more detailed comment, see Jacobs, 'A Fresh Look at *Gwarchan Adebon*'. This poem has no claim to be as old as the sixth century in its present form (see on 7 for evidence of its date), but some lines may be genuinely ancient; see on 8, 11, 13, and above, Language, C 2(a). Two of the other three poems are clearly heroic elegies (see Jarman, *Gododdin*, pp. lxv-lxviii, 68-75, 153-6), and the same has been recently argued for the third (see Isaac, '*Gwarchan Maeldderw*') These can be associated with the subject-matter of the *Gododdin,* though not all of them have any connexion with the battle of Catraeth. *Gwarchan Adebon* has hitherto been seen as an exception. At first sight, certainly, it is a short gnomic composition; such was the unequivocal view of Ifor Williams, *CA*, pp. lviii-lix, and subsequent editors of the *Gododdin* have gone beyond him to the extent of not editing it at all. Short as it is, Ifor Williams suggested that it was a mere fragment of a longer poem similar to *Gossymdeith Llefoet Wynebclawr*. But it contains several lines which suggest a heroic context, and most of these cannot easily be interpreted as gnomic, whereas the gnomic lines are for the most part easily read as comment on the death of a hero. *Gwarchan Adebon* may thus be seen as an example, unique in Welsh, of a heroic elegy with gnomic elements; compare the frequent use of gnomic lines in the 'saga englynion' of *Canu Llywarch Hen* and the like.

1 **pell**: adverb modifying the following verb. If temporal 'long' (*sc.* in falling), the line may be a metaphor for the brevity of life, which is compatible with an elegiac poem; if spatial 'far', for the limited extent of the consequences of an action, an attitude uncharacteristic of gnomic poetry. Marged Haycock suggests (private communication) a sense that a kin-group is affected by the death of a loved one, but the implication in a heroic elegy that only they are so affected would be equally odd.

2 **cy[m]yd**, for MS *cynnyd*, explained by Ifor Williams as 'succeed'. For the emendation, cf IX.9, 28. The line then becomes a generalisation about envy.

4 **yt ball**: since *yd* is followed by soft mutation (see *GMW* §190 N.) this must be from *pallu* 'fail' rather than *ballu* 'perish', but the sense is the same.

5 As the line stands it suggests a poet mourning his patron. For heroic or elegiac elements in gnomic poetry, cf. II.21c, VII.9c.; it is difficult to read the line otherwise. **gar**: obscure; hardly 'O friend!'. Emendation to *garw* would keep the metre, give fair sense and provide a rhyme on *marw*, but the error would be hard to explain.

6 **byd[ir]**: MS *byd*. An impersonal form is needed for the sense ('one does not die …'), and a sixth syllable is required for the second part of a *toddaid byr*. Both could be supplied by emending to *bydir*; this form is not recorded in *GMW*, but occurs at least twice in proverb-collections.

7 **amsud**: evidently 'varied' from the prefix *am-*, denoting variety and *sud* 'form, manner'. The latter is a borrowing from Norman French *sute* (which later, perhaps about 1300, gave rise to English *suit*). The word is unlikely to have been borrowed into Welsh before 1100, and some time is needed for it to have become sufficiently acclimatised to give a compound of this kind; as a result the line, and the poem in its present form, can hardly be much earlier than 1200. The spelling of this word and of *mud* suggests an exemplar in the orthography of the Black Book of Carmarthen, but that is not incompatible with the date suggested.

8 **ceri**: 3 sg. impf. ind.; an old form, more commonly *carai*. **cyvyeith**: the subject is mutated because the object stands between it and the verb, see *GMW* §21(a). Given the normal force of the imperfect, this looks like another heroic line 'our compatriot did not love to cause terror [*sc.* to his fellow-countrymen]', For the word order, which suggests that the line is an early one, see *GMW* §199 N(b).

9 **em[y]s**: Ifor Williams's correction for *e mis*; this is etymologically a singular (Lat. *AMMISSVS), but the existence of a re-formed singular *amws* suggests that it may have been taken as a plural. **amwyn**: either 'white (*sc.* with foam)' suggesting speed, or 'pure white', on the assumption that such horses were highly valued. Since *gwyn* is not used of horses in early poetry, *can* being the

appropriate term (cf. on I.27c), the latter is unlikely. The line could be a gnomic observation about the kind of horse appropriate to a young hero, or an elegiac recollection of a particular man. For the syntax, cf. VI.22b.

10 **Kuhelyn**: evidently a lord famed for his hospitality, for which *corn* serves as a metonym. Among the historical possibilities are the ninth-century figure *Cuhelyn mab Bleidiud* or *Cuhelyn Fardd fab Gwynfardd Dyfed* (fl. 1100-1130); among legendary dignitaries, Geoffrey of Monmouth's *Guithelinus* or *Cuhelyn fab Gwrgant*; see P. C. Bartrum, *A Welsh Classical Dictionary*, pp. 150-51. Is this a historical reference to an actual hero, or a gnomic observation about the popularity of a generous man? Such a hero, or one of his retainers, may have been the subject of the elegy, if that is what it is.

11 **adef**: usually in combination with *nef* 'heaven', but cf *EWSP* 410, 37b, where it is clearly used of an earthly home. **collit**: if 3 sg. pr. ind., this must be intransitive 'is lost'; if with the more usual sense 'lose', it must be the impers. impf. The tense would then be difficult. The point in either case would be that wars begin in a social context, as in the story of Branwen; a general observation is applied to the career of the hero. Note the archaic word order subject-verb.

12 The line is probably corrupt. Lines 11-12 can be translated as they stand as a heroic or elegiac reference, taking (with Ifor Williams) *led* for *lledd* 'scar': 'your scar proves that you were brave (*or* a lion) in the day of battle', but the lenition of *led* and *lew* is unexplained.

13 **rudvyt**: perhaps for *rhudd* + *mid* 'bloody battle'. **keissyessit**: strictly the independent form of the preterite, see *GMW* §133 N.1, but Ifor Williams, *CA*, p.142, on l. 262, suggests that it may also have served as 3 sg. impf. The sense would be 'the ambitious sought *or* used to seek bloody battle', and appears heroic rather than gnomic. On the word-order, cf. 8.

14 **medel**: here 'a reaper', not, as normally, 'band of reapers'. **mein uchel**: adjectives used substantivally as subject in a 'hanging' construction. This may be a gnomic observation or praise of a particular hero, cf. 9. In combination with *mein* 'slim, slender', 'tall' would give better sense for *uchel* than 'high-ranking', but there seems to be no parallel for the usage, where *hir* is normal.

15 **dy ven**: obscure as it stands. Three interpretations are proposed by Ifor Williams: (1) for *dy wên* 'your smile', hence 'your blessing'; (2) for *diben* 'end'; (3) for *dy fen* 'your mark' (*sc.* of approval). None is convincing, but the second is less unsatisfactory than the others, and as 13-15 is the only section with an uneven number of rhyming lines it is quite likely that this line is a colophon mistakenly copied as part of the text.

## XI. Neud Calan Ionawr

Unlike the fifteenth-century *'Englynion' y Misoedd* or Stanzas of the Months (XII), which survive in over sixty manuscripts, all post-mediaeval, this version, dated by its editor on linguistic grounds early in the twelfth century, survives in only one copy, and that probably in fragmentary form, in National Library of Wales, MS Peniarth 182. This manuscript was written by Sir Huw Pennant about 1513; for an edition, see Thomas, 'An Early Welsh Seasonal Poem'. Additional notes have subsequently been supplied by the present author, 'Nodiadau ar y Canu Gwirebol II'. The first page is heavily rubbed and the microfilm barely legible in places; almost everything that Dr Thomas was able to read can be made out with the eye of faith, but without the help of his edition it would have been hard to decipher. Like *'Englynion' y Misoedd* the poem is written in eight-line monorhymed stanzas and combines natural description with generally gloomy moral reflections, chiefly on the brevity and uncertainty of human life, but unlike all the other poems edited here it is written in lines of nine or ten syllables, some of them with internal rhyme, and in two of the three stanzas there are some words or phrases in Latin, sometimes integrated into the syntax of the Welsh and sometimes not, in a quite unsystematic way. This is reminiscent of some of the poems in the Book of Taliesin. Only the stanzas for January, June and November are preserved. The poem is something of a curiosity, and the interpretation of many of its lines is debatable, but it deserves to be read as a possible prototype for the later and much more accomplished *'Englynion' y Misoedd*. For convenience of comparison with the latter the stanzas are numbered as if they were part of a full cycle of months, though there is no way of knowing whether such ever existed.

1a **neud**: as copula, followed by the predicate with radical consonant. The subject is unexpressed. **kras**: for the sense 'dried herbage', cf. V.7a.

1b **amdud**: verb, according to Thomas, but perhaps better taken as an adj. in a pure nominal sentence. see *GPC* for other such early formations as *amdrai, amdwll, amlys, amrwusg, amwall*. †**lliuvawr**† 'colourful': surprising as an epithet for lakes; a noun is needed here to go with *gwyrddlas* on the chiastic pattern seen in I.3c and elsewhere. Some form of *llif* 'flood, stream' is possible. *-awr* may be under the influence of the internal rhymes of the preceding line. *Llifiau* would give an internal rhyme here too, but the form is not recorded. 'Flood' would give good sense: a river fed by melting snow or ice can appear greenish blue in colour.

1c *grandin[i]s ymber* 'shower of hail': Thomas's correction for MS nom. pl. *grandines* 'hailstorms'. *super terras* 'over the land'. Hail is more commonly associated with summer storms, cf XII.7b, and (at least in present-day Wales) seems more frequent in March and April than in January.

1d *aper inter silvas*: 'the wild boar ... through the woods', perhaps in contrast to domestic swine, turned out only in the autumn, the season of acorns; cf III.2a, XII.11(B)a.

1e **periklid**: 3 sg. pr. ind. absolute, not impers. impf., as the unvoicing of *g* shows; see *GMW* §129 (d) (1). It must therefore be intransitive. *homo per pecunias*: 'man ... through [love of] money'. The point is made in more general terms in the next line.

1g **a chennym oes bresswyl**: taking *presswyl* as adj., perhaps 'given that we have eternal life...' **yn vas**: i.e. worldly thoughts. The whole line is in loose apposition to the line before, and expands on it. Thomas suggests the translation 'that we shall have a continuous lifetime is a shallow thought', but the noun clause is hard to construe.

1h **mor vychod**: *mor* with substantive presumably on the analogy of *ychydig*, which can be either substantive or adj., with the latter of which *mor* is normal. **mors rydadlas**: 'death has determined *or* confirmed it'; for the form, see *GMW* §133(a)(1).

6a **dymkawn**: 3 sg.pres. ind. *digoni* 'make, bring about', with nasal infix so far unexplained; for discussion, see *Dwned* 11 (2005), 12–15.

6b **dygw[yl]**: Thomas's supplement at a point where the MS is torn, and the only likely one. One of two feast-days might be referred to: St John the Baptist (Midsummer Day, 24 June) or St Peter (29 June). The benefit is presumably that described in the next line.

6c *segites*: 'corn', incorrectly for *segetes*. A flourishing cornfield at the end of June is a necessary, even if not a sufficient condition for a good harvest. **buches lawn**: contrast XII.1d *gwac buches*.

6d *equs*: 'horse', for *equus*. **maës**: a disyllabic pronunciation is required to give the internal rhyme and the full count of syllables, and since the word is monosyllabic in the poetry of the *Gogynfeirdd*, who are generally pedantic in such matters, this text is unlikely to be much later than the beginning of the twelfth century. **dawn**: the repeated rhyme (cf 6b, h) is suspicious, but the verse technique in this stanza may simply be inadequate; cf. *iawn* twice in 6e, g. *Grawn* 'grain' is a possibility, given that at this time of the year a war-horse was required to be kept in its stable and fed on oats (see Jenkins, 'The Horse in the Welsh Law-Tracts'); *rhawn* 'horsehair' is less persuasive, though a luxuriant mane suggests a healthy horse.

6e **rihyd**: 'eternal glory' in IX.10, 78, but the context here (cf. 11e) requires 'worldly glory'.

6g **a[e] h[a]edd[wy gan] Dduw**: *a heddiw Dduw* MS. Thomas justifies the soft mutation in *Dduw* as a vocative 'O God', but given that the line is unusually short and that *heddiw* 'today' makes little sense, it is likely that the line is corrupt. The suggested reading implies auditory corruption.

6h **nis deruydd [d]awn**: *nis derfyddawn* MS. The verb is certainly *darfod*. Thomas sees here an old 1 pl. consuetudinal present or future, presumably on the model of the 3 sg. in *(h)awt* and 3 pl. in *(h)awnt* ; see *GMW* §§129(d)(3), 130(b)(2). This, though not inconceivable, is unparalleled, and it is not clear how the verb (glossed 'to end, finish, complete, die, fade, decline, perish') is to be construed with *nis*. It would be simpler to take the other sense of *darfod*, 'happen, befall', reading *nis deruyd dawn* and translating 'and as for him who does not deserve it, no benefit will befall him'; for infixed pronoun in dative function, see *GMW* §61, and cf. 11e below. The only objection here is that it leaves a third line out of eight rhyming on the same word.

11 The rhyme in this stanza is the same as that in the corresponding stanza of *'Englynion' y Misoedd* (XII[A].11); the rhyme-words are, however, different, and too much should not be read into the parallel.

11a **deuawd**: does this refer to traditional ceremonies at the beginning of the year (*Calan Gaeaf*), or, given the poem's general preoccupation with mortality, to those of All Souls' Day (2 November)?

11b **dedwydd**: see on II.3c.

11c **ffrwyth yn hely**: Thomas renders 'the fruit of our hunting', but this lacks a complement. *Ffrwyth* may be figurative for 'profit, success'; is an adjectival sense 'successful' possible? Better might be to take *yn* as representing *i'n* and translate 'truly there is profit in our hunting'. Or read *ffrwythynt* 'profitable pursuit' as complement? *hely* is monosyllabic; cf I.5a on *eiry*.

11d **oer tes mynydd**: *tes* originally 'heat', then 'a mist' (generated by hot weather). Here either a violent oxymoron, or an extension of the latter sense.

11e **o'i vawr rïydd**: parenthetic; see on 6e.

11f **er edmig** 'for honouring', qualifying *awr* in the preceding line.

## XII. 'Englynion' y Misoedd

The two main versions of this set of stanzas, known, following Jackson, as A and B are edited here. The text probably dates originally to the early or middle years of the fifteenth century, though no MS exists earlier than the sixteenth. More than sixty manuscripts survive. The two versions are substantially the same down to the end of August, but the four remaining stanzas are entirely different. Some twenty-two manuscripts give the B stanzas whole or in part. There is some internal evidence that the B version of these stanzas is later than A, and may have been composed about 1486. A period of oral, or at least of memorial transmission at an early stage is indicated by the frequent disturbance of the order of the lines within the stanza throughout the A version, though this occurs only in one manuscript in the stanzas peculiar to B. Oral transmission is again indicated by a good deal of variation within the line, as well as by the existence in three MSS of a set of marginalia detailing the variants from a third version, Jackson's C, of which no copy exists: this is based roughly on A for most of the text but almost entirely different from it in the stanzas for July and November. The A version is edited by Jackson in *EWGP*, pp. 37–42, and, together with an entertaining parody by the sixteenth-century Flintshire poet Siôn Tudur, by T. H. Parry-Williams in *Canu Rhydd Cynnar*, pp. 244–53. The B and C versions are edited by the present author in, respectively, '"Englynion" y Misoedd: Testun B', and '"Englynion" y Misoedd: Testun C', together with a new commentary on A, "Nodiadau ar y Canu Gwirebol. I'; see also ' "Stanzas of the Months" '.

1a **myglyd dyffryn**: the combined effect of domestic fires and still, damp weather.

1b **blin trulliad**: *sc.* after the many feasts of the Christmas season.

1d **gwac buches**: the summer milking-enclosure is said to be deserted in January because the cows were being milked in their stalls; contrast XI.6c. **diwres odyn**: because the grain or malt had been dried by January.

1e: 'degraded is the man who is not worthy to be asked for anything' (Jackson), but, since *gofyn* is used transitively only in the sense 'question', not of 'request', perhaps better 'wretched is the man who makes an unworthy request'.

1f **i dri gelyn**: the world, the flesh and the Devil?

1g **gwir**: see on V.8c. **Kynvelyn**: probably the patron saint of Llangynfelyn, Ceredigion. He is not otherwise known as a source of proverbial wisdom, and, as in the case of the other quotations in the text, there is no justification for the attribution.

2a **ancwyn**: commonly 'feast', but here 'fruit', as a delicacy served at table. Balliol College, Oxford, MS 343 glosses as 'ffrwyth ney aeron' (fruit or berries).

2b **pal**: for clearing ditches? **olwyn**: presumably a mill-wheel; both imply floods, cf. the English saying 'February fill-dyke'. But there may also be a reference to grinding the corn to which there is an implied reference in 1d.

2c **knawd**: this variant of *gnawd* appears in the sixteenth century, apparently through a false etymology whereby *gnawd* in the sense of 'natural' was identified with *cnawd* 'flesh' in its figurative sense; see *GPC* s.v. *gnawd*.

2d 'woe to him who complains without a cause' rather than 'needless misery is caused by complaint', which does not account for the subjunctive.

2e **a vac**: preferable to Jackson's *a dry*, which looks like an anticipation of the following word. **drygwenwyn**: the precise sense of the compound (*drwg* + *gwenwyn* 'poison') is unknown. Something like 'disaster' or 'tribulation' would fit.

2f **murn a chynllwyn**: to be taken together as the second element of the triad.

2g **pen ki**: a portion of a solar halo with weak rainbow colouring, now called *ci haul*, i.e. 'sun-dog', an expression used also in English, together with 'wind-dog' (*madra gaoithe*) or 'weather-dog' in Ireland. **gwanwyn**: the mutated form suggests an adverb, but it may be for *o wanwyn*.

2h-i. No other example of a nine-line stanza exists in A or B, and most MSS end at 2h. One of the two lines is probably an addition, most probably that referring to the killing of a *morwyn*. Unless this word (generally used of a maidservant; see on VII.4c) can mean 'virgin daughter', with reference to the story of Jephthah (Judges xi:30–40) as a warning against rash promises, this looks like a topical reference intruded into the text, with the original final line dropped in most versions so as to keep the stanza to its proper length. The final maxim can be taken in a number of ways: 'the benefit of a day's work comes (only) with finishing it' or 'a day's work done is its own reward'; alternatively, assuming a pause after *dydd*, 'the end of a day — it is good to enjoy it' or, taking *mwyn* as adj. 'gracious, agreeable, pleasant' used substantivally, 'the end of the day — it is good for the gracious man'.

3c: properly a summer maxim: the corn supply is apt to run out in the good weather before harvest-time. In context, a general warning against trusting in prosperity lest prodigality lead to destitution, or else an exhortation to work hard at ploughing-time.

3h **mawr i garchar**: Jackson takes this as an exclamation 'great is his prison!', but it may be an adjectival phrase 'whose prison is great'.

4b: the effects of ploughing, cf. on 3c.

4c **gwael hydd**: stags cast their antlers in April and thus could be considered a sorry sight at that time.

4h: a favourite maxim. It is found in the *Seithennin* sequence (see *EWSP*, p. 464, 4b) and in *Englynion y Clyweit* 23c (see Haycock, *BBGCC*, no. 31).

5a **difrodus geilwad**: the function of the ploughboy was to walk ahead of the oxen and call them on. He is despised in May because there is no longer need for his services.

5c **diarchenad**: not 'lightly clad' (Jackson) but 'without shoes' (cf. [B].12a *tomlyd archan*). He is happy because the ground is drying out; by June even the peat-bogs are passable, see 6d.

5g-h: not a seasonal observation but a proverb. Its significance is explained by a traditional stanza printed by T. H. Parry-Williams, *Hen Benillion*, no. 92: *Mae gyn amled ar y farchnad Groen yr oen â chroen y ddafad, A chyn amled yn y llan Gladdu'r ferch a chladdu'r fam* 'It is as common in the market to find a lambskin as a sheepskin; it is as common in the churchyard to see the daughter buried as the mother'. Here the studied understatement of *nid hwyrach* 'no slower' implies the prevalence of such untimely deaths. The variant *mynd i'r farchnad* was originally copied in W; it occurs only in two other early manuscripts, but since both are copies by John Jones, Gellilyfdy, whose text is often reliable, this is very probably a genuine early variant; Jackson prints it in his text. The further variant *yr â i'r farchnad* looks like a derivative of this.

6b **marannedd**: there are numerous variants on this word, which the copyists have largely failed to understand. *GPC* gives 'wealth, treasure', but this gives no sense with *llawen*. Some aquatic creature seems indicated; an anonymous gloss in Balliol College, Oxford, MS 353 gives *morveirch* 'sea-horses', probably 'porpoises, dolphins', and that, even if only a guess, is the best yet. Jackson's preference for *mariannedd* 'sandy places, seashores' is puzzling.

6c **heinif**: the earlier form of *heini*, and probably original, as Jackson presumed, though the *-f* survives in only three MSS.

6d **hylawn**: because the lambs are growing apace.

7a **hyglvd** 'ready for carrying': though the reading is preserved only in W, this is preferable to *hyglyd* 'ready to be put under cover', probably not the practice at the time of composition. But as W elsewhere writes *v* for *y*, as in [A]9a *mvdr*, this argument is not unassailable.

7b **toddedig kessair**: i.e. hail falls in a summer thunderstorm, but melts quickly.

7e **dielid**: the old absolute form of the 3 sg. pr. ind., common in the earlier texts (see Language B 1(a), C 2(b)) but a linguistic fossil by the fifteenth century, preserved in the maxim.

7f **kronffair**: an obscure term; perhaps a small fair held at the time of haymaking, little visited because offering short-time employment for a meagre wage. See N. Jacobs, '*Lledwag kronffair*: what kind of fair?'.

7g-h **mab maeth Mair**: evidently Christ, though John the Evangelist might be expected on the basis of John xix: 26–27. Either way, the quotation is not authentic; cf. 1g-h.

8a **molwynoc**: another word which has troubled the copyists. *GPC* gives 'rich, fertile', though not on strong authority. **morva**: perhaps any low-lying land near the sea, as some place-names suggest, rather than the more common 'salt-marsh'; if so, the translation of *molwynog* in *GPC* is acceptable. Jackson favours *malwenog* and translates 'the salt-marsh is full of snails'; this may well be factually true, but in the context it is an odd observation.

8d: Jackson explains 'i.e. the greens have been turned into rickyards?'

8e: two rel. clauses, cf. XI.6h.

8f **nid teilwng**: the expected form in a copula sentence; see Language C 1(c). The anomalous *ni* in W and three other early MSS is probably under the influence of the same particle used twice in the previous line, though it could represent an oral corruption.

8g-h: cf. 1g-h, 7g-h. **Sain Brenda**: a very dubious saint, perhaps originally a corruption of *Brendan* or *Beda* (i.e. the Venerable Bede); but the name does appear in some sixteenth-century genealogies. The maxim here attributed to him argues no great profundity of thought.

9[A]a-b **mydr ynGhanon**: a very obscure allusion. *Canon* appears to be for the ecclesiastical calendar (originally that part of it concerned with determining the dates of movable feasts). In some MSS of the Sarum Missal each month is provided with a set of Latin verses on medical or dietary topics: that for September includes the line *Fructus maturi Septembris sunt valituri* 'the ripe fruits of September will be beneficial', and if *valituri* were mistranslated 'abundant', something like 9[A]b would be the result.

9[A]b **addved oed**: i.e. the time of ripening. Cf. 9[B]d.

9[A]c: a surprising intrusion of personal feeling, which unlike those in the Red Book cannot be attributed to a saga origin. *Gwae* is the safer reading, though *gwaew* or *gwayw* is the harder reading and might thus be preferred. *Gwaew* 'spear', figuratively 'pain', would then have to be taken as an adj.; see 1b *trallawd* for a possible parallel. Jackson would emend to *gwyw*, citing a line from the saga *englynion* (see *EWSP* 449, 14c). A generalised statement may underlie the text.

9[A]d **golwc**: in the sense 'kindly or gracious look'. In the absence of a verb it is not clear whether this is a statement or a wish.

9[A]e: i.e. although it is true, it is bad to reveal it.

9[A]f: i.e. though an oath is broken for a greater good, the means corrupt the end.

10[A]a **echel**: *sc.* of a grindstone, after sharpening shears, scythes and sickles through summer and autumn?

10[A]b **chwareus hydd**: October is the rutting season for red deer.

10[A]c **ysbeilwynt**: *ysbail* 'plunder' + *gwynt*. The sense is that the wind carries the smell of burning buildings or crops; on balance this powerful image of devastation is to be preferred to the trivial majority reading *ysbeilwyr* 'spoilers'.

10[A] e **diriaid**: see on II.3c.

10[A]f **trychni**: see on II.33c. **nid hawdd**: it is hard to decide between *hawdd* as in W and the majority reading *rrwydd*, but *nid* is required in place of *ni* (cf. 8f), and all the MSS with *rrwydd* have it.

11[A]c **drwy**: 'with', Jackson. This is difficult, since the usage seems otherwise to be restricted to culinary or medical recipes, but the overall sense of the line, taken with the following line, is clear.

11[A]d **dyfydd**: synonymous with *derfydd* 'happens'. This is the effective reading of only three MSS and a correction in a fourth, but is likely to be correct in view of the repetition of *derfydd* (in the sense 'perishes') as rhyme-word in the same stanza.

11[A]f **rrydd**; the subjunctive *rhoddo*, which is the reading of almost all the MSS, is more idiomatic than the indicative, but it gives an octosyllabic line, even when <a'i> is excised. For this reason Jackson in his second edition opted for *rhydd*. The subjunctive may have arisen under influence of *eiddo* in the previous line. There is much variation in this line, which suggests that the syntax of *pieu* (see *GMW* §88) was by this time not well understood.

12[A]a **byrddydd, hirnos**: apparently a double predicate in a 'hanging' construction.

12[A]b **brain**: 'rooks', rather than 'crows' or (as translated by Jackson) 'ravens', neither of which would be expected to feed in an arable field. **egin**: the cultivation of winter wheat is unusual but not inconceivable at this period.

12[A]d: the choice between this reading, with its suggestion that the kind of party which goes on till morning is particularly likely to end in a fight, and that favoured by Jackson, *trin yn niwedd kyfeddnos*, which suggests that parties in general end in trouble, is finely balanced. The first is preferred here as being more pointed, though if *trin* = 'battle' Jackson's preference may be upheld as echoing the heroic commonplace that feasting should precede and be paid for with battle.

12[A]e-f: note the juxtaposition of *dedwydd* and *diriaid*, and see on II.3c.

12[A]h **yn nydd a nos**: 'in a day and a night', Jackson; but the MS variants *yn nos* and *ag yn nos* suggest rather 'both day and night', 'constantly'.

9[B]a **Menni**: a rare variant on *Medi*. **maneg**: the reading of P[4], a possible 3 sg. pres. ind. of *mynegi, manegi* 'show'; as an early reading this is preferable to *mynaig* as printed in the present author's edition in *Dwned, 6*. **planed**: this may refer to the planet Mercury, which formed part of a rare configuration with Venus and the moon on or about 19 September 1486, and may even have been, unusually, visible in the evening sky; the astronomical details are given in the *Dwned* article at 12–13.

9[B]c: i.e. after the hay harvest?

9[B]d: cf 9[A]b.

9[B]e-f **mab darogan ... a'n dwg**: the two complete texts (Ll[2] and P[5]) have *merch frenhinol. ... an dug* 'a royal daughter ... who has brought', with probable reference to the Virgin Mary, whose nativity is celebrated on 8 September. The version printed appears to refer to Arthur, elder son of Henry VII, born 19 September 1486 (see on a); if not, it is hard to interpret. The reference to Mary may still be rejected as the easier reading; it can be explained as an alteration consequent on Arthur's death in 1502. The kind of prophecy referred to is evidently to be distinguished from the activities of the *drygddarogan* or false prophet condemned in XII.12[B]h.

9[B]g-h: yet another spurious quotation; cf. VIII.25d.

10[B]a: see on 10[A]b.

10[B]b **gweddw havod**: see on V.3b.

10[B]d **lleilai laeth**: note mutation of *llaeth*, which suggests that the cow and goats are the subject and *lleilai laeth* (as a loose adjectival collocation) the predicate. **gavrod**: a possibly dialectal plural first recorded here for standard *geifr*.

10[B]e **[by]chod**: only in two eighteenth-century MSS associated with the antiquarian William Morris (1705–63), once as a correction, and probably his emendation on the basis of V.3c.

11[B]a **mehinvawr**: i.e. after being turned out to feed on acorns.

11[B]b: the musician is to be expected at winter feasts (for which cf. XII[A]1b), but the dismissal of the shepherd is puzzling. The last quarter of the fifteenth century seems very early for a reference to pastoral poetry.

11[B]c **gwaedlyd**: after the slaughter of the pigs of the first line.

11[B]d **llonn**: 'rough' is unparalleled, but *lonn* is used in Irish in the same sense and may have influenced the semantic development. **merllyd**: i.e. after boiling down for lard those parts of the pig suitable neither for salting nor for immediate consumption.

11[B]f: this line occurs only in eighteenth-century MSS associated with the Morris brothers, though Peniarth 155 (1561–62) leaves it blank. It is in all probability a late supplement for something lost early on.

12[B]a **archan**; cf. 5c *diarchenad*.

12[B]b **trym<b>luog**: the form without *b* is historically correct, though the *-b-* may be a genuine phonological development. Alternatively it may be the product of a false etymology involving *plu* 'feathers' in an image of sluggish flight.

12]B]c **llwm gwydd**: perhaps with an echo of the masts in I.10b, but a simple reference to trees is perfectly satisfactory. **llywaethan**: obscure. Ifor Williams suggested a connexion with *llyweth* 'curl, ringlet'; a sense 'coiled serpent' may be postulated, and this might explain its use for 'eel' (the only sense by the sixteenth century), but it had evidently earlier been confused with the Leviathan of the Old Testament and acquired an additional sense 'whale'. 'Snake' seems plausible here, since these are torpid by December. On the other hand there may be a connexion with *llywaeth* (< *llawfaeth* 'hand-reared') with some such sense as 'pet dog'.

12[B]d-f **llon**: here with its normal sense 'cheerful' (contrast 11[B]d). A folk-belief of this kind regarding the cock is not recorded, but, for the owl, cf. the Middle English poem (? c. 1200) *The Owl and the Nightingale*, ed. Stanley, 481–84, *&*

*hure and hure to Cristes masse þane riche and poure, more & lasse, Singeþ cundut niȝt & dai, Ich hom helpe what ich mai* 'and especially at Christmas, when rich and poor, high and low, sing carols night and day, I help them as best I can'. It was believed in parts of Germany that the cry of an owl foretold the birth of a child, though there appears to be no record of such a belief in Wales.

12[B]g **Ysgolan**: see *EWSP*, pp. 465–66: a traditional figure noted for wisdom, used to introduce yet another spurious quotation.

12[B]h **drygddarogan**: the harder reading as against *drwg ddarogan* 'evil prophecy'. The compound adj. should refer to someone who prophesies evil, or who prophesies by evil means, and the sense is probably 'false prophet' or 'soothsayer'.

# GLOSSARY

The Glossary is intended for the convenience of readers with little or no knowledge of Modern Welsh, and for that reason I have not shrunk from glossing even the commonest words. For similar reasons, though perfect consistency would be hard to achieve, the head-words are given as far as possible as they occur in the manuscripts. For the most part, therefore, they are given in the Middle Welsh orthography of the Red Book of Hergest, from which the majority of the texts are drawn. Any word occurring in the texts preserved there appears under a head-word spelt according to the Red Book conventions, nouns being given in their singular form and verbs as verbal nouns; in addition, other forms of these words, where their head-word is not obvious, are listed separately with cross-references. Where a word or form of a word appears also in the idiosyncratic orthography of the Black Book of Carmarthen or in the Early Modern Welsh orthography of later manuscripts, or in an otherwise deviant spelling, it is given its manuscript spelling in brackets after the line-reference. Such forms, if their identity is not self-evident, are again listed separately with cross-references to the Red Book head-words.

Where no form in Red Book orthography is recorded, the manuscript forms themselves are used as the head-words. In the case of words in Black Book orthography, many of which are potentially confusing to the beginner, the Modern Welsh equivalent, where there is one, is supplied in brackets *at the end of the full entry* with the annotation 'ModW'; otherwise an equivalent is given with an identity sign (≡). The same has been done with many words in Red Book orthography, in the hope that the student will speedily acquire familiarity with the different spelling-systems.

The glossary is not exhaustive: where a word or a form occurs more than once, the first two or three instances are given in the order in which they occur in the text of this edition. Where a word occurs at a particular place in a form significantly different from the head-word, the manuscript form is supplied in brackets *after the relevant line-reference*. Where a word printed in the text is the product of an emendation, the form cited in the Glossary is marked with an asterisk. The circumflex accent (^) and the diaeresis (¨) have been used according to the modern convention to indicate, respectively, a long vowel in a monosyllabic word or the pronunciation of the diphthongs spelt <wy>, and a disyllabic pronunciation of two consecutive vowels.

Words are for the most part listed in the order of the English rather than the Welsh alphabet, with the exception that Ch follows C and Ff follows F. Perverse though the result will seem to those already thoroughly familiar with Middle Welsh, the convenience of the beginner must take first place. Note, in addition, that C and K are treated as interchangeable and are listed together, as are Chw and (rare) Wh, and R, Rh and (rare) Rr, all three of which correspond to modern Welsh Rh.

Verbs are listed under the verbal noun, cross-referenced where necessary, the stem being separated from the termination where appropriate by a vertical stroke, for example **can|u**. In such cases **-af, -o** etc. represent **canaf, cano** etc.; where no termination is given the form cited consists of the bare stem.

For more detailed study, *Geiriadur Prifysgol Cymru: A Dictionary of the Welsh Language* (Cardiff, 1950–2002) is indispensible; this provides glosses in both Welsh and English and covers the entire alphabet, the earlier letters being currently under revision in a second edition, of which nine fascicles have so far appeared (2003-). A still more detailed treatment is available in J. Lloyd-Jones, *Geirfa Barddoniaeth Gynnar Gymraeg* (Cardiff, 1931–63), though this extends only down to the beginning of the letter H and is entirely in Welsh. The former gives head-words in Modern Welsh spelling and lists verbs under the first person singular; the latter gives head-words in standard Middle Welsh spelling and lists verbs under their verbal nouns.

The Glossary is followed by a short index of words discussed in the Commentary, in particular those whose interpretation here deviates from that of Jackson.

# A

**a** (1) (**ac, ag**) conj. + spirant mut. *and* I.23a, XI.6d etc.; (2) (**ac**) prep. + spirant mut. *with* II.1b, IV.9b, IX.42?, 52?, XI. 6d; (3) rel. pron. (subject) + soft mut. (*he/she/that*) *who/which* II.33b, III.3c etc.; (4) rel. pron. (object) + soft mut. (*he/she/that*) *whom/which* I.29a, II.6b etc.; (5) affirmative particle + soft mut. separating subj. or obj. from following verb I.16c, II.22b etc.; (6) particle + soft mut. separating adj. from noun VII.8c; (7) vocative particle + soft mut. II.10c etc.; (8) preverbal particle supporting infixed pronoun IX.48, 66; (9) see **mynd, mynet**

**acdo** see **agdo**

**aches** n.m. *flood* II.5b

**achos** n. *cause* XII[A] 12f

**achwyn** n.m. *complaint* XII.2d

**adar** n.coll. *birds* I.12a, IV.10b, XII.3a

**adaw** (1) n.m. *promise* IX.27; (2) v.tr. *promise*; pres. ind. 3 sg. **edeu** IV.11c (ModW addo) addail n.coll. *leaves* or adj. *leafless* VI.7b (≡ ad-ddail)

addas adj. *proper*; as n. *reward* XI.1f

addfed adj. *ripe* XII[A].9b, [B].9d (addved) (ModW aeddfed)

addfwyn adj. *amiable, gracious* III.21c

addved see addfed

Adebon ? pers. n. X title, 15

adef (1) n.m. *home, habitation* X.11; (2) v.tr. *confess*; pres. ind. 3 sg. X.12?? impv. 2 sg. VII.4c etc.

adeil (1) n. *dwelling* XII[A].12e; (2) see adeilyat (≡ adail)

adeilyat v. *build*; pres.ind. 3 sg. adeil IV.10b

adnabot v.tr. *know (person)*; pres. ind. 1 sg. atwen II.6d, 3 sg. edwyn XII.3f (ModW adnabod, pres. ind. 1 sg adwaen)

adneu see atneu

adoet n.m. *harm* II.29c (≡ addoed)

adwy n.f. *gap, pass* III.4b

adwyth n.m. *death, calamity* XII[B].12f

adysc n.f. *education* VIII.3c. (ModW addysg)

äe adj.? III.14a

a'e (1) = a (2) + 'e (1) (m.) IX.66, (f) III.16c, XII[B].12e (a'i); (2) = a (3) + 'e (2) III.10c (2x), VI.10b, VIII.6b, XII[B].11g (a'i); (3) = a (5) + 'e (2) II.3a, III.1c, 11c, 18b.

aed see mynd, mynet

aeleu adj. *sad* III.14a

aelwyt n.f. *hearth* IV.8c, VI.22c (aelwyd)

aeron n.coll. *berries* XII[A].9b, [B].9d

aeth n.m. *grief* VIII.24c

aflawen adj. *miserable* III.19c

aflwyd n.m. *failure* III.2c (ModW aflwydd)

afrifed adj. *broad? countless? (sc.its waves)* XII[B].9b

agarw adj. *rough* V.5a\*, VI.5a\*

agdo n.m. *covering* I.13a , *veil* IX.14 (acdo) (≡ angdo)

agheluydyt n.m. *clumsiness* VIII.30c (ModW anghelfyddyd)

aghen n.m. *want, need* IX.3 (Mod W angen)

aghywir adj. *faithless* VIII.17c (ModW angh-)

aglew adj. *very brave*; as n. XI.6

agoret adj. *open* VIII.25b; see under awr.

ai ... ai conj. *whether ... or* XI.11h

a'i see a'e

alaf n.coll. *cattle* II.17b, VI.2a*, *property* IX.107

alaw n. *water-lily* II.31b

allan(n) adv. *outside* I.2c, 21c , VII.8a

allt n.f. *(wooded) slope* VII.10b

alltut n.m. *exile (person)* II.4c, III.12a etc.

alltuded n.m. *exile (state)* VIII.8c

am prep. *about, for* II.28c etc.; *around* I.11a

a'm see a, 'm

amav n.m. *uncertainty*; as adj. XII[A].10h (ModW amau)

amdud adj. *covered (with ice)* XI.1b

amgall adj. *prudent* VIII.13a

amgeled n.m. *anxiety, grief* VIII.19c

aml adj. *frequent* XII.4e, [B].11g; comp. **amlach** XII.8d

amlwc adj. *conspicuous, prominent* III.6a (ModW amlwg)

amsud adj. *varied?* X. 7

amswrn n.m. *throng?* X.10

amwyn adj. *white with foam? pure white?* X.9

anaf n.m. *wound* I.8c (anaw) (fig.) *misfortune* II.22c; *fault* VIII.11c

anaml adj. *infrequent* XII.1c. 2a etc.

anauus adj. *wounded*; as n. II.15c

anaw n.m.(1) *wealth* VIII.33a, IX.9; (2) see **anaf**.

ancwyn n.m. *feast* III.21c; *fruit* XII.2a

angad n.f. *hand* VI.17a

angav n. *death* XII[A].10g

angawr n.m. *miser* VIII.25a*; as adj.*grasping* XII[B].12h

anghyfaelywr n.m. *unreliable ally* IX.33

anghyfyeith adj. *speaking another language, alien* IX.99

anghyfyrdelit adj. *half-hearted* IX. 33

anhaut adj. *difficult* I.1a (ModW anodd)

anhebic adj. *unlike* II.9c, V.5b (ModW annhebyg)

anhuned n.m. *sleeplessness*, (fig.) *tumult* VIII.7a

anhygar adj. *disagreeable, disobliging* III.21a

aniueil n.m. *beast* II.16b (ModW anifail)

**anllad** adj. *wanton, lustful* XII.5d

**anllwyth** n.m. *flood* IV.8a

**annerth** n.m. *weakness* VIII.30c

**an(n)oeth** adj. *unwise, foolish* II.36c, VIII.4b

**anniweir** adj. *faithless, unchaste* III.5c, 7c, XII.7d

**an(n)wadal** adj. *fickle , half-hearted* III.10a; as n., III.5a

**annuyd** see **annwyt**

**annwyt** n.f. *nature* I.9c (annuyd); *vigour? cold (sickness)?* IX.28; *cold (temperature)* IX.72 .

**annyanawl** adj. *lively* III.1a (≡ anianol)

**anoeth** see **annoeth**

**anreith** n.f. *plunder, treasure* IX.95, X.5 (ModW anrhaith)

**anrrydedd** n. *honour* XII.6g

**anudon** n.m. *perjury* XII.9f

**anuoes** n.f. *discourtesy, oafishness* VIII.11c

**anwaws** adj. *without danger* IX.37

**anwiw** adj. *unworthy* XII.1e

**anyan** n. *nature* VIII.3c

*aper* (Lat.) n. *wild boar* XI.1d

**ar** (1) prep. *on* I.1c etc., 2 sg. **arnad** I.28a, 3 sg. m. **arnaw** IX.7, 3 sg. f. **erni** VII.7a; in adverbial phrase expressing physical movement and/or mental state II.5a, 6a, 8a, 11a, 31a, V.1b, VI.15a; (2) rel. pron. 3 sg. III.10c, IX.83, 108, 109; (3) **ar lles** see **er.**

**aradyr** n.f. *plough* V.9b, VI.4b (aradr); pl. **ereidr** VI.11a

**araf** (1) adj. *slow, still* II.25b; (2) see **arf**

**aral** n. *vigour* I.23a (≡ arial)

**arall** pron. *other* VIII.13b; pl. **ereill** VIII.25b

**archan** n. *shoe* XII[B].12a

**ardal** n.f. *region* III.5a

**areith** n. *speech* X.7

**aren** n.m. *hoar-frost* I.6a (≡ arien)

**arf** n. *weapon* II.8b (araf); pl. I.28a (ariweu)

**arglwyd(d)** n.m. *lord* VI.16c, IX.62

**ariweu** see **arf**

**arlwy** n. or v.tr. *(make) provision for* IV.3c

**arnad** see **ar** (1)

**aros** v. *last, remain*; vn. XII[A].12g

**artu** n? *darkness* (or place-name?) I.25b (≡ arddu)

**aruaeth** n. *plan, intention* II.24c, IX.25 etc.

**aruoll** (1) n.m. *promise* VIII.15c; (2) v.tr. *receive*; pres. ind. 3 sg **erwyll** XI.6g

**Aruul** name of horse I.25a (≡ Arfwl)

**aryant** n.m. *money* IV.9b

**arynaig** v.tr. *fear*; pres. ind. 3 sg. XII.3e

**athreidu** v.intr. *visit* II.34c

**atneir** n.m. *reproach* IX.79 (≡ adnair)

**atneu** n.m. ? *place of burial*, ? *treasury, store* III.9c (adneu), IV.1a (ModW adnau)

**atuant** adj. *fragile, vain* IX.22, 27 (≡ adfant)

**atwaed** adj. *loud, shrill* IX.22 (≡ adwaedd)

**atwen** see adnabot

**auall** n.f. *apple-tree* VIII.13a, X.1 (avall)

**auir** see awyr

**auon** n.f. *river* I.17c (awon), II.19a etc.; pl. **awonit** I.18a (ModW afon, afonydd)

**aval** n.m. *apple* X.1.

**avall** see auall

**aw** see mynd, mynet

**awel** n.f. *wind, breeze* I.1a, 3c, 21d, VI.9b

**awirtul** adj. *sad, despondent* I.25b (≡ afrddwl)

**awon** see auon

**awr** (1) n.f. *hour, time* XI.11a, e, XII [A].11c,d; (2) n.m. ? *gold*; **awr agoret** *generous*, VIII.25b*

**Awst** n.m. *August* VI.16a, XII.8a

**awyr** n.f. *sky* I.11b (auir), II.23b


## B

**bacwyawc** adj. *curly-haired?* II.20b; *budding* VIII.12b (≡ bagwyawg)

**baglawc** adj. *bearing a (pastoral) staff* III.7a; ? *serried*, ? *armed with spears or staves* VII.1a

**bagwy** adj. *budding?* VII.1a

**bai** n.m. *blame* XII.4e

**balch** adj. *proud* II.20b, IV.2a

**banadyl** n.coll. *broom* VIII.12a

**bann** (1) n.f. *top* pl. **banev** I.2b; (2) adj. *high, loud* I.21d, III.15a

**banw** n. *young pig* IV.4b

**bâr** n.m. *anger* II.8d

**bara** n.m. *bread* XII.8f

**bard** n.m. *poet* III.3c (ModW bardd)

**barf** n.f. *beard*; (fig.) *honour* II.8d\* (baraf)

**bargawt** n. *eaves* II.10b (ModW bargod)

**barn|u** v.tr. and intr.*judge*; pres. ind. 3 sg. XII.7h

**baryflwyd** adj. *grey-bearded* II.25c (≡ barflwyd)

**barywhaud** verbal adj. *bearded* I.4b (≡ barfawd)

**bas** adj. *shallow* II.32b, VIII.12c, XI.1g

**bechan** see **bychan**

**bedw** n.coll. *birches* V.3b, VII.4a, XII[B].10b

**bei** (1) conj. *if* (with unfulfilled condition) II.35b (cf. Mod W pe); (2) see **bot**

**beidyat** n.m. *challenger* IX.19

**beidyawt** adj.? *fearless* IX.95

**Bened** pers. name *Benedict* XII[B].9g

**berwr** n.coll. *watercress* VIII.29a

**betwerw** n.f. *birchwood* VIII.24b

**bir** see **byrr**

**bit** see **bot**

**biv** see **biw**

**biw** n.coll. *cattle* I.9b (biv), III.8a, VI.7b, VIII.24b

**blaen** n.m. *top* I.7b, 11c, II.12b etc.

**bleid** n.m. wolf II.22a, III.6c etc, (fig.) III.4b (ModW blaidd)

**blin** adj. *weary* XII.1b

**bluch** see **imbluch**

**blwng** adj. *surly*; as n. XII[B].11h

**bore** n.m. *morning* V.1c, VI.13c, XII.2g

**bot** v. *to be*; pres. ind. 2 sg vid I.19a, 26c **wyt** IX. 69, 84 (≡ wyd) 3 sg. **yw** VI.1a; (future) 3 sg. **byd** V.7b, XI.1g (vydd), **bit** I.16c, 17c (≡ bydd); impers. **bydir** X.6\*; (consuetudinal) 3 sg. **byd** II.7c, V.4c, VIII.15b, 27a, 27c etc., XII.2h (fydd) **bit** II.36b, III.1a etc. (≡ bid); (copula) **ys** II.34b, IX.112, 116, affirmative **neud** I.18c, XI.1a etc., neg. **nid** I.9c, II.23a, **ni** VI.8b, IX.56; (substantive) **mae** XI.1f; with neg. and indefinite noun **oes** VIII.4c, IX.94; rel. **sy** XII[A].10g; 3 pl **bydant** VIII.1a; pres. subj. 1 sg. **bwyf** II.26c, 3 sg. **bo** I.13b, II.6d etc., **boet**

IV.10a; impv. 3 sg **bit** IX.91; imperf. ind. 3 sg. **oed** II.4c (with modal sense); conditional 3 sg **bydei** II.35c; pret 2 sg **buost** I.19c, X.12

**brain** see **brân**

**braint** n.f. *privilege, right of access*? VI.6b

**brân** n.f. *raven* II.1b, V.7b etc.; *rook*, pl. **brein** IV.2d, XII[A].12b (brain).

**bras** adj. *fat* VI.3b, XII[A].11b

**braw** n.m. *fear, terror* VI.15c*

**brawt** n.m. *brother*; pl. **brodyr** II.21c

**bre** n.f. *hill, upland* I.2b, III.14c, VII. 15a

**breich** n.f. *arm* II.26b

**brein** see **brân**

**breit** n. ? *wonder, exception* (or as adj.? *exceptional*) I.2c, 21e (ModW braidd)

**breith** see **brith**

**Brenda** pers. name *Brendan*? XII.8g

**breyenin** n.m. *king* IX.95 (≡ breienin, ModW brenin)

**bric** n.m. *tip, shoot* VIII.9a (≡ brig)

**briclas** adj. *with green shoots* VII.4a (≡ briglas)

**brigawc** adj. *prickly* VIII.27a

**brith** adj. *speckled, of various colours* I.35b, II.16a etc.; fem. **breith** I.21a,b

**brin** n.m. *hill* I.1a, 12c (≡ bryn).

**briuhid** see **briwaw**

**briw|aw** v.intr. *break, shatter* pres. 3 sg **briuhid** I.20b, 21c

**bro** n.f. *valley* II.12b, *native haunt* IV.5a, *country* IX.17, 26; pl. **brooet** I.20b

**brodyr** see **brawt**

**brolit** n.m. *public strife* IX.34 (= bro + llid)

**bron(n)** n.f. *breast* I.21a,b; (fig.) *heart* IX.34; *side, face* II.16a, 17a, VI.21b, etc.; (of sea) *swell* I.35b; *hill* II.30a; see also under **rac**

**bronnvit** n. *tribulation* IX.48

**bronnwaly** n.f. *heart's sufficiency* VIII.1c

**bronrein** adj. *stiff-chested, boastful, puffed-up* IV.2a (≡ -rhain)

**bronureith** n. *thrush* I.21a,b (ModW bronfraith)

**brooet** see **bro**

**brwyn** n.coll. *rushes* II.15a, VIII.19a, XII[A].12b

**bryt** n.m. *mind* II.6b, VIII.29c, IX.89

**brythuch** n.m. *tumult* I.3a (≡ -wch)

buan adj. *swift* II. 14b, 22a, III.5a etc.

buches n. f. *milking-enclosure* XI.6c, XII.1d

budugawl adj. *victorious* III.1b (ModW buddugol)

bugeil n.m. *shepherd* III.6c, XII[B].11b

bun n.f. *girl* VIII.2c

buost see **bot**

buwch n.f. *cow* XII[B].10d

bwa n.m. *bow* XII.8c

bwyeit n.m. *psalm, Beatitudes* XI.18*

bychan adj. *small, petty* IV.10a etc.; fem. **vechan** VI.18c; comp. **llai**, as adv. *less* XII.8h

bychot n.m. *small thing, trifle* V.3c, XI.1h, XII[B].10e*; *(low estate)* IX.118

byd (1) see **bot**; (2) see **byt** .

bydar adj. *deaf* III.9a etc. (ModW byddar)

bydin n.f. *army* III.14a (ModW byddin)

bydinawr n.m. *campaigner, companion of armies*? VIII.29a

bydir see **bot**

byrddydd adj. *with short days* XII[A].12a

byrr adj. *short* I.4c (birr), 11c, 22c (bir), XI.11c.

byt n.m. *world* II. 33b, IX.1 etc.XI.11g (byd); see also **gwynn y uyt** (ModW byd)

byth adv. *ever* VII.7c; see also **pyth**

bytheiad n.m. *hound* XII.5f

byw adj. *living* IX.91; as n. *living thing* XII.3e.


## C (K)

kad n.f. *battle* I.8b (cad), VI. 17c*; *host* I.28b; pl. **kadeu** III.9b

kadarn adj. *firm, strong* II.26b, VIII.15c, XII.6h

kadawarth n.m. ? *charlock* VIII.20a

kadir adj. *fine* I.7c (≡ cadr)

cadw v.tr. *keep* VIII. 15c; pres. ind. 3 sg. **keidw** III.4c; impv 3 sg. **katwet** VIII.11b

cadwent n.f. *battle, battlefield* VI.22b

cadwyn n.f. *chain* VII.5b

kaeth adj. *captive, slave* II.13c, IX.25

caethiwed n. *captivity* XII[B].9f

**caff|ael** v.tr. *obtain, find* I.1a; **kael** IV.2d, 5b, V.5b; pres. ind. 3 sg. **keiff** II.20c; impers. **ceffir** IX.40; pres. subj. 3 sg. **-o** II.16c

**kalaf** n.m. *reed, stalk* I.3b (calaw), II. 17b, IV.9a

**kalan** n.m. *first day of month* V.1a, VI.1a, XI.1a etc.; **Kalangaeaf** *first day of winter (1 November)* I.22a (-w) etc.

**calaw** see **kalaf**

**caled** see **kalet**

**caledi** n.m. *miserliness* VIII.11a

**kalet** adj. *hard* I.14b (caled), V.1a, 7a etc.

**call** adj. *wise, prudent*; as n. VIII.6c; *clever, skilled, crafty?* IX.55

**callawr** n. *cauldron* XII[B].11d

**callet** n.coll. ? *greenery*, ? *trees* I.17b

**callonn** see **calon**

**callwedd** adj. *prudent of manner*: as n. VIII.7b

**calon** n.f. *heart* III.15c (callonn) , VI.14c etc.

**cam** adj. *crooked* I.21c; as n. *wrong* VI.5c

**camp** n.f. *exploit* VII.11c

**can, kan** (1) adj. *white*; as n. *(horse)* I.27c (can); (2) prep. = **gan**; 1 pl. **cennym** XI.1g; (3) conj. *since* I.26a, 30a, XI. 6f, 11g.

**kangeu** see **keinc**

**kanlin** v.tr. *follow* I.27c (≡ canlyn)

**kannmlwyd** adj. *a hundred years old* II.26c

**cannwyll** n.f. *candle* VII.8c, IX.72, XII.1h

**canon** n.m. *canon table* ? XII[A].9a

**kant** n.m. *hundred* V.9c, VII.1c

**kan|u** v.intr. *sing, give voice* II.1b; pres. ind. impers. **kenir** IX.18

**kar** (1) n.m. *friend* II.34b, ?X.5 (2) see **karu**

**carchar** n.m. *prison* I.29a, XII.3h; *chain, fetter* VII.6b

**karcharawr** n.m. *prisoner* I.9b (-aur), XII[B].11e; (fig.) VIII.14c (ModW carcharor)

**cardod** n.f. *almsgiving* XII[B].10h

**kariad** n.m. *love* XII.5e

**carn** n.m. *hoof* I.21c

**car|u, kar|u** (1) v.tr. *love* VIII.6c; pres. ind. 3 sg. III.10c, IV.7c, VIII.23c, IX.103, XII.6e; pres. ind. impers. **kerir** XII.4e **-awr** (? future) VIII.29c, 32c, IX.101; pres. subj. 3 sg. **-o** II.6b, III.3c, XII.1f; impf. ind. 1 sg. **carwn** X.5, 3 sg. **-ei** X.5, **ceri** X.8; (2) see **carv**

carv n.m. *stag* I.20a, 21c, 24b (caru) (ModW carw)

kas adj. *hateful* II.7c

kassulwin adj. *cloaked in white* I.12c* (≡ casulwyn)

caun see cawn

cawdd see coddi

cawn n.coll. *reeds, grass* I.3b, 4b (caun) etc., II.27a, VII.11b; sg. conin I.1c

kedic adj. *fierce, violent* I.3c

kedwir n.coll. *warriors* I.5b, 8b (keduir)

kedymdeith n.m. *companion* V.9c, VI.4c (cydymddaith) (cf. ModW cydymaith)

keffir see caffael

keidw see kadw

keiff see caffael

keilyawc n.m. *cock* III.1a, XII[B].12d (ModW ceiliog)

kein adj. *fine* V.2a, IX.70 (ModW cain) ; see also kyfreu

keinc n.f. *branch*; pl. kangeu VIII.12c (cf. ModW cangen)

keinmyg|u v.tr. *admire*; pres.ind. impers. -ir VIII.2b

keinyadu v.tr. *seek*; impv. 1 pl. keinyathwn IX.31 (≡ cennadu)

keissyat n.m. *sergeant of the peace, catchpole* III.3a; *striver*, pl. keissyadon X.13

keissy|aw v.tr. *seek*; pret. (? impf.) 3 sg. -essyt X.13

keithiw see igkeithiw

kelli n.f. *wood* VIII.23a

kel|u v.tr. *conceal* V.2c; pres. ind. 3 sg. VIII.10c; impv. 3 sg. -et II.24c

keluyd adj. *skilled*; ? as adv. IV.10a; as n. II.24c, V.2c (ModW celfydd)

kelwyd n.m. *lie* IX.24 (ModW celwydd)

kelwydawc adj. *lying*; as n. VII.7c (ModW celwyddog)

kelyn n.coll. *holly-trees* VIII.25a

kenin n.coll. *leeks* III.12c (ModW cennin)

kennat n.m. *messenger* VIII.28c

cennym see can (2)

kerd n.f. *song, poem* IX.92

kerddawr n.m. *minstrel, musician* XII[B].11b

kerennyd n. *reconciliation, friendship* IX.32 (krennyd), 55, 74, 102

kerd|et v.intr. *walk*; pres. ind. 3 sg. -a II.29b; pres.subj. 3 sg. -o VI.14b

kerir see karu

kerth adj. *certain* XI.6f

**kerwyn** n.f. *tub* II.15b

**kerwyt** n.m. *stag* V.8a, VI.13b

**kessair** n.m. *hail* XII.7b

**ket** see **kyt**

**ketrwyf** adj. *living on gifts* IX.92* (≡ cedrwyf)

**keu** adj. *hollow* I.15b (cev); ? as n. *belly* III.9a

**keudawt** n. *heart* II.35b, III.5b; *mind* IX.81

**ceugant** adj. *certain* VI.18a

**keunant** n.m. *ravine* II.2a

**cev** see **keu**

**kewin** n.m. *back, ridge* I.12c (ModW cefn)

**ki** n.m. *dog* XII.2g (see also **pen**)

**kic** n.m. *meat* IV.2d

**kighor** see **kyghor**

**kilyd** n.m. *companion*; as pron. **y gilyd** *each other* VIII.26c

**kin** conj. *though* I.25a etc. (≡ cyn)

**Kindilic** pers. *name* Cynddylig

**kinteic** adj. *swift* I.24a (≡ cyntëig)

**kirchid** see **kyrchu**

**kirn** see **corn**

**kis(s)caud** n.m. *shelter* I.4a, 23a (ModW cysgod)

**kiuaethlauc** adj. *turbulent* I.17a* (≡ cywaethlog)

**claf** adj. *sick* II.36b, III.13b

**klawdd** n.m. *dyke, hedge* XII.5b

**cleirch** n.m. *(decrepit) old man* III.18c

**klerddyn** n.m. *minstrel* XII.1b

**clidur** see **clydwr**

**clid** see **clyt**

**clot** n. *praise* IX.24, 117

**cluir** n.m. *company, host* ? I.11a (≡ clwyr)

**clustir** adj. *long-eared*; as n. *hare* XII.4c (clust + hir)

**clyt** adj. *sheltered* I.20a (clid), II.7b; as n. *shelter* I.1a (clid), XII.5b (klyd)

**klyd** see **clyt**

**clydwr** n.m. *shelter* I.15a (clidur), II.16b, VII.9a

**knawd** see **gnawd**

cnes n.m. *covering* I.5a

cnifiat n.m. *fighter;* as adj. *truculent* III.3a

cnu n.m. *fleece* II.34a

koc see cog

coch adj. *red* I.12c, II.21a etc.

codd|i v.tr. *anger;* pres. ind. 3 sg. cawdd VI.20c

koet n.coll. *trees, wood* I.3c, 24a (coed), II.29a, IX.70; pl. koydydd XII[A].11b (ModW coed)

coeth see rhygoeth

cog n.f. *cuckoo* VI.12a, XII.5f (koc); pl. cogeu V.6b

colofn n.f. *pillar,* ? *peak* VI.9b

colwyn n.m. *young dog* III.13c, 20a

coll n.coll. *hazels* VIII.15a

coll|i v.tr. *lose, destroy, miss;* pres. ind. 3 sg. -yt II.13b, -it X.11 (or impf. impers.?), kyll IX.60.

conin see cawn

korff n.m. *body* XII.7d

corn n.m. *horn (drinking-horn),* X.10 ; pl. cyrn I.11a (cirn),

corof n. *saddle-bow* II.8c (≡ corf)

cors n.f. *bog, marsh;* pl. corsyd VIII.16a

kowir see kywir

cowyll n.m. *covering* IX.70

koydydd see koet

crauangawc adj. *clawed* III.17a (ModW crafangog)

cranclef III.11b (see note)

cras adj. *parched;* as n. *dry vegetation* V.7a, XI.1a

cred see cretu

kreic n.f. *rock* II.17a (ModW craig)

creilum adj. *bare, bleak* I.24a

krennydd see kerennydd

cret|u v.tr & intr. *believe;* pres. ind. 3 sg. VI.20c (cred), IX.45

creu n. *blood* IX.6

creuyd n.f. *religion, monasticism* IV.5c, IX.26; ? *piety* IX.31 (ModW crefydd)

crib n.m. *comb* III.1a

krin adj. *withered* I.3b, II. 17b, IV.9a etc.; as n. IX.54

Crist pers. name *Christ* IX.32

croen n.m. *skin* XII.5h

kronffair n.f. *petty fair* ? XII.7f

crwm adj. *convex, rounded* III.9a*; *bent, hunched* I.20a (crum), II.27b, III.8a,V.4a

crwybyr n.m. *froth* VIII.8b, *hoar-frost* VIII.14c

krymman n.m. *sickle* XII.8c (ModW cryman)

crynnwryaeth n.f. *churlishness, mean-spiritedness* IV.6a

ku adj. *dear, beloved, agreeable* II.34b

Kuhelyn pers. name *Cuhelyn* X.10

kuhudyat n.m. *accuser* III.3a

cul adj. *narrow, slender, thin* I.4b etc, XII.1e (kvl)

Kulaethwy ? pers. n. (? cf. *Gilfaethwy*) VI.11c

culgrwm adj. *thin and hunched* I.21c (-grum), II.28b

cum see cwm

cunlleit n.coll. *herbage?* I.15b (≡ cunllaidd)

cwm n.m. *valley* I.20a (cum), II.28b

cwnneu v.tr. *kindle*; pres. ind. 3 sg. (fig.) IX.76 (ModW cynnau)

cwsg see kysgu

cwt, kwt interrog. adv. *where* IX.16, 82

cwyd|o v.intr. *fall*; pres. ind. 3 sg. X.1 (≡ cwyddo)

cwymp n.m. *fall* V.7c, VI.3c

cwyn n. *complaint* II.15c; as adj. *querulous* III.13b, 19b

cwynuanus adj. *querulous* VII.10b

cwyn|o v.intr. *complain, grieve*; pres. ind. 3 sg. II.14c

kybydd n.m. *miser* XII[A].11e, [B].11h

kychwyn v. tr. & intr. *start, move*; *ar gychwyn* ? *spinning,whirling, ? about to depart* V.1b, *on the move* VI.15a

cydymddaith see kedymdeith

kyfa adj., *whole* IX.110

kyfaruot v.intr. *meet*; pres.ind. 3 pl. **cyfaruydant** II.2d

kyfarweith n.m. ? *effort* IX.98

kyfedd n.m. *feast, revelry* XII[A].12d

kyflwyt adj. *successful* IX.104 (≡ cyflwydd)

kyfnewit v.intr. *exchange, bargain* IV.9b

cyfnod n.m. *period, time* VI.16a

**kyfofni** v.tr.& intr. *terrify, cause fear* X.8

**kyfreu** n.m. *words, song, sound, voice*; **kein g.** compound adj. *of fine song, melodious* V.6a, VIII.29b, 31a

**kyfret** adj. eq. *as swift* V.2b (≡ cyfred)

**kyfrin** adj. *secret (shared)* ; as n. V.2a, VIII.4a

**kyfyrdy** n.m. *ale-house* IV.7b

**kyghein** see **kynghenni**

**kyghor** n.m. *counsel, advice* I.10c, 20c (kighor), XII.2f (kyngor) (ModW cyngor)

**kyhafal** adj. *equal, well-balanced* IX.5

**kylched** n.m. *bed* VIII.25c

**kyll** see **colli**

**kylor** n.coll. *pignuts* IV.4c

**kymanua** n.f. *assembly* VII.2b

**kymar** n.m. *mate* XII.3f

**kymot** v.intr. *go together, be at peace*; pres. ind. 3 sg. **cymyd** IX.28, X.2*; as n. *agreement, reconciliation* XII.5e      (ModW cymod)

**kymwyn** adj. *fruitful* VIII.19a

**cymyd** see **kymot**

**kymydawc** n.m. *neighbour* II.35c (ModW cymydog)

**kynddrygedd** n. *dissension* XII.6f

**kynghenn|i** v.intr. *prevail, be accepted*; pres. ind. 3 sg. **kyghein** VIII.32c

**kynglhennyd** n.f. *liverwort?, waterweed?* II.19a (≡ cynghlennydd)

**kyngor** see **kyghor**

**kyngrair** n. *agreement, peace* XII.7c (ModW cynghrair)

**kyngrwn** adj. *hunched* II.9a

**cynhauaf** n.m. *harvest* (fig.) VI.22 b (ModW cynhaeaf)

**kyni** n.m. *suffering, misery* IV.6c

**kynllwyn** n.m. *plot, conspiracy* XII.2f

**kynnadyl** n.f. *meeting-place* VIII.12a

**kynneuin** adj. *familiar, accustomed* II.1b

**kynnic** n.m. *venture, exploit* IX.86 (ModW cynnig)

**kynnlleith** adj. *soft, mild*; ? as n. *mild (spell of) weather* IV.8a

**kynnvidyd** n.m. *fighter in front line* IX.53

**kynnwys** v.tr. *receive*; as n. *reception, acceptance* III.3b kynnyd(d) v.intr. *prosper*; pres. ind. 3 sg. (*in spiritual sense*) VI.14c, IX.30; as n. *success* II.19b

kynran n.m. *chieftain* II.8b; pl. kynrein II.4b, kynreinyon IV.8b

kynrwytieith adj. ?*loquacious* IV.8b (≡ cynrhwyddiaith)

kynteuin n.m. *early summer, spring* V.5b

Kynuit place name *Cynwyd* I.28b

Kynvelyn pers. name *Cynfelyn* XII.1g

kyrbwyll v.tr. *speak of, invoke* IX.69; pres. ind. impers. -ir IX.48 (ModW crybwyll)

kyrawal n.coll. *rowan-berries,* ? *-trees* VIII.21a (cf. ModW criafol)

cyrch n.m. *sortie, attack* VI.13c

kyrch|u v.tr. *seek* I.27b, pres. ind. 3 sg. -it I.20a (kirchid), VIII.24b, impers. -ir XII.8h

cyrn see corn

kysg|u v.intr. *sleep*; pres. ind. 3 sg. kwsc VIII.25d etc. -yt II.18b, subj. 3 sg. -o VI.14c, VIII.25c

kyssul n.m. *counsel* VII.1c

kysswyn n.m. *plot, conspiracy* XII.2c

kystud n.m. *affliction* VIII.10c

kyt conj. *although* II.6c, IV.10a, IX.2 (ket) (≡ cyd)

kytuot v.intr. *agree*; pres. ind. 3 sg. kytuyd II.18c (kytuyt), VII.2c (ModW cydfod)

kytuyt see kytuot

kyueillt n.m. *friend* III.6c (ModW cyfaill)

kyvaethlaw v.intr. *contend, quarrel* IX.5

kyvan adj. *entire, whole, (unbroken)* VIII.18c

kyvarwit adj. *familiar, well-informed* I.26c (≡ cyfarwydd)

kyuoet adj. *of the same age*; ? as n. *companion* IV.10c (Mod W cyfoed)

kyvyeith adj. *of the same language*; as n. *fellow-countryman* X.8

kyweith n.m. *colleague, collaborator* IX.104

kywir adj. *true, faithful* III.7a; as n. VIII.18c, XII.4f (kowir)

kywreint adj. *skilful, clever* VIII.2b, IX.30; as n. VI.8b (cywraint)

kywren(n)hin adj. *strong, mighty*; as n. IX.53, 69.

## CHW (WH)

chwaer|u v.intr. *fall*; pres. ind. 3 sg. chwerit IX.6

chwal|u v.tr. & intr. *disperse*; pres. ind. 3 sg. chwelit IX.14

chwaneg|u v.tr. *increase*; pres. ind. 3 sg. **chwenneckyt** II.32c; see also **ychwanegu**.

chwannawc adj. ? *greedy,* ? *eager* III.7b, 18c, IX.20; *prone* III.12b

chwant n.m *desire* IX.22

chwareus adj. *playful* XII.4c (gwareus), [A].10b

chwarwyva n.f. *playing-place* XII.8d

chwec, whec adj. *sweet* IV.3a, VIII.10b*, 13b* (whec), IX.37 (≡ chweg)

chwedyl n.f. *tale* II.6c; pl. **chwedleu** IV.1c

Chwefrawr n.m. *February* VI.10a, XII.2a (Chwefrol)

whefris ? adj. ? *rough, perilous* VIII.8b

Chwefrol see **Chwefrawr**

chwelit see **chwalu**

chwenneckyt see **chwanegu**

chwenych|u v.tr. *desire*; pres. ind. 3 sg. **chwennych** XII.6g

chwerdit, -yt see **chwerthin**

chwerit see **chwaeru**

chwerthin v.tr. & intr. *laugh, smile* III.12b, IX.52; pres. ind. 3 sg. **chwerdyt** II.6b, V.7c (-it), VI.3c (chwerddid), VIII.29c (-yt)

chwerthinat n.m. *laugher*; as adj. VIII.10b (≡ chwerthiniad)

chwerw adj. *bitter* VIII.9a, 10a; (fig.) VI.10a, IX.38, XII.3b

chwiban n. *whistle*; as adj. VI.11b

chwyrn adj. *fierce* III.13c, XII[A].10b

chwyrniad n.m. *snarler* III.20a


## D

da adj. *good*; comp. **gwell** III.20c; superl. **goreu** V.6c, IX.104 etc; as n. *good man* IV.10c, VII.12c *benefit* II.1c, IX.40, XI.11b, *goods, property* XII[A].11e, g, *goodness, grace* 11h.

dadl|u v.tr. & intr. *determine* ; pret. 3 sg. -as XI.1h

daffar n.m. *provision* V.6c, VIII.31c, 33c

daiar n.f. *earth* XII.3e; ? *solid ground* VI.1c (ModW daear)

dall adj. *blind*, as n. VIII.14c ; pl. **deillon** VIII.20b

dan prep. *under* VIII.27b

dâr n.f. *oak* IV.7a, VIII.22a; pl. **deri** VIII.23b

**darfod** v.intr. (1) *die, perish, terminate*; pres. ind. 3 sg. (future) **derfydd** XII[A].11g, 12h; (2) *happen*; pres. ind. 3 sg. (future) **derfydd** XI.6h* XII[A].11g, 12h; impv. 3 sg. **deruhid** I.22c (≡ derffid)

**darogan** n.f. *prophecy* XII[B].9e; see **mab darogan**

**darpar|u** v.tr. *provide*; pres. subj. 3 sg. -o IX.12

**das** n. *rick* VI.2b, XII.8d

**davad** n.f. *sheep* XII.5h

**daw** see **dyuot**

**dawn** n.f. *talent* V.4c, VI.19c, VIII.31b; *excellence* XI.6d; *benefit* II.27c, VII.11c, XI.6b, 6h*

**dawr** see **dori**

**deall** v.tr. *understand*; as n. *understanding* II.4c

**dedwyd** see **detwyd**

**deheu** n.m. *south* IV.1a

**deigyr** n.m. *tear* VIII.19b

**deil** n.coll. *leaves* IV.5d, V.1b etc.

**deilyar** adj. *with rustling leaves* VII.6a

**deilyedig** adj. *captive*; as n. *prisoner? serf?* VIII.26b

**deillon** see **dall**

**dêl, deled** see **dyuot**

**denghyn** adj. *strong, mighty* IX.67*

**deon** n.coll. *fighting men* VI.15a

**deri** see **dâr**

**derfydd** see **darfod**

**derllydd|u** v.tr. *deserve*; pres. subj. 3 sg. -wy XI.6h

**deruhit** see **darfod**

**derw** n.coll. *oak-trees* VII.5a, VII.9a etc.

**detwyd** adj. *fortunate* III.10c, VIII.13a, IX.73; as n. II.29b, IV.10c, VII.3c, IX.9, XI.11b, XII[A].12e (ModW dedwydd)

**detwyn** ?adj. *returning* (or v.intr.) IX.64

**deu** num. *two*; as n. *couple* II.2c

**deuawd** n.f. *ceremony* XI.11a (ModW defod)

**deudde(n)g** num. *twelve* XII[B].12e

**deueiriawc** adj. *duplicitous* III.7c

**deur** adj. *brave* I.23b (≡ dewr)

**deweint** n.m. *small hours of morning* VIII.2a

**dewin** n.m. *worker of wonders* V.5c, VIII.4c, IX.61

**diaele** adj. *without a care, untroubled* VIII.15b

**dial** v.tr. *avenge*; vn. as n. VI.10c, VIII. 21c; pres. ind. 3 sg. **dieil** II.19c, **dielid** XII.7e

**dialwr** n.m. *avenger* VI.9c

**dianc** v.intr. *escape*; pres. ind. 3 sg. **dieigc** I.20c (≡ dieinc), **diang** VI.17c; (future) impers. **diangawr** VI.10b

**diarchar** adj. *brave* I.23b

**diarchenad** adj. *unshod*; as n. XII.5c

**diaspat** n.f. *cry* ; ? as adj. *vociferous* III.14a (ModW diasbad)

**diawc** adj. *lazy* III.6c (ModW diog)

**diawl** n.m. *Devil* XII.6f

**dichleic** adj. *dry-shod* II.17b

**didar** adj. *noisy* VIII.22

**didor|i (didarbot)** v.tr. & intr. *interest, care*; pres. ind. 3 sg. **didawr** IX.16, XII[B].11g (diddawr)

**didos** adj. *sheltered, snug* II.18b, XII[A].12e (ModW diddos)

**dieid** adj.? *apathetic, sluggish* II.22c (≡ -aidd)

**dieigc** see **dianc**

**dieil, dielid** see **dial**

**dien** n.coll. *grass* I.6c

**difenw|i** v.tr. *despise, slander* VI.8b; pres. ind. 3 sg **difanw** VI.18c, impers. -ir IX.109 (divennwir)

**diffaith, diffeith** adj. *desolate, waste, deserted* IV.8c, VI. 22c (diffaith), IX.100; as n. *wilderness* VI.22a (diffaith)

**diffeithwch** n.m. *wilderness* II.22b

**diffreidad** n.m. *defender* I.28b

**diffrint** see **dyffryn(t)**

**diffwys** n.m. *precipice*; as adj. *precipitous* VII.10b

**diffyd(d)** adj. *without faith* IX.29, 109; as n. IV.8c, VI.22c (diffydd), IX.100

**difrawd** n.m. *destruction* XII.4g; *harm* XII[B].10f (difrod)

**difro** adj. *homeless, exiled*; as n. VI.16b

**difrod** see **difrawd**

**difrodus** adj. *despised* XII.5a

**difrys** see **dyfrysiaw**

**dig** n.m. *anger, bitterness, grief* VI.16b (or as adj.)

**digallon** adj. *disheartened* VIII.5a (≡ digalon)

**digarad** adj. *unloved*; as n. XII.5b

**digawn** pron. *enough* (or see **digoni**) IX.12

**Digoll** pl. n. VIII.15a

**digon|i** v.tr. *be capable of, provide, perform*; pres. ind. 3 sg. **digawn** VIII.6b, IX.12; (with unexplained infix) **dymkawn** XI.6a

**digu** adj. *loveless* IV.9c

**diguit** see **dygwyd**

**dihawl** adj. *not liable to legal action* II.3c

**dillat** n.coll. *clothes* III.3b

**dinas** n.f. *stronghold, city* IX.100

**dinaw** v.tr. *provoke* IX.6, 114

**diobeith** adj. *hopeless*; as n. IX.103

**diofn** adj. *fearless* VI.9c

**diogel** adj. *assured* XII[A].10g

**dioryuic** adj. *?stubborn* IX.15 (≡ diorfyg)

**dir** adj. *certain* IX.96, 116

**diriaid, dirieit** adj. *ill-starred* II.3c; as n. II.31c (diryeit), III.2c (diryeit), 21a (diriaid), V.4b, VII.2c (diryeit), XII[A].10e, 12f (diriaid)

**dirmyg|u** v.tr. *despise* ; pres. ind. 3 sg. **dirmic** VIII.2c, impers. -jr IX.107

**diryeit** see **dirieit**

**disgethrin** adj. *surly, truculent*; as n. VIII.4b

**disgynn|u** v. intr. *fall, descend* II.8d

**dit** see **dyd**

**diuedit** n.m. *end of day* I.4c,11c (≡ diwedydd)

**diulith** see **divlit**

**diuo** (1) adj. *destructive* IX.20; (2) see **dyuot** (1)

? **diuot** v. intr. *avail*: 3 sg. **diw** VIII.19c*

**diuryssint** see **dyfrysiaw**

**diva** v. tr. *destroy, ruin*; pres. ind. 3 sg. XII[A].9h.

**divlit** adj. *bleak, bitter* I.12b (diulith), 14c (≡ diwlydd)

**diw** see ? **diuot**

**diwall** adj. *contented*; as n. X.2*

**diwarth** adj. *without shame* III.16a, VIII.20b

**diwc** see **diwyn**

**diwedd** n.m. *end* XII.2i, 6h

**diweddnos** n. *end of night* XII[A].12d

**diweir** adj. *faithful* IX.46

**diwestyl** adj. *without legal claim* ? IX.107

**diwres** adj. *devoid of heat* XII.1d

**diwyt** adj. *diligent* VIII.28c

**diwyn** v.tr & intr. *make amends*; pres. ind. 3 sg. diwc IX.79

**diymgel** adj. *manifest* XII[A].10d

**doeth** (1) adj. *wise* III.11c, IX.88; as n. VIII.4a (2) see **dyuot**

**dofydd** see **dovyd**

**dor|i** v. impers. *concern*; pres. ind. 3 sg. dawr IX.16, XII[A].10e

**dovyd** n.m. *lord (God)* VI.10c (dofydd), IX.74, 103

**drein** n.coll. *thorns* IV.2b

**driccin** see **dryccin**

**dricweuet** n.m. *evil property* I.15c (≡ drygfeuedd)

**dros** prep. *for, for the sake of, in return for* VI.5c; 3 sg.f. drosti XII[A].11d

**drut** adj. *brave* II.4b; *rash* III.14c; as n. *fool* III.12b, IX.45, 99

**drwc** adj. *bad* III.16c, IV.6b etc.; as n. *evil* II.12c etc.; compar. **gwaeth**, as adv. (g)**waethwaeth** *worse and worse* IV.6c; superl. **gwaethaf** VIII.11c, XII[A] 9e,f (gwaetha)

**drwy** see **trwy**

**drycanyan** n. *evil nature*; or as adj. then as n. *ill-natured man* VII.3c

**dryccor** n. *wrongful agreement, conspiracy* IX.38

**dryccin** n.f. *foul weather, storm* I.18a (driccin), V.2b (dryckin), VIII.22a (drychin)

**drycdrem** n.f. *poor sight* II.13c

**drychin** see **dryccin**

**drycwr** n.m. *bad husband* II.16c

**drycwreic** n.f. *bad wife* II.17c

**drycwryaeth** n.f. *wickedness* IX. 91

**drygddarogan** adj. *ill-prophesying*; as n. *false prophet, ? soothsayer* XII[B].12h

**drygwenwyn** n.m. *disaster, tribulation?* XII.2e

**dryssi** n.coll. *brambles* VII.7a

**du** adj. *black* VI.3b

**Duv** see **Duw**

**duvin** see **dwfyn**

**Duw** n.m. *God* I.29a (Duv), III.1c, V.5c etc.

dwc see dwyn

dwfyr n.m. *water* II.32b, VIII.18b etc.

dwfyn (1) adj. *deep; profound* I.35c (duvin); (2) n.m. *world* IX.41 (≡ dwfn)

dwg see dwyn

dwyn v.tr. *take; bring;* pres. ind. 3 sg. dwc VIII.33c, XII[B].9f (dwg), impers. dygir
    IX.113

dwyrein n.m. *east* IV.2a

dwyweith adv. *twice* X.6

dy ven X.15 (see note)

dyad|u v.tr. *let go;* pres. subj. impers. dyatter IX.8

dybyd see dyuot

dychwyn|aw v.intr. *complain;* pres. ind. impers. -ir IX.114

dychyfyaw n. ? *security,* ? *comradeship* IX.3

dychyffre v.tr. *scatter, sprinkle, cause to flow;* pres. ind. 3 sg. IX.57

dychymot v.intr. *go together;* pres. ind. 3 sg. dychymmyd IX.9

dychynneit|yaw v.intr. *compete;* pres. ind. 3 sg. IX.23

dychynnydd adj. *growing* IX.23

dychystud|iaw v.tr. *wear away, damage,* pres. ind. 3 sg. IX.3, 34

dychyuaruot v.intr. *meet, go together;* pres. ind. 3 sg. dychyveruyd IX.58

dyd n.m. *day* I.12b, 19b (dit), II.36a, X.12, XII[B].12e (dydd) etc.

dydaw, dydo see dydyuot

dydyuot v.intr. *come;* pres. ind. 3 sg. dydaw IX.1, dydo IX.11

dyfrys|iaw v.intr. *hasten;* pres. ind. 3 sg. IX.4 (difrys), 63; 3 pl. diuryssint I.8b

dyffryn(t) n.m. *watercourse* I.17a (diffrint), XII.1a.

dyffust|iaw v.tr. *beat;* pres. ind. 3 sg. -it IX.49

dyfod see dywedyd

dyfydd see dyuot (1)

dygir see dwyn

dygn adj. *severe, harsh* XII[B].9f

dygweste VI.17b (see note)

dygwrthryn|u v.tr. *pound;* pres. ind. 3 sg. IX.63

dygwydd v.intr. *fall;* pres. ind. 3 sg. I.26b (diguit); -yt II.23b, VIII.23b (cf. ModW
    digwydd, with figurative sense)

dygyuor n.m. *surge* IV.4a

dygynnull v.tr. *gather together* XI.11b

**dygwyl** n.m. *feast-day* XI.6b

**dylif** n. *weft*; (fig.) *nature* XI.11c

**dyly|u** v.tr. *owe*; pres. ind. 3 sg. **dyly** VIII.2c

**dymkawn** see **digoni**

**dyn** n.m. *man* II.3c,13c, III.1c etc; pl. **dynion** XII [A].9f

**dyppo** see **dyuot**

**dyre** adj. *skittish* III.14b, *vigorous* VI.13a

**dysc, dysg** n. *learning* II.27c, V.4c, VI.19c

**dysgedyd** n.m. *pupil* VIII.16b

**dyuot** (1) v. intr. *come, happen*; pres. ind. 3 sg. **daw** II.1c etc., consuetudinal pres./ future 3 sg. **dybyd** IX.4, 21, **dyfydd** XII[A].11d*, subj. 3 sg. **dyppo** I.13c (future sense?) **diuo** IX.74, 75 **dyvo** XI.11e **dêl** XII[A].10h, impv. 3 sg. **deled** XII[B].11b; pret. 3 sg. **doeth** II.36a* (ModW dyfod, dod); (2) see **dywedyt**.

**dyvn** adj. *at one* VI.8c (≡ duun)

**dyvo** see **dyuot** (1)

**dyvrys** see **dyfrysiaw**

**dywal** adj. *fierce*; as n. IX.96, X.2*

**dywallaw** v.tr. *share, dispense*; pres. ind. 3 sg. IX.10

**dywed|yt** v.tr. *say, tell*; pres. subj. impers. **dywetter** II.6c; pret.1 sg -eis II.9b; pret. 3 sg. **dyvod, dyfod** (< dywawd) XII.1g, 7g, [B].9g etc.


### E

**e, 'e** (after vowel) (1) poss. pron. 3 sg. m.+ soft mut. X.7, 14; (with a (2)) **a'e** (m.) IX.66*, (with no) **no'e** V.1c, (with o (1)) **o'e** IX.6, 43, 87, **o'i** XI.6e, 11e; (2) poss. pron. 3 sg. f. (with a (2)) **a'e** III.16c, **a'i** XII[B].12e; (3) poss. pron. 3 pl. (with o (2)) **o'e** I.5b; (4) infixed pers. pron. (obj.) 3 sg. m. + asp. of foll. vowel (with a (4)) **a'e** III.10c (twice), VI.10b*, VIII.6b, **a'i** XII[B].11g; (with a (5)) **a'e** II.3a, III.1c, 11c, 18b.

**Ebrill** n.m. *April* VI.12a, XII.4a

**echel** n.f. *axle* XII[A].10a

**echwenic** see **ychwanegu**

**edëin** adj. *alien* III.12a (≡ -dd-)

**edeu** see **adaw**

**edewit** n. *promise* IX.35 (≡ -dd-; cf. ModW addewid)

**edmig** n.m. *reverence, praise* XI.11f

**edn** n.m. *bird* XII.3f

**edrych** v. intr. *look* IX.71

**edwyn** see **adnabot**

**edyn** n.m. *rascal* IX.76 (cf. ModW adyn)

**ef** (1) pers. pron. 3 sg. m. IX.10, 60?; (2) preverbal particle II.20c, IX. 68, 88, 102, ?X.5, with soft mutation IX.88

**efrifed** adj. *countless* VI.21b

**eglur** adj. *clear* IX.71

**egin** n.coll. *shoots, sprouts* VI.13a, XII[A].12b

**egroes** n. coll. *rose-hips* VIII.11a

**egwa** n.m. *speech* IX.75; see also **prif egwa**

**ehedydd** n. *skylark* VI.11b*

**ehovyn** adj. *fearless* IX.89, X.3 (ModW eofn)

**ehud** adj. *foolhardy* III.10a

**ei** see **i** (1)

**eiddo** n.m. *property* XII[A].11e

**eidic** adj. *greedy, jealous* VIII.6a; as n., pl. **eidigyon** VIII.5b

**eidil** adj. *weak, feeble*; as n. VIII.5c, IX.54, 64 (eidyl)

**eidun|aw** v.tr. *desire, pray* ; pres. ind. 1 sg. -af II.26c

**eidyl** see **eidil**

**eigiawn** n. *ocean* II.27b, VI.5b, VII.11a

**eilic** adj. *lively* VIII.3a

**eilion** n.m. *stag* II.24a

**eillyaeth** n.f. *support, sustenance* IX.92 (≡ eiliaeth)

**eilwyddgar** adj. *sociable* VI.13b

**ein** see **genni**

**eing** see **engi**

**eirch** see **erchi**

**eirchyat** n.m. *petitioner* III.16a

**eirvg** v.intr. *be deserving* ?; pres. ind. 3 sg. VI.1c (≡ eirwng)

**eiry** n.m. *snow* I.5a etc., II.1a etc.

**eiryan** adj. *bright, shining. splendid* II.8b

**eiryawl** v. intr. *intercede, entreat*; as vn. VIII.32c, IX.101

**eiryoes** n.f. *faith* VIII.11b

**eithin** n.coll. *furze, whin, gorse* III.12a, VIII.4a

**eleic** adj. ? *grey-haired* I.19a (≡ -aig)

elein n. *young deer* VIII.32a (≡ -ain)

elestyr n.coll. *flags (yellow iris)* VIII.17a

eluit n. *land, world* I.14c, 18c (≡ elfydd)

elwig adj. *prosperous, prized,* VI.1b, VIII.26a

emriv n.f. ? *embankment* I.16b (≡ emriw)

emwythwas n.m. ? *fierce young man* X.9

emys n.m. *war-horse* X.9 (or pl.)

eneit n.m. *soul* IV.9c

en see yn

eng|i v. intr. *escape*; pres. ind. 3 sg. eing IX.97, -hit IX.98

ennaint n. *bath* VI.8a

en(n)wir adj. *terrible* IX.106; *faithless, disloyal* I.24c (enuir), XII.4g; as n. IX.60

eos n.f. *nightingale* XII[A].12c

*equs* (Lat., for equus) n. *horse* XI.6d

er (1) prep. *for (sake of)* V.3b (yr), XI.6b (ar), XII[B].10e; *despite* I.13c (ir); (2) conj. *although* XII.4d

erbyn prep. *by (time)* XI.6b

erch|i v.tr. *request* IX.112; pres. ind. 3 sg. eirch III.18b, impers. -ir IX.111*

erchwynn n.m. ? *defender* II.25c

ereidr see aradr

ereill see arall

erlit v.tr. *pursue* IX.43

erlynnyat n.m. *pursuer* VIII.28b

erni see ar

erwein n.coll. *meadowsweet* VIII.32a

erwyll see aruoll (2)

eryr n. *eagle* IV.7a

escar n.m. *enemy* I.23c, XII.3e (ysgar)

escussawt n.m. *excuse* IX.39 (ModW esgusod)

escut adj. *swift* II.4a, III.8b (esgut), VI.13b (esgud)

esgud, esgut see escut

esgwit adj. *ready, facile* IX.39

estrawn adj. *strange*; as n. *stranger* V.1d

ethiw see myned

etifedd n.m. *heir*; pl. -ion XII[A].9h

eu poss. pron. 3 pl *their* I.5c

eurdwrn n.m. ? *gold handle*; pl. eurtirn I.11a

euwr n.coll. *kex, cow-parsley* I.15b (ewur), VII.9b (≡ efwr)

evras adj. *vigorous, in his prime* V.7b*

eweint adj. *lively, spirited*; as n. *young man* III.21a

ewig n.f. *hind* VI.1b

ewur see euwr

ewynn n.m. *foam* VII.8c

eyt see myned

### F, Ff

ffer adj. *fierce, wild* III.21a; as n. IX.8

ffisscau v.tr. *attack* I.23c (≡ ffysgo)

ffo n.m. *flight* IX.18

ffoi v.intr. *flee*; impv. 2 pl. fouch I.30b

ffôl adj. *foolish*; as n. *fool* VIII.16c

ffoll adj. *puffed-up*; as n. *coxcomb, pompous ass* VIII.15b

ffonn n.f. *staff, stick* II.30c

ffos n.f. *ditch* II.18a

ffraeth adj. *lively* II.24a

ffrwd n. *stream* VI.1c

ffrwyth n. *fruit, success* XI.11c

ffyd n.f. *faith* VIII.16c (ModW ffydd)

ffysgod see pysg

fouch see ffoi

fydd see bot

### G

gad|u v.tr. *leave* VIII.13c; *allow, permit*; pres. ind. 3 sg. I.8c

gaeafrawt n.m. *winter storm* IX.77

gaeaw see gayaf

gafr n.f. *goat*; pl. gavrod XII[B].10d

gal n.m. *enemy*; pl. -on X.14

galar n.m. *mourning, grief* III.17c, XII.3d

galon see gal

galarus adj. *lamenting*; as n. *mourner* III.19b

galw v.tr. *call*; pres. ind. impers. gelwir I.19b (geluir), VI.11c

gan prep. *by, with, from* II.8b, XI.6g etc.; *because of* I.21c

ganed see geni

gar ? X.5

garv adj. *rough* I.16c (≡ garw)

gau see geu

gauaf see gayaf

gaur see gawr

gavrod see gafr

gavwy adj. *ardent, zealous* III.4a

gawr n. *noise* I.12a (gaur), IX.106; *battle-cry* III.11b

gayaf n.m. *winter* I.3a,15a (gaeaw), IV.8a, V.1a, VI.1a etc. (gauaf)

geilwad n.m. *ploughboy* XII.5a

gein see genni

geir (1) n.m. *word, promise* VIII.17b; (2) prep. *by, beside* VIII.15a

geluir, gelwir see galw

gelyn n.m. *enemy* XII.1f

gen|i v.tr. *bear* XII[B].12f; pres. ind. impers. -ir IX.88; pret. impers. ganed XII[B].9e

genn|i v.intr. *be contained, be accepted*; pres. ind. 3 sg. gein IX.17

geu adj. *false* IX.35; as n. VI.6c (gau)

geublant n.coll. *false (unacknowledged) children* IV.9c

geufel n. *an unidentified plant, perhaps ragwort* VIII.22b

glan(n) n.f. *bank* I.16b, VIII.18b

glas adj.*green* I.15b etc., II.3b etc.

glaw n.m. *rain* I.16c (glau),VII.8a etc.

glew adj. *brave*; as n. I.7c, 20c (glev), II.25c, III.4a?, IX.98, X.12? etc.

glwth adj. *greedy* III.18c

glynn n.m. *valley* II.25a

gnawt adj. *usual, common, natural, characteristic* II.4a, 8b etc., III.2c, IV.1a etc.; XII.2a, 4c etc (knawd); superl. gnotaf VI.13c*

gnif n.m. *tribulation* IX.45

gnotaf see gnawt

go adv. *somewhat, rather* IV.1b

**goaflwm** adj. *rich, fertile* IX.105

**gobeith** n.m. *hope* IX.47

**gobennyd** n. *pillow* VIII.27b

**gobwyll|aw** v.intr. *take thought*; pres. ind. 3 sg. IX.29

**gochel** v.tr. *avoid* XII[A].10f

**gochlyw|et** v.tr. *hear*; pres. ind. impers. -ir IX.117

**gochwiban** adj. *whistling* II.10b etc., VII.3b etc.

**gocled** n.m. *north* IV.3a (ModW gogledd)

**goddaith** see **godeith**

**godeith** n. *(mountain) fire* IX.90; ? *ground for burning* V.9a, VI.4a (goddaith)

**godo** n.m. *cover* I.13a

**godoli** see **gwaddoli**

**gofag** see **yngofag**

**gofwy** v.tr. *visit, frequent*; pres. ind. 3 sg. VI.10b

**gofyn** v.tr. *ask (request)* IV.1c, XII.1e

**goffryn|u** v.tr. *achieve*; impv. I pl. **gofrynwn** IX.31

**gofrynu** see **goffrynu**

**gogaur** n. *shelter, winter quarters* I.12a

**gogelawc** adj. *furtive, surreptitious* III.6a

**gogo** n.f. *cave, recess* (ModW ogof) II.7b

**gogyhyt** adj. *of equal height* VIII.23a

**goleith** n.m. (1) *evasion* I.13c, IX.42; (2) *death* IX.96

**goleu** adj. *bright; conspicuous* VIII.31b

**golut** n. *wealth* IX.1

**goludawc** adj. *rich* ; as n. III.6b

**golwc** n.f. *look, sight, demeanour* IV.7c, XII[A].9d

**gorawenus** adj. *boisterous* III.19a*

**gordin** n.m. *violence, oppression* IX.50

**gordiwes** v.tr. *overtake* II.5c

**gordugor** n.m. ? *dress* I.22a

**gordyfn|u** v.intr. *become accustomed, reconciled*; pres. ind. 3 sg. **gordyfyn** IX.66

**gordyar** adj. *loud, resounding* VII.2a etc.

**goreilyd|iaw** v.tr. & intr. *pester, cause trouble*; pres. subj. 3 sg. **goreilytto** II. 7c (ModW goreilidio).

**goreu** see **da**

goreuynawc adj. *topped with foam* I.22b (≡ gorewynawg)

gorffwys v.intr. *(be at) rest*; pres. ind. 3 sing. gorffowys XI.11d

goror n. *edge, fringe* I.10, VII.8b

Gorphennaf n.m. *July* VI.15a, XII.7a (Gorffennaf)

gorthir n.m. *uplands* XII.4a

goruchel adj. *very loud* I.2b

goruelyn adj. *very yellow* VIII.12b

goruit see gorwyd [ŵ]

gorun adj. *noisy* III.18a*

gorwyd [ŵ] n.m. *horse, steed* I.9b, 23a (goruit), III. 7a, 9b, VI.9a, 13b etc. (gorwydd)

gorwyd [ŷ] n.m. *edge of forest* IV.10b

gorwyddfeith adj. *swift with staying-power* VI.22a

gorwyn adj. *bright; delightful* VIII.1a etc.; ? *very white* VIII.7a, 8a

gorwyr n.m. *great-grandson* IV.6c

gorymdeith v.intr. *wander*; pres. ind. 3 sg. gworymdaa IX.81

gosgub|aw v.tr. *sweep (bare)*; pres. ind. 3 sg. gosgupid I.7b

gosgymon n. *fuel*; (fig.) IX.50

goual n.m. *care, anxiety* III.5b, VIII.21a; pl. goualon VIII.5c

govit n.m. *trouble, grief* IX.42

govrys n.m. *haste; instability* IX.82

gowlych|u v.tr. *wet*; pres. ind. 3 sg. -yt II.24b

goyewin adj. *brave?*; as n. IX.51

graen(n)wyn(n) adj.*wondrously white? white-capped?* II.7a, VII.1b

*grandinis* (Lat.) n., gen. sg. of grando *hail* XI.1c*

grawn n.coll. *grain, seed* III.8c, 9c, V.1a, XI.6d*

grid n.m. *tumult, uproar, conflict* I.35a (≡ gryd)

gro n.m. *gravel, shingle* II.7a, IX.13, 63

gruc n.coll. *heather* I.22a etc. (≡ grug)

grud n. *cheek* VIII.10c

guaet, gwaeteu see gwaed

guan see gwan(n)

gueilgi see gweilgi

gueled see gwelet

guely see gwely

guenin see gwenyn

guilan see gwylan

guir see gwir, gŵr

guit see gwyd

gulichid see gwlychu

gulip see gwlyb

gulybur n.m. *wet, damp* I.15a (≡ gwlybwr)

guna, gunaei see gwneuthur

gur see gŵr

gureic see gwreic

gurim adj. *brown* I.22a (≡ gwrm)

gvenin see gwenyn

gvit see gwyd

gvir adj. *bent* I.11c (≡ gwyr)

gvyrhaud adj. *bent* I.4c (≡ gwyrawd)

gwac adj. *empty* IX.26 (fig.), XII.1d

gwaddol|i v.tr. *endow, provide for*; *reward* pres. ind. impers. -ir VI.7c, IX.118 (godolir)

gwae n. *misery*; as interj.+ soft mut. *woe betide* II.16c, V.1d etc.

gwaeannwyn n.m. *spring* IX.105, XII.2f (gwanwyn)

gwaed n.f. *roar* I.21d (guaet), IX. 13, pl. guaetev I.2b (ModW gwaedd)

gwaeddgreg fem.adj. *harsh-voiced* VI.20a, 21a

gwaedlyd adj. *bloody* XII[B].11c

gwael adj. *wretched, mean* XII.1e, 4c

gwaet, gwaeteu see gwaed

gwaetha, gwaethwaeth see drwg

gwaetlin n.m. *(stream of) blood* IX.57

gwaetvann adj. *loud-roaring* I.21d (≡ gwaedd-)

gwaew n. *spear* IX.57; pl. gwaewawr III.11a

gwag see gwac

gwahodd v.tr. *invite*; pres. ind. impers. -ir XII.4d

gwair n.m. *hay* XII.7a

gwaith see gweith

gwall n.m. *fault* VIII.8c; as adj. *faulty* IX.108

gwallt n.coll. *hair* VII.10a

gwanas n. *peg, fixture for chain* VII.4b

**gwanec, -eg** n.f. *wave* VI.20a, IX.13 etc

**gwan(n)** adj. *weak* I.12a (guan), IV.1b, XII.6h (gwan); as n. V.8b, VII.10b

**gwanwyn** see **gwaeannwyn**

**gwarandaw** v.intr. *listen* II.31c

**gwarchan** n.f. ? *song* X title, 15

**gwaret** v.tr. & intr. *help, avail*; pres. ind. 3 sg. **gweryt** II.28c, VI.2c (-d), IX.72; as n. *deliverance* VIII.25d, XII[B].9h

**gwareus** see **chwareus**

**gwarth** n. *shame, reproach* III.16c, XII.2c

**gwarthaw** n.m. *top* I.7a (≡ gwarthaf)

**gwarthrudd** n. *shame* XII[A].9e

**gwas** n.m. *young man* V.7c, VI.3e, VII.4c

**gwasgarawg** adj. ? *far-spreading* VI.20b

**gwasgar|u** v. tr.& intr. *scatter*; pres. ind. 3 sg. **gwesgerit** VIII.9b

**gwasgawt** n.m. *shelter* V.7b

**gwasg|u** v.tr. *press*; pres. ind. 3 sg. **gwesgyt** III.9c

**gwastat** adj. *level; settled* II.25b; *stable, sober* IX.111

**gwastra** adj. ? *useless,* ? *fierce* IX.36

**gwaur** see **gwawr**

**gwawn** n.m. *gossamer* III.8c, 9c

**gwawr** n.f. *dawn* I.12c (gwaur), VIII.14c

**gweddi** n.f. *prayer* XII[B].10h

**gweddï|o** v.intr. *pray*; pres. ind. 3 sing. -a XII.8e

**gweddawt** n.m. *widowhood* IX.112 (≡ gwedd-dawd, ModW gweddwdod)

**gwedawc** adj. *subjected*; as n. *subject, bondman* II.19*.

**gwedw** adj. *widowed,* (fig.) *deserted* V.3b, XII[B].10b, *useless* VII.11c (ModW gweddw)

**gwedy** prep. *after* I.30c (gwydi), IV.3d etc.; as conj. IX.38

**gweilgi** n.f. *sea* I.18c (gueilgi), III.19a, VII.10c etc.

**gweilid** adj. ? *reckless, without anxiety*; as n. IX.36

**gweinydd|u** v.tr. *serve*; pres. ind. 3 sg. XI.6e

**gweith** n.m. *work* V.2c, 9b, IX.102 etc.

**gweithret** n.f. *act* VIII.6c, 15c

**gwel|et** v.tr. *see*; pres. ind. 3 sg. **gwyl** III.10c, impers. -ir IX.108 etc; ? as n. *appearance* I.18c (gueled)

gwell see **da**

gwelwgan adj. *pale* VII.10c

gwely n.m. *bed* I.3a\*, 4a (guely), III.1b

gwên n.f. *smile* V.7c , VI.3c

gwenbleit n.f. *white fence* II.11b

gwen(n) see **gwyn(n)**

gwenwyn n.m. *poison*; as n. *poisonous* III.20a, *peevish* III.13c

gwenyn n.coll. *bees* I.12a (gvenin), 13a etc. (guenin), II.18b etc.

gwerin n.f. *company, troop* IX.60

gwerthevin adj. *supreme* IX.62

gweryd, -t see **gwaret**

gwesgerit see **gwasgaru**

gwesgyt see **gwasgu**

gweun n.f. *marsh*; pl. **gweunyd** IV.5b (ModW gwaun)

gwialen n.f. *rod, sapling*; pl. **gwyeil** IV.5d

gwic n.f. *wood* IV.2d

gwilliad n.m. *brigand* XII.7c (ModW gwylliad)

gwir adj. *true* V.8c, XII.1g; *just*, as n. *justice, just amends* VI.6c, IX.17; as adv. *very*
? I.21e (guir)

gwirion adj. *innocent* XII[A].9g

gwirtliv adj. *green* I.14a (≡ gwyrddliw)

gwisg|aw v.tr. *put on*; pres. ind. 3 sg. (future) -awt IX.70

gwlatlwyd adj. *bringing prosperity to the land* IX.62

gwled n.f. *feast* IV.3c

gwlyb adj. *wet* I.17a (gulip), III.13a, VI.6a

gwlych|u v.tr. *wet, flood*; pres. ind. 3 sg.-yd I.18b (gulichid), VII.8a etc.

gwneuthur v.tr. *do, make*; pres. ind. 2 sg. **gwnehyd** IX.27; 3 sg. **gwna** I.27a (guna),
IX.76 **gwnelit** VIII.24c, 28c, 30c (gwnelyt), rel. **gwneyd** IX.17; subj. 3 sg.
**gwnel** VI.5c, XII.2d, [A].10e; impf. ind. 3 sg. **gunaei** I.25b

gwnn see **gwybot**, and under **os**.

gworymdaa see **gorymdeith**

gŵr n.m. *man* I.1c (gur), IV.1b etc.; pl. **gwŷr** I.23b (guir), 35a (gwir), IV.7b etc.

gwrach n.f. *old woman* III.13c

gwreic n.f. *woman* I.19c (gureic), III.16c etc., XII.2f (gwraic); pl. **gwraged** IV.6b, XII.
6c (gwragedd) (ModW gwraig)

gwreid n.m. *root* III.8c (ModW gwraidd)

**gwrda** n.m. *noble lord* IX.84

**gwrysc** n.coll. *herbage* II.27b, V.4a, VI. 5b (gwrysg) etc.

**gwst** n. *sickness* IX.64

**gwyar** n.m. *blood* III.15b

**gwybot** v.tr. *know*; pres. ind. 1 sg. **gwnn** II.9b (see also **os**), 3 sg **gŵyr** XI.6f, impers. **gwŷs** IX.82; impf. subj. 3 sg. **gwypei** II.35b

**gwychyr** adj. *violent; blustery* VIII.32b

**gwyd** (ŵy) (1) n.f. *goose; gander* III.3a (2) see **cwydo**.

**gwyd** (wŷ) n.coll. *trees* I.4c, 7b (guit), 11c (gvit), II.26a, VII.3b, VIII.23a; *masts* I.10b (guit)

**gwyeil** see **gwialen**

**gwyl** see **gwelet**

**gwylan** n.f. *seagull* I.16b (guilan), III.15a, VI.21a

**gwyled** n.m. *modesty, courtesy* VIII.7c

**gwyluein** adj. ? *quiet and gentle* IX.51

**gwyn(n)** adj. *white* I.5a,6a (guin), II.1a etc., fem. **gwenn** III.15a; **gwynn y uyt** adj. phr. *blessed* VIII.23c, IX.119, XII.4f

**Gwyned** place name *Gwynedd* IV.3b

**gwynnawn** n.coll. *dry grass* IX.90

**gwynt** n.m. *wind* I. 7b, 24a (guint), II.2b etc.

**gwynwyl** n.f. *rut* (of animals) VI.18b

**gwypei** see **gwybot**

**gwyr** (ŵy) see **gwybot**

**gwyr** (wŷ) see **gŵr**

**gwyry|aw** v. tr. & intr. *bend*; pres. ind. 3 pl. -**ant** II.2b (cf ModW gwyro)

**gwyrdd** adj. *green* III.19a, VI.21a

**gwyrddlas** adj. *greenish blue* XI.1b

**gwys** see **gwybot**

**gwyth** n.m. *strife* IX.50

**gwythlawn** adj. *angry, fierce* VIII.6a

**gyt a** prep. *(together) with* II.34c, VIII.30b (ModW gyda)

**gynn no** prep. *before* V.1c

**gynnin** n.coll. *Norsemen?* IX.55

# H

haed|u v.tr. *deserve, earn*; pres. ind. 3 sg. V.3c, XII[B].10e, subj. 3 sg. **haeddwy** XI.6g*

hael adj. *generous*; as n. XII[A].11f

haf n.m. *summer* II.25b

hafdyd n.m. *summer's day* I.9c (hawdit), II.9c (≡ hafddydd)

haha adj. ? *given to saying 'Eh? Eh?'* III.10a

haint see **heint**

hallt adj. *salt* VII.10c

hanes n. ? *speech* IX.51

hard adj. *beautiful* XII.6a (hardd) , *excellent* III.3c

haul n. *sun* VI.17b

hauot n.f. *summer farmstead, shieling* V.3b, XII[B].10b (havod) (ModW hafod)

hawd adj. *easy* II.5c, XII.5e etc. (ModW hawdd)

hawdweith n.m. *easy matter* IX.101

hawdit see **hafdyd**

heb prep. *without* I.5c, VII.11c, IX.40 etc.

hebawc n. *hawk* II.20b (ModW hebog)

hediw adv. *today* I.9c, 14c, 16c (hetiv) etc, VIII.19b etc.

hegarwch n.m. *graciousness* V.7c (≡ hygarwch)

heibyaw adv. *past* IX.8

heid n.coll. *barley* III.8b (ModW haidd)

heiniar n. *crop* XII.3c

heinif adj. *lively* XII.6c

heint n. *sickness* VI.8c (haint), VIII.2c etc.

heintus adj. *sickly* III.19c

heinvs adj. *sickly, languishing* XII[B].11e (≡ -us)

heli n.m. *salt water, sea* VII.10c

helic n.coll. *willows* VIII.3a, 26a (ModW helyg)

hellawt adj. *hunted* II.10a (≡ hel-lawd)

hely v.tr. & intr. *hunt* ; as vn. XI.11c

hen adj. *old*; as n. *old man* I. 6b, II.5c, 13b etc.

heneint n.m. *old age* III.21c, VIII.1c

heno adv. *tonight* I.27a

henoeth adv. *tonight* VI.1a

hetiv see **heddiw**

hid see **hyd**

**hil** n. *seed, offspring* XII.7d

**hin** n.f. *weather* V.5a

**hindda** n.f. *fair weather* XII.3c

**hinon** n.f. *fair weather* I.17c, IX.4

hint see **hynt**

**hir** adj. *long* I.16a, II.18c etc.; comp. **hwy** XII.3c,d.

**hiraeth** n.m *regret* II.21c, 28c, VII.1c etc.

**hirbla** n. *long affliction* IV.11c

**hirbwyll** n. *long thought (consideration, prudence)* IV.11c

**hirdyd** n.m. *long (summer) day* VIII.26b

**hirgain** adj. *long and fair* XII.6c

**hiroes** n.f. *long life* XI.11h

**hirnos** adj. *with long nights* XII[A].12a

**hirwynn** adj. *tall and bright*; pl. -yon VIII.1a

hit see **hyd** (3)

**hoed(y)l** n.f. *life-span* VI.21c (hoedl), IX.120, XII[A].12g (hoydl)

**hoffder** n.m. *favourite thing* III.18b

**hoian** v.intr. *call* XII[B].12e

*homo* (Lat.) *man, mankind* XI.1e

**hôr** n.coll. *lice* IV.4b

hoydl see **hoedl**

**huan** n. *sun* XII[B].12b

**hun** (1) n.f. *sleep* VI.8c, VIII.2c (2) see **hwn**

**hunawc** adj. *sleepy (able to sleep well)* VIII.12c

**hwn** demonstrative pron. *this* I.24c (hun), II.9c

hwy see **hir**

**hwyat** n.f. *duck*; pl. **hwyeit** II.5b, VIII.9b

**hwylyat** n.m. *course* VIII.28a

**hwyr** adj. *slow* II.5c,19b* 23a; comp. -ach XII.5g

**hyd** (1) n. *length* XI.11g, XII[A].12g; see also **pa** (1) (ModW hyd) (2) see **hyt** (3) n.m. *stag* I.17b (hit), II.4a, VI.XIc (hydd) etc. (ModW hydd).; pl. **hydot** V.3a, XII[B].10a (hyddod)

**hydraidd** adj. *aggressive (in rutting)* XII[B].10a

hydravl adj. *worn* XII[A].10a (≡ hydraul)

Hydref n.m. *October* VI.18a (Hyfref), XII[AB].10a

hyddail adj. *leafy* XII.5d

hyddgant n. *herd of deer* VI.18b, 22a

hydyr adj. *strong* VIII.8a, 18b, ? *great* VIII.33a (≡ hydr)

hyffordd adj. *passable* XII.6d

Hyfref see Hydref

hyfryt adj. *pleasant, agreeable*; as n. VIII.12c; *merry* XII.5d

hyglvd adj. *ready to be brought in* XII.7a (≡ hyglud)

hylawn adj. *abundant, prolific* XII.6d

hynt n. *path* I.17a (hint*), course, flight* VI.12b

hyt prep. *up to, as far as, until* I.25a (hid), IX.32, XI.6f (hyd) (Mod W hyd)

hyuagyl adj. *staining, blotchy* III.15b (≡ hyfagl)

hyvysgwr adj. *resolute, strong* IX.93

hywerth adj. *readily sold,* VIII.30a


# I (J)

i (1) pers. pron 1 sg. (?)X.5 (y); (2) poss. pron. 3 sg. masc. I.5a (y), II.30c (y), IX.60 (y), XII.1e.f etc. (3) infixed pers. pron. 3 sg. m., see e (4); (4) prep. *to, for* I.23c, II.9c, 30c, III.1c; inflected 2 sg. it IX.45, 3 sg. masc. iddo XII.8f, 1 pl. yn IX.47; with infixed poss.pron. 3 pl. o'e I.5b; (5) prep. with infixed poss. pron. *in*; 1 sg. y'm VIII.9c, 3 sg. y'w IX.36; (6) in compound prepositions i ar *upon* I.27c, y ar *from on, away from, off* VII.7b*, y gan prep. *out of* VII.9a; (7) see yn (2)

'i see e, 'e (1, 2, 4)

iâ n.m. *ice* I. 20b, IV.11a

iach adj. *healthy* III.13b, (fig.) II.14c

iäen n.f. *sheet of ice* I.4a

iäenuawr adj. *icy* XI.1a

iâr n.f. *hen* III.17a; pl. ieir II.32a

iawn n.m. *right, justice* VI.5c, XI.6e, *recompense* XI.6g; as adj. *right, proper* VIII.6c

iddo see i (4)

ieir see iâr

ieuanc adj. *young* VIII.16b; pl. ieueinc IX.23

ig see yn (2)

igkeithiv verbal adj. *captive* I.14a (≡ yngheithiw)

igniw verbal adj. *contending, turbulent* I.18a (≡ yngnif)

igodo, igogaur, igrid see yn (2), godo, gogaur, grid.

*imber* (Lat.) n. *shower* XI.1c (ymber)

imbluch verbal adj. *stripped bare?* I.3c* (≡ ymlwch)

imtuin v.tr. *bear* I.28a (≡ ymddwyn)

in see yn (1)

*inter* (Lat.) prep. *between, amid* XI.1d

Ionawr n.m. *January* VI.9a, XI.1a, XII.1a (Jonor)

ir see er

irgig n.m. *fresh meat* VI.16a*

iscolheic n.m. *cleric* I.19a (ModW ysgolhaig)

iscuit see ysgwyd

iscun see ysgwn

istrad n.f. *level valley* I.8a (≡ ystrad)

it see i (4)

Iwerit pers. name *Iwerydd* I.30a

jyrchwyn n.m. *roebuck* II.14b


K see C


L

led see lled
lew see glew or llew


Ll

lladd v.tr. *kill*; pret. 3 sg. -odd XII.2h

llaeth n.m. *milk* IV.5c, XII[B].10d

llafn n. *blade* XII[B].11c

llafur|o v.intr. *labour* ; pres. ind. 3 sg. XII.8e

llafurus adj. *hard-working* VI.17a, XII.2b

llai see bychan

llais n. *voice* XII.1c

llam|u v.intr. *leap*; pres. ind. impers. llemittor IX.7*

llann n.f. *churchyard* IV.1a, *church* IX.33

llanw n.m. *(rising) tide* IV.4a

llauar adj. *loud, vociferous, garrulous* IV.7b, XII.5f; as n. *chatterbox* VII.6c

llauer see llawer

llaur see llawr

llaw n.f. *hand* VIII.33c (?), IX.20

llawen adj. *happy, joyful* III.2a, XII.5c etc.

llawenydd n.m. *happiness, joy* III.1c (llewenyd), XII[A].11c

llawer pron. *much* II.9b; adj. *many* I.10c, 20c (llauer), II.2c

llawn adj. *full* V.1b, XI.6c etc.

llawr (1) n.m. *ground* I.18b (llaur); (2) adj. *solitary*; as n. VIII.29b

lle n.m. *place* I.3a(?), II.12c; as conj. *where* II.6d, 27c, V.4c, XII.4e

lled n. *wound, scar* (?)X.11

llednoeth see lletnoeth

lledrad n.m. *theft* XII[A].10d

lledwag adj. *half-empty* XII.7f

llef n. *call* III.1a, VI.11b*

llefar|u v.intr. *speak*; pres. ind. 3 sg. lleueir II.32b (fig.), XII.7h (llefair)

lleidyr n.m. *thief* II.18c, III.6a etc.

lleilai adj. *less and less* XII[B].10d

llein n.m. *sword* IX.20*

lleith n. *death* I.13c, IX.97

llemittor see llamu

llên n.f. *learning* III.7b; see also mab llên

lles n.m. *benefit* XI.6b

llesc adj. *feeble* IX.54

lletnoeth adj. *half-naked* XII[A]11b (-d-) ; as n. II.36b

lleturyt n.m. *faint-heartedness* II.23c (≡ lledfryd)

lleturyded n.m. *low spirits* IV.3d

lleueir see llefaru

llew n.m. *lion* III.4b?, X.12

llewenyd see llawenydd

lliaws n. *abundance* XI.6d

llicrid see llygru

llid n.m. *anger, resentment* XII.3d

llidiawc adj. *fierce* II.21b (ModW -og)

llif n.m. *flood* I.17c (llyw), 18b (lliw), IV.9

llin, llinneu see llynn

lliw see llif

lliuvawr adj. *colourful* XI.1b? (ModW lliwfawr)

lloergan n.m. *moonlight* II.3b

llon(n) adj. *lively* XII.8b, [B].12d; *rough (of sea)* XII[B].11d

llong n.f. *ship* I.10b (llog), IX.89

llonydd adj. *calm, sluggish* XII[B].12c

llownfras adj. *well-fed* XII[B].10c (≡ llawnfras)

llu n.m. *host* I.25c (llv), IX.52

lluarth n.m. *vegetable garden* III.16a

lluch n.m. *lake* I.3a (≡ llwch)

lluchedic adj. *full of lightning* I.11b

lludded adj. *weary* XII[B].9c

lludedic adj. *weary* VIII.5b, XII.4b (lluddedig)

lluid see llwyd

llum see llwm(m)

lluossawc adj. *numerous* II.21b

llv see llu

llvwyr see llwuyr

llwdn n.m. *young beast*; pl. **llydnod** XII[A].11b

llwfyr see llwuyr

llwm(m) adj. *bare* I.1a, 10b (llum) II.27a, XII.4b

llwrw n.m. *path*; pl. **llyri** I.11b

llwuyr adj. *cowardly*; as n. I.10c (llvwyr), II.29c, VII.9c (llyvwr), VIII.5a (llyfwr) etc.

llwydd|o v.intr. *succeed*; pres. ind. 3 sg. XII.7d

llwyn n.m. *wood, bushes* II.14a, VII.5a etc.

llwyr adj. *complete* II.23c; as adv. XII.7e

llwyt adj. *grey* I.16a (lluid), III.8a etc.; *old*; as n. IX.28

llydan adj. *broad; extensive* II.3b

llydnod see llwdn

llyfeithin n.m. *coward* IX.59

llyfn adj. *smooth, calm* XII.6b

**llyfyrder** n.m. *cowardice* IX.97

**llyfwr** see **llwuyr**

**llygr|u** v.tr. and intr. *foul, become foul* ; pres. ind. 3 sg. **llicrid** I.1b

**llynges** n.f. *fleet* XI.11d

**llym** adj. *sharp* I.1a, III.11a etc.

**llynn** (1) n.m. *lake* I.1b (llin), 24b\*, II.5b, 25b (llynn) etc., VII.1b etc.; pl. **llinneu** I.5c, **llynniav** XI.1b; (2) n.m. *drink* IV.3d

**llynnwynn** n.m. *pond* V.1b

**llyri** see **llwrw**

**llyu** n.m. *colour* I.5c (ModW lliw)

**llyvrder** see **llyfyrder**

**llyvwr** see **llwuyr**

**llyw** see **llif**

**llywaethan** n.m. *snake* (?), *eel* (?), *pet dog* (?) XII[B].12c

## M

**'m**, infixed pron. 1 sg. II.26b, 33b.

**mab** n.m. *son, boy* IX.46, XII.7g; pl. **meibon** VIII.20c; **mab darogan** *prophesied deliverer* XII[B]. 9e; **mab llên** *clerical student* III.7b

**mach** n.m. *surety* III.13a

**mabolaeth** n. *youth* II.13b

**mäes** n.m. *field* XI.6c

**maeth** (1) n.m. *fosterage* IV.1d, *sustenance* IV.5c; (2) adj. *reared,* ? *born* XII.7g; (3) see **magu**

**mag|u** v.tr. *breed* IV.4b; pres. ind. 3 sg. **mac** XII.2e, **meccid** I.10c (fig.), **megyt** II.23c **meckyt** 29c; pret. ind. 3 sg. **ryvaeth** I.29c , impers. **-uid** I.28c

**Mai** n.m. *May* VI.13a, XII.5a

**Mair** see **Meir**

**mall** adj. *wicked, depraved* VIII.14b; *dishonest, false* IX.55

**mam** n.f. *mother* IV.9c, VI.18c

**man** n.f. *place*; as conj. *where* XI.1f

**mân** adj. *small* VIII.3b

**manawc** adj. *freckled* VIII.20c (≡ mannog)

**maneg** see **mynegi**

**man|u** v.intr. *prosper, succeed*; pres. ind. 3 sg. (future) **menhit** IX.46

maon n.m.pl. *heroes* IX.65

marannedd n. *?porpoises, dolphins* XII.6b

march n.m. *stallion; horse;* pl. meirch XII.B9c

marchawc n.m. *rider, horseman* III.6a (ModW -og)

marchnad n.f. *market* XII.5g

marchogaeth n.f. *riding, horsemanship* IX.86

marchwieil n.coll. *stout saplings* VII.4a etc.

marw adj. *dead* IX.54, 115, X.6; as n. II.28c, XII.3h

mawl see moli

mawr adj. *great* VI.10c, IX.84

mawreir n.m. *boast* II.32c, IX.80, XII.7f (mowrair)

Mawrth n.m. *March* VI.11a, XII.3a

meccid, meckyt see magu

med (1) n.m. *mead* I.30c (met), II.15b etc. (2) see medu

medel n.m. *reaper* X.15

Medi n.m. *September* XII[A].1a; VI.17a, XI[B].1a, XII[B].1a (Menni)

medlyn n.m. *mead* IX.65

medr|u v. tr. *find, hit on;* pres. ind. 2 sg. -it I.26a

med|u v.tr. *possess, control;* pres. ind. 3 sg. IX.87, XII[B].11f (medd), subj. 3 sg. -o VI.16c (- dd-)

meduaeth adj. *nourished on mead* IV.6b (≡ meddfaeth)

medw adj. *drunken* IX.99

medwl n.m. *mind* VIII.27c

mefl see meuyl

megyt see magu

Mehefin n.m. *June* VI.14a, XI.6a, XII.6a

mehinvawr adj. *lardy, fat* XII[B].11a

meibon see mab

meichyat n.m. *swineherd;* pl. meichyeit III.2a

meillyon n.coll. *clover* VIII.5a

mein adj. *slim* X.14

Meir pers. n. *(Virgin) Mary* IX.46, XII.7g (Mair)

meirch see march

melyn adj. *yellow* I.25a ('bay') (melin), V.3a, XII[B].10b

menechtit n.f. *monastic life, monastery* IX.44

**menestyr** n.m. *butler* (fig.) VIII.17a

**menhit** see **manu**

**Menni** see **Medi**

**merllyd** adj. *greasy* XII[B].11d

**meryd** adj. *sluggish*; as n. *sluggard* II.19c, VIII.14b, XII[A].11a

**met** see **med**

**methl|u** v.intr. *fail*; pres. ind. 3 sg. -a IX.80

**meuil** see **meuyl**

**meuyl** n.m. *shame, reproach, fault* I.30c (meuil), II.6d, V.3d, IX.112, XII.7e etc. (mefl)

**mi** pers. pron. 1 sg.; followed by a (5) II.6d; emphatic *I myself* I.8c.

**mign** n.f. *marsh, bog* ; pl. -ed II.15b, -edd XII.6d

**mir** see **môr**

**mis** n.m. *month* XII.1a etc.

**mit** n. *battle* X.12

**moch** (1) n.coll. *pigs* IV.4c, XII[B].11a (2) adv. *soon, quickly* II.19c, IX.62, 115

**mochddwyreawg** adj. *early rising* VI.14a

**modryda(f)** n. *colony of bees, hive* XII.8b

**moes** n. *(good) manners* VIII.11a

**moeth** n.m. *luxury, pampering*; pl. moetheu IV.1d

**mol|i** v.tr. *praise*; pres. ind. 3 sg. **mawl** III.1c, impers. -ir IX.102

**molwynoc** adj. ? *rich, fertile* XII.8a

**mor** eq. particle *as*; with adj. I.26a, with n. XI.1h; exclamatory particle with v. *how!* VIII.20b, IX.69, 84

**môr** n.m. *sea* I.10b, 14a etc., VII.8b, XII[B].9b etc.; pl. **mir** I.16c (≡ mŷr)

*mors* (Lat.) n. *death* XI.1h

**morua** n.m. *salt-marsh, land by sea* VII.2a, IX.77, XII.8a (morva)

**morwyn** n.f. *girl, maidservant* VII.5c, XII.2h

**mowrair** see **mawreir**

**mvrn** n. *deceit* XII.2f (≡ murn)

**mut** adj. *dumb, speechless* IX.99; as n. X.7

**mwyalch** n.f. *blackbird* IV.2b, VII.7b

**mwyar** n.coll. *blackberries* VII.7a

**mwyn** (1) n.m. *benefit, enjoyment* ? XII.2i (2) adj. *pleasant, gentle, gracious* ? XII.2i. (see note).

mwynieithus adj. *with gentle voice* XII[B].9b

mydr n.m. *verse* XII[A].9a

mygedus adj. *misty? smoky?* VI.11a

myglyd adj. *smoky* XII.1a

myn conj. *where* II.32b

mynaig see mynegi

mynawc adj. *excellent* IX.92; *noble*; as n. IX.86

mynd, mynet v.intr. *go* V.1c, XII.5g (mynd); pres. ind. 1 sg. aw I.8c (≡ af), 3 sg. â I.5b, IX.82 eyt IX.1, 11, 21, impv. 3 sg. aed XII[B].11b; perf. 3 sg. ethiw I.30a

myneg|i v.tr. *show*; pres. ind. 3 sg. maneg XII[B].9a

mynit see mynyd

mynn|u v.tr. *demand*; pres. ind. 3 sg. II.20c; with neg. *will not* II.31c; impv. 2 pl. mynuch I.30c (≡ mynnwch)

mynuch see mynnu

mynut adj. *courteous* IV.7c

mynych adj. *frequent* II.34c, III.13a, XII.2c etc.; as adv. IX.108

mynyd n.m. *mountain* I.10a, 18a (mynit), II.1a etc.; pl. -ed VIII.7a etc.

mywn prep. *in* II.15a, 25a, VII.5a (ModW mewn)


# N

'n infixed pers. pron. 1 pl. IX.32

na neg. preverbal particle, cf. Lat. *ne* (1) introducing subordinate clause IX.94 (nat); (2) in subordinate clause after conj., with infixed pron. 3 sg. nas XII.4d; (3) introducing wish or command I.19c, VII.4c (nac)

nac (1) preverbal particle = na (2) before vowel; (2) as n. *refusal* IX.35

namwyn prep. *except* V.5c, VIII.4c (namyn), IX.61

namyn see namwyn

nant n. *stream, dingle* IV.9a; pl. neint VI.6b, VIII.1b

nas see na (2)

nat preverbal particle = na (1) before vowel

naw n.m. *swimming*; ar naw adj. phr. *swimming* II.31a

nawd see noddi

nawn n.m. *mid-afternoon* VI.5a, XI.6f

naws n. *temper* XI.6d

nawt see gnawt

**neb** indef. pron. *anyone* II.35c; (*'everyone'*) IX.87; as adj. *any* I.13c (nep)

**nebawt** indef. pron. *anyone* IX.69

**nef** n. *heaven* IX.68

**nefol** adj. *heavenly* XII[A].11h

**neges** n. *task, business* I.5b, VI.12c

**neidr** n.f. *adder* III.20a

**neint** see **nant**

**neit** n. *leap*: **ar neit** adj. phr. *leaping* II.11a (ModW naid)

**nep** see **neb**

**nerth** n. *strength,* ? *fortitude* VIII.30b

**neut, neud** (1) preverbal particle XI.1a, 1b, 1d, 11b, 11d; (2) affirmative copula, see **bot**

**newyn** n.m. *hunger, starvation* VIII.7c

**ni** (1) neg. preverbal particle + spirant or soft mut., cf. Lat. *non*: in main clause, II.1c, III.4c etc.; in subordinate clause V.4c; with infixed pron. 1 sg ni'm I. 8c, 25b, 2 sg. ny'th I.19b, IV.11b, 3 sg. nis XI.6h; (2) neg. copula, see **bot**; (3) neg. rel. particle + soft mut. IX.74, 83, 113; with infixed pron. 3 sg. nis VI.20c, XI.6h, nwy IX.73, 75

**nid** (1) see **nyt** (2) neg. copula, see **bot**

**nim, nis** see **ni** (1,3)

**no** conj. *than* III.20c, V.1c etc. (cf ModW na)

**noc** = **no** before vowel

**nodd|i** v.tr. *protect*; pres. ind. 3 sg. **nawd** III.11c

**no'e** see **no**.

**noeth** adj. *naked*; as n. X.3; (fig.) *destitute* IX.93, as n. VI.1c

**nof|iaw** v.tr. & intr.. *swim; wade* III.20b

**nos** n.f. *night* I.16a, 23c, II.18c etc.

**nug|yaw** v.intr. *tremble:* ? pres.ind 3 pl. **nugyein** VIII.32b

**nwy** see **ni**

**nyt** neg. preverbal particle = **ni** before vowel I.5b, 8c etc. (nid), II.20c

**nyth** n. *nest* IV.7a, VII.7c

**ny'th** see **ni**

# O

**o** (1) prep.+ soft mut. *from, of, as result of* I.20c, II.1c; (with e (1)) o'e IX.6, 43, 87; 3 sg. masc. **ohonaw** IX.2; with subj. of preceding vn. IV.2d; **o du** *on the side of* I.9a (o dv), II.8c; separating adjectival phrase from n. I.29b, from pron. III.10c (o'r a) (2) prep. *to* (only with infixed poss. pronoun 'e) I.5b; see **e**, **'e** (3); (3) conj. *if*; (combined with **ry**) or I.2c, 21e; see also **ry**

**och** interj.+ soft mut. *alas!* I.19c, II.21c

**od|i** v.intr. *fall* (usually of snow) pres. ind. 3 sg. **ottid** I.5a etc., pl. **otynt** IX.106; impf. (conditional) ind. 3 sg. **ottei** I.25a

**odidawc** adj. *unusual* II.34b (ModW godidog)

**odit** n.m. *rare thing* II.3b, 33b, V.9c, IX.37

**odwr** n.m. *receiver of stolen goods* II.20c

**odyn** n.f. *kiln* XII.1d

**o'e** (1) see **i** (1); (2) see **o** (1).

**oed** (1) (≡ oed) n. *time, season* XII[A].9b; (2) (≡ oedd) see **bod**

**oen** n.m. *lamb* XII.5h

**oer** adj. *cold* I.3a etc., II.15b etc.

**oes** (1) n.f. *age, life* XI.1g,h; (2) see **bod**

**oerlas** adj. *cold and blue* IV.11a

**oeruel** n. *cold* VIII.8a

**oeruelauc** adj. *cold* I.35b (ModW oerfelog)

**oeruerw** n.m. *cold bubbling* or adj. *cold and bubbling* VIII.24a

**oerwlyb** adj. *cold and wet* IV.11a

**oerwynt** n.m. *cold wind* XII.3b

**ogo** see **gogo**

**ohonaw** see **o** (1)

**o'i** see **o'e**

**olwyn** n. *wheel* XII.2b

**ongyr** n.coll. *spears* II.21b

**onn** n.coll. *ash-trees* II.30b, VII.1a etc.; *spears* III.15b.

**ond** conj. *but, except* XII.3h

**or** see **o** (3), **ry**

**o'r a** = prep. *o* + demonstrative *a* + rel.pron *a* III.10c; see **o** (1), **ar** (2), **a** (3/4)

**os** conj. *if*; **os gwnn** *to be sure* II.9b (see note)

**osb** n.m. *guest* XII.4d

**ottei, ottid, otynt** see **odi**

**Owein** pers. name I.27c, 29c

## P

pa (1) interrog. adj. & pron. *what?* I.24c, 28c, XII[A].10e; **pa hyd** *how long* XI.11g; (2) interrog. adv. *why?* II.14c

pair see peri

pâl n. *spade* XII.2b

paladr n.m. *staff*, pl. peleidr III.20b

pall|u v.intr. *fail, come to end*; pres. ind. 3 sg. X.4

pan (1) conj. *when* I.13b, VIII.1b, 25cd, 27b, IX.14, X.4; (2) interrog. adv. *whence?* I.26c

pâr n. *spear* I.29b

para v.intr. *continue, persist*; pres. ind. 3 sg. pery XII.3d

parchus adj. *respected* XII[B].11f*

pastardaeth n.f. *bastardy* IV.6a

pawb distrib. pron. *all, everyone* II.20c, VI.16c etc.

pechawt n.m. *sin* II.10c, XII[B].10g (ModW pechod)

*pecunias* (Lat.) n., acc. pl. of **pecunia** *money* XI.1e

pedryfan adj. *four-cornered* IX.41

pedrychwelit adj. *four-sided* IX.41

peleidr see paladr

Pelis pers. name I.24c

pell adj. *far, long; long-lasting* VI.16b, VIII.9c, IX.56; as adv. *far* IX.43, X.1 ?, *long* VI.7c, X.1?

pen(n) n.m. *head* V.4b, *end* XII.3b; as adj. *chief* XI.11f; **pen ki** *fragment of solar halo* XII.2g

pendefig n.m. *prince* VI.12c

pen(n)aeth n.m. *chieftain* I.29b, IX.94

*per* (Lat.) prep. *through, by means of* XI.1e

perchen n.m. *ruler, lord* XI.11f

per|i v. tr. *create*; pres. ind. 3 sg. pair XII.6f, pret. 2 sg. -eist VII.9c

periklid see peryglu

perth n.f. *bush, hedge* VIII.30a; pl. -i VIII.31a

pery see para

perygl|u v. intr. *run into danger*; pres. ind. 3 sg. periklid XI.1e

pesg|i v.tr. *feed*; pres. ind. impers. -ittor III.14b, -itawr VI.9a

peth n.m. *thing* XII.2e, 3g; **triffeth** *three things* XII[B].10g piau v. tr. *own*; fut. 3 sg. **pieifydd** XII[A].11f

pisscaud see pysc

plant n.coll. *children* VI.18c etc.

planed n.f. *planet* XII[B].9a

plith see ymhlith

plygein n. *matins, early Mass* VI.10a

plu n.coll. *plumage* VI.3b

pob distrib. adj. *every* II.1a etc., VII.11c, XII.3e etc.

pobl n.f. *people* IX.99

porth|i v.tr. *support, ? practise* IX.44

praidd n. *flock, herd* XII.6d

presswyl adj. *permanent , everlasting* XI.1g

prif adj. *chief* I.27b (priw); **prif egwa** *prominent in talk; blusterer, windbag* IX.75

prit n.m. *price* IX.40

priw see prif

Prydein place name *Britain* I.27a, II.4b

pryder n.m. *anxiety* I.27a

pryn|u v.tr. *purchase*; pres. subj. 3 sg. -wy IX.68*

pryt n.m. *appearance* V.8c (ModW -d)

puch|o v.tr. *desire, require*; pres. ind. impers. -ir IX.110

purdu adj. *jet-black* II.14b, V.7b

pwyll n. *sense, consideration* VII.8c, IX.73, 75 etc.; as adj. *deliberate?* IX.52

pwyllad v.intr. *think* XI.1g

pwyth n.m. *due, fee* VIII.2c

py interrog. adv. *why?* VII.9c

pybyr adj. *bright*; (fig.) *excellent* VIII.9c

pydiw rel. pron. *to whom* IX.119

pŷr n. *? pear-tree* II.21a

pysc n.m. *fish* II.7b etc., VIII.3a; coll. **pisscaud** I.4a, XII[B].10c (pysgod)

pyth adv. *always, for ever* II.2d (see also byth)

## R (Rh, Rr)

rac (1) n. *front line* VI.12c (2); prep. *before, against, in face of* I.3a, 15a, II.2b, IX.79 etc.; **rac bronn** *against* I.2b raid see **reit**

raith see **reith**

rann n.f. *part, portion* IX.110

redegawc adj. *running* VIII.20c; *flowing* VIII.19b

redeint (1) n. *course, pace* IX.85; (2) ? n.coll. ? *young stags* III.5a

redyn n.coll. *fern, bracken* VII.8a etc

rëen n.m. *lord* I.35c*, VII.9c

rei indef. pron. *some* II.35c

reid see **reit**

reinyat n.m. *sharer, (generous) lord* III.16b

reit n.m. *necessity* I.19b (reid), VI.6c (rhaid), XII.2d (raid); as adj. *necessary* II.4c

reith (1) n.f. *law* IX.94; (2) ? n. *violence* VI.22b, ?IX.42

reo see **rew**

reu(h)id see **rewi**

rev see **rew**

rew n.m. *ice* I.7a (reo), 13b (rev); *frost* II.25c; as adj. *frozen* III.14c

rew|i v. intr. *freeze*; pres. ind. 3 sg. reuhid I.1b, 6b, reuid I.13b; impers. -ittor I.35a

rewyd n.m. *passion. desire, wantonness* VIII.13b*; as adj. *lustful, lewd*; as secondary n. *lecher, oaf* VIII.22c, IX.56 (≡ rhewydd)

rhaeadr n. *cataract*; pl. rheieidr VI.6b

rhag see **rac**

Rhagfyr n.m. *December* XII[A,B].12a

rhagorawl adj. *magnificent, ? powerful* VI.20a*

rhaid see **reit**

rhann|u v.tr. *distribute; allot*; pres. ind. 3 sg. VI.21c

rheieidr see **rhaeadr**

rhiw n.f. *slope* I.9a, 16a (riv), VI.7b

rhoddi, roddi v.tr. *give*; pres.ind. 3 sg. ryd VIII.25d, XII[A].11f (rrydd), impers. -ir IX.119; subj. 3 sg. -wy III.4c, -o XII[A].11f, ro XII[B].9h; impv. 3 sg. rothid I.30c.

rhos see **ros**

rhybudd see **rybud**

rhychau see **rych**

rhyd see **ryt**

rhyddhau v.tr. *deliver*; pres. subj. 3 sg. rithao I.29a

**rhyfelfawr**, adj. *warlike*; (fig.) *turbulent* VI.2b

**rhyfic** n.m. *boisterousness,* ? *clamour* XII.3a (ModW -yg 'impertinence')

**rhygoeth** adj. *excellent* ; as n. VI.1b

**rianed** see **riein**

**rid** see **ryt**

**riein** n.f. *girl*; pl. **rianed** IV.3a

**rigaeth** adj. *excessively severe* I.29a (rhygaeth)

**rihyd** n.m. *glory* IX.10, 78; *vainglory* XI.6e, 11e (riydd)

**rin** n. *secret* VII.4c, IX.56

**rithao** see **rhyddhau**

**riv** (1) see **rhiw**; (2) indef. adj. *such, whatever* I.26b

**rynn|u** ? v.tr. intr. *chill, freeze*; ? pres. ind. 3 sg.(future sense) **rynawd** VI.7a (see also **rynawd**)

**riydd** see **rihyd**

**ro** see **rhoddi**

**rodwit, -ut** n.m. *dyke* I.26a, (in place name) 30a (-ut) (≡ rhodwydd)

**rodwy** see **rhoddi**

**rodyat** n.m *giver* III.3c (≡ rhoddiad)

**ros** n.f. *moor* I.16a, III.12c, XII.12b (rhos)

**rothid** see **rhoddi**

**Rragfyr** see **Rhagfyr**

**rrydd** see **rhoddi**

**rryfel** n.m. *war* XII[A].10c

**rudvyt** n. ? *bloody battle* X.13 (≡ rhuddfid)

**ruit** see **rwyd**

**ruiw** n.m. *lord* I.30a (≡ rhwyf)

**rut** adj. *red* I.29b (ModW rhudd)

**ruthur** n. *onrush* II.2b (ModW rhuthr)

**rwyd** adj. *smooth, easy* I.26a (ruit), IX.85 (ModW rhwydd)

**ry** preverbal particle (1) expressing completed action I.29c, X.4 (fut. perf. sense), XI.1h; (2) expressing possibility I.1c, 20c, IX.65, 68, 110, 113; combined with o (2) as **or** I.2c*, 21e*

**rybud** n. *warning* II.33c, VI.2c (rhybudd)

**rych** n. *furrow* III.13a, V.9b, VI.4b; pl. **rhychau** VI.6a

**rychwerthin** n. *excessive laughter* VIII.22c

ryd adj. *free* ; as noun *free man* II.14c, IX.25 (ModW rhydd)

rydd see **rhoddi**

rygyngawc adj. *ambling* III.7a (≡ rhygyngog)

ryn n.m. *cold*; as adj. *cold, frost* VI.7a

rynawd ? n. *space of time*; as adv. VI.7a? (see also **rhynnu**)

ryngawc adj. ? *interfering* III.18c

ryssedha v.intr. *behave excessively* IX.78 (≡ rhysedda)

ryt n.f. *ford* I.1b, 13a etc. (rid) II.7b, VI.2b (rhyd) etc.

ryuaeth see **magu, ry**

ryvawr adj. *very great* I.6c (≡ rhyfawr)

ryuedot n. *wonder* II.14c (ModW rhyfeddod)


# S

saeth n. *arrow*; (fig.) VIII.24c

Sain, n., with pers. n. *Saint* XII.8g, [B].9g

Satan pers. name XII[B].12f

*segites* (Lat.) n. nom.pl. of **seges,** correctly **segetes** *corn* XI.6c

segur adj. *idle* I.6b

seirch n.coll. *armour* III.18a

Seis n.m. *Englishman* IV.9b

seithuc adj. *futile, useless*; ? as n. VIII.18a (ModW seithug)

seiw see **seuyll**

serchawc adj. *amorous*; as n. VIII.12a, 27c, 28b

seuir see **seuyll**

seu|yll, v.intr. *stand*; pres. ind. 3 sg. **seiw** I.1c, impers.-**ir** I.2c, 21e (ModW sefyll)

sich adj. *dry* I.17a ( ≡ sych)

*siluas* (Lat.) n. acc. pl. of **silua** *woods* XI.1d

sorr|i v. intr. *take offence*; pres. ind. 3 sg. **syrr** V.8b

*super* (Lat.) prep. *over* XI.1c

swydd n.f. *public office*; *(legal) institution*, ? *process*; pl. **swyddau\*** VI.6b

sy see **bot**

syberw adj. *proud, noble* VIII.24c, 27c

synn|u v.intr. *wonder*; *be confounded*; pres. ind. 3 sg. IX.68

syrr see **sorri**

sywedydd n.m. *wise one* XI.11f

# T

Tachwedd n.m. *November* VI.8a, XI.11a etc.

taer adj. *intense* XII.7b

tafl|u v.tr. *throw*; pres. ind. 3 sg. **tawl** II.3a (ModW taflu, (dialectal) towlu).

tâl n.m. *end* I.20a; *face* I.21c; (fig.) VIII.18b

talar n.f. *head-land (of field)* XII.3b

tal|u v.tr. *pay* VI.6c; ? intr. *make amends*; pres. ind. 3 sg. IX.83

tangdef n. *peace* X.11 (-dd-)

tangnevedd n.m. *peace* XII.6e

tangnef|u v.intr. *be at peace*; pres. ind. 3 sg. IX.90

tann|u v.tr. *spread*; pres. subj. impers. -er VIII.27b

tarf, -af n.m. *scattering, flight, alarm*; **ar daraf** *scattering, in flight* II.8a (cf Mod W tarfu 'disturb')

tauawt n. *tongue* II.35b (ModW tafod)

tauawl n.coll. *dock (plant)* II.3b (ModW tafol)

tawdd see **toddi**

tawel adj. *quiet, silent*; as n. *quiet man* II.11c, III.2b etc.

tawl see **taflu**

tec adj. *fair* I.23c, IV.3b etc. (ModW teg).

tech|u v.intr. *retreat*; pres. subj. 3 sg. -o IX.113

tei see **tŷ**

teilwng adj. *fit, worthy* XII.8f

teleit adj. *excellent* II.11c, III.2b ($\equiv$ -aid)

teneu adj. *thin* IV.1b

*terras* (Lat.) n. acc. pl. of **terra** *land* XI.1c

terth n. *terce, 9 a.m.* XI.6f

teruyn n.m. *end, limit* VI.21c (terfyn), IX.66

teruysc n. *trouble* V.4b, VI.19b etc. (ModW terfysg)

tes n.m. *heat* I.5c, XII.7b; *temperature* XI.11d; (fig.) *excitement, agitation*; **ar des** *frisky, in rut?* II.5a

teu see **tewi**

teulu n.m. *war-band, company* I.30b etc.

tev adj. *thick* I.7b (≡ tew)

tew|i v.intr. *be silent*; pres. ind. 3 sg. **teu** VII.7c

tëyrn n.m. *king* IV.3c

tîn n.f. *rump, crupper* I.25a*

tir n.m. *land* I.2a, 24c, 28c, IX.105 etc.; pl. **tiredd** XII.6a

tlawd, tlawt adj. *poor* VI.7c, (fig.) IX.77; pl. **tylodion** XII[A].9d

to n.m. *roof* II.12b, VI.2b etc.; (thatch) IV.5b

toddedic adj. *(quickly) melted* XII.7b

todd|i v.tr. *melt*; pres. ind. 3 sg. **tawdd** XII[B].10g

tohid see **töi**

tö|i v.tr. *cover*; pres. ind. 3 sg -**id** I.2a, -**hid** I.8a

tomlyd adj. *dung-covered, muddy* XII[B].12a

ton(n) (1) n.f. *wave* I.2a, 35b, VI.20a etc.; *water* VIII.10b; pl. **tonneu** II.24b; **tonnawr** IX.106; (2) see **twnn**

torr|i v.tr. & intr.. *break, lose strength*; pres. ind. 3 sg. -**it** IX.67, **tyrr** VIII.16c.

tost adj. *bitter, pungent* III.12c

towissun see **tywys**

tra prep. *over, on, after* I.2a

trachysc|u v.intr. *sleep excessively* II.1c

traet see **troet**

traeth n.m. *strand, shore* II.13a, IX.49 etc.; pl. **treith** IX.89

traeth|u v.tr. *speak, pronounce*; impf. subj. 3 sg. -**ei** II.35b

tragwyddol adj. *eternal* XII[A].11h

traha n. *arrogance* IV.2c, IX.109, XII.4h etc.; ? as adj. *presumptuous* IX.83

trallawd n.m. *misery*; as adj. *wretched* XII.2b

tralleu|ein vn. *lamentation* IV.2c (ModW -llefain)

tranck n.m. *death* XII.4h

trech comp. adj. *stronger* VII.1c, VIII.3c

tref n.f. *town, village*; pl. **trewit** I.18b (≡ trefydd)

treid|iaw v.tr. *visit*; pres. ind. 3 sg. II.22b

treisio see **treissyaw**

treissig adj. *forceful, masterful* VIII.33b

treiss|yaw v. tr. & intr. *do violence (to)* VIII.33b, XII[A].9g (treisio)

tremyn|u v.intr. *wander*; pres. ind. 3 sg. XI.1d

treng|i v.intr. *die*; pres. ind. 3 sg. -hit IX.38, -hyt IX.67

trewit see tref

tri num. *three* XII.2e; in compound triffeth XII[B].10g

triffeth see tri, peth

trîn n.f. *contention, trouble* IX.58, XII[A].12d

Trindawt n.f. *Trinity* IX.83 (ModW Trindod)

trist adj. *sad* XII[A].11d; as n. XII[B].11h

tristit n.m. *sadness* II.23c

tro n.m. *movement*; ar dro *moving, active* II.6a

troet n.f. *foot* II.29b, VII.4b etc.; pl. traet II.32a

truch see trwch

trugar adj. *merciful* V.6c, VIII.31c

trulliad n.m. *cup-bearer, butler* XII.1b

trum see trwm

trwch adj. *broken* I.3b (truch); *incorrigible*, as n. II.33c, VI.2c, IX.58

trwm adj. *heavy*; (of soil) XII[B].12b; *burdensome, grave* II.10c; *sad, sorrowful, miserable* III.9a, VIII.16a, as n. II.36b; *serious, sober* VIII.7b; as n. *difficulty* I.20c (trum).

trwy prep. *through* XII.3g (drwy); (fig.) *by means of* XII[A].9f (drwy), ? *accompanied by* XII[A].11c (drwy); with vn. *while* XI.52

trychni n.m. *disaster* XII[A].10f

trydar n. *battle, contention* III.17a

trydyd adj. *third* II.30c

trymluog adj. *sluggish, torpid* XII[B].12b*

trysawr n.m. *treasure* XII[B].11f

tu n.m. *side* I.2a, II.8c, (of hill) II.1a

tvchan v.intr. *complain*; pres. ind. 3 sg. XII[A].11a (≡ tuchan)

tudded n. *covering* VI.20b

tur|yaw v.tr. *root up* IV.4c

twn(n) adj. *shattered, broken* VI.2b*, VIII.17c; fem. tonn III.17c

tŵr n.m. *tower* II.10c, III.18a; ? *steep mountain* II.16b.

twyll n. *deception* IX.52

twyll|aw v.tr. *deceive*; pres. ind. 3 sg. VII.3c, IX. 74, -a IV.11b, -yt III.6b; subj. 3 sg. -o IX.19*

twym adj. *hot* VI.8a*

tŷ n.m. *house*; pl. tei II.35a

tylodedd n.m. *poverty* III.21b (≡ tlodedd)

tylodion see tlawd

tylluan n.f. *owl* XII[B].12d

tyng|u v.tr. *determine (by fate), destine*; pres. ind. impers. -ir X.4

tynn|u v.tr. *draw, pull*; pres. ind. 3 sg. VII.4b etc.

tyrr see torri

Tytul place name I.25c (≡ Tyddwl)

tyu|u v.i. *grow*; pres. ind. 3 pl. -ant VIII.1b (ModW tyfu)

tywyll see yntywyll.

tywys v.tr. *lead*; impf. ind. 1 sg. towissun I.25c*

## Th

'th, infixed pers. pron. 2 sg. I.28c, IX.48

## U (V)

uanw see banw

uchel adj. *high* II.11b, VIII.22b; ? *tall*, ? *high-ranking* X.14

ucheneit n.m. *howling* III.2a (cf ModW ochenaid)

vid see bot

uit see bot

vn num. *one* I.1c, XI.11h; as adj. *the same* IX.25

unben(n) n.m. *chieftain* I.19a, III.4a; pl. unbynn II.20b

unic adj. *solitary, single*; as n. VIII.33a (≡ unig)

vo see bot

vy (1) poss. pron. 1 sg. + nasal mut. *my* II.26b, VII.4b (uyn), 5b (vynn), 6b (vyn), 10b (vyg) (2) pers. pron. 3 pl. I.19a (≡ hwy)

vyg see vy (≡ vy ng-)

uyn, vyn(n) see vy

vyth see byth

## W

'w, infixed pers. pron. 3 sg. m. IX.36

waethwaeth see drwc

wedy see **gwedy**

**whec, whefris** see under **chw-**

**wrth** prep. *at, by, to* II.6b; 1 sg. **wrthyf** II.6c, 2 sg. **wrthit** IX.47

**worymdaa** see **gorymdaith**

**wybraidd** adj. *cloudy* XII.4a

**wyneb** n.f. *face* II.34b; (fig.) *dignity* III.4c

**ŵyr** n.m. *grandson* IV.6c

## Y

**y** (1) def. article I.26a, 29a, VI.4c (-'r), 5c (yr), 6c ; (2) poss. pron. 3 sg. masc. I.5a,
 II.30c, IX.60, XII.1e.f etc.(i); (3) see **i** (4); (4) preverbal particle VI.11c?, 18c ;
 (4) relative particle I.28c

**y ar** see **i** (6)

**ych** (1) n.m. *ox* V.9b, VI.4b, pl. -en XII.4b (ModW ych) (2) poss. pron. 3 pl. I.22a
 (ModW eich)

**ychwaneg|u** v.tr. *increase, add*; pres. ind. 3 sg. **echwenic** IX.24

**ŷd** n.m. *corn* XII[A].9b

**ydd** preverbal particle XI.6g

**ydlan** n.f. *rickyard* XII.7f

**yf|et** v.tr. *drink*; pres. ind. 3 pl. -ant IX.65 (ModW yfed)

**yg** before velar = **yng**; see **yn** (2)

**y gan** see **i** (6)

**yghyuarth** verbal adj. *at bay* (fig.) III.16b (≡ ynghyfarth, cf. ModW cyfarth 'bark')

**ym** see **i** (4)

*ymber* see *imber*

**ymdiryet** v.i. *trust* IV.11b; pres. ind. 3 sg. **ymdiret** V.1d (ModW ymddiried)

**ymgar|u** v.refl. *love each other*; pres. ind. 3 pl. -ant II.2c

**ymgeinmyg|u** v.refl. *pride oneself*; pres. subj. impers. **ymgeinmycker** IX.2

**ymgel|u** v.refl. *hide* II.12c

**ymladgar** adj. *pugnacious* III.10b

**ym plith** prep. *among* IV.2b (≡ ymhlith)

**ympryd** n.m. *fast* XII[B].10h

**yn** (1) poss. pron. 1 pl. IX.47, XI.1f, 1h (in), XI. 11c (?) (ModW ein); (2) prep. (nasal
 mut.) *in* I.4a (yg), 12a (i), 13a (i), 14a (ig), 15a (ig), 16b (in), IV.8c, IV.2d (yg),
 VI.17c X.3 (en); (3) predicative particle with adj. (soft mut.) III.2c, V.1d,
 VIII.12c, 16a; (4) see **i** (3); (5) **yn y** conj. *where* VI.19c

y'n = y (4) + 'n

ynghad see yn (2), kad

yngkynnyd verbal adj. *successful* II.19b

yngofag verbal adj. *breeding, multiplying* VI.12b

yntywyll ?verbal adj. *in darkness, benighted* IX.71? (≡ ynhywyll)

ynuyt adj. *foolish, hot-headed*; as n. III.10b etc. (ModW ynfyd)

ynyal adj. *waste*; as n. *wilderness* VIII.21b (cf. ModW anial)

yr (1) see y (1); (2) = y(4) + ry; (3) see er

ys see bot

ysbaid n.f. *space of time, duration* XI.6f (ysbayd), 11h.

ysbeiliwr n.m. *despoiler* XII[B].12f

ysbeilwynt n.m. *wind of plunder* (i.e. *smell of devastation*) XII[A].10c

yscubawr n.f. *barn* XII[B].11c (ModW ysgubor)

yscuid n. *shield* I.6b, 7c , 23a, 28a (ModW ysgwyd)

ysgall n.coll. *thistles* X.3

ysgar see esgar

ysgaw n.coll. *elder-trees* VIII.33

Ysgolan pers. n. XII[B].12g

ysgwn adj. *steadfast* VIII.17b; *swift* I.24b (iscun)

ysgwyd n.f. *shoulder* I.6b (iscuit), 7c (yscuit), II.26b (ModW ysgwydd)

ysgynn|u v.i. *mount* II.8c

yspydat n.coll. *thorn-bushes* VIII.28a (≡ ysbyddad)

ystlys n. *flank* (fig.) II.22b

yt preverbal particle + soft mut. II.32b, X.4 (≡ yd)

y'th see y (4), 'th

yw see bot

y'w = i (5) + 'w

ywch prep. *above* II.10b etc., VII.3b etc. (ModW uwch)

# INDEX TO COMMENTARY

CPSIA information can be obtained
at www.ICGtesting.com
Printed in the USA
LVHW041520170423
744556LV00004B/161